Classroom Discussions

Classroom Discussions
Using Math Talk to Help Students Learn

GRADES 1–6

≋

Suzanne H. Chapin
Catherine O'Connor
Nancy Canavan Anderson

≋

MATH SOLUTIONS PUBLICATIONS
Sausalito, CA

Math Solutions Publications
A division of
Marilyn Burns Education Associates
150 Gate 5 Road, Suite 101
Sausalito, CA 94965
www.mathsolutions.com

The publisher would like to acknowledge adapted material:

Chapter 12: Mrs. Robert's lesson plan is an adaptation of a lesson in Economopoulos et al. 1995.
Chapter 13: Mr. Donnell's lesson plan is an adaptation of a lesson in Lappan et al. 2002.

Library of Congress Cataloging-in-Publication Data
Chapin, Suzanne H.
    Classroom discussions using math to help students learn, grades 1–6 / Suzanne
H. Chapin, Catherine O'Connor, Nancy Canavan Anderson.
       p. cm.
Includes bibliographical references and index.
    ISBN 0-941355-53-5 (acid-free paper)
    1. Mathematics—Study and teaching (Elementary) I. O'Connor, Catherine.
II. Anderson, Nancy Canavan. III. Title.
    QA135.6.C47 2003
    372.7—dc21

                             2003010787

ISBN-13: 978-0-941355-53-7
ISBN-10: 0-941355-53-5

Editor: Toby Gordon
Production: Melissa L. Inglis
Cover design: Linda Knowles
Interior design: Joni Doherty Design
Composition: Tom Allen/Pear Graphic Design

Printed in the United States of America on acid-free paper
07 06   ML   6 7 8 9 10

A Message from Marilyn Burns

We at Math Solutions Professional Development believe that teaching math well calls for increasing our understanding of the math we teach, seeking deeper insights into how children learn mathematics, and refining our lessons to best promote students' learning.

Math Solutions Publications shares classroom-tested lessons and teaching expertise from our faculty of Math Solutions Inservice instructors as well as from other respected math educators. Our publications are part of the nationwide effort we've made since 1984 that now includes

- more than five hundred face-to-face inservice programs each year for teachers and administrators in districts across the country;
- annually publishing professional development books, now totaling more than fifty titles and spanning the teaching of all math topics in kindergarten through grade 8;
- four series of videotapes for teachers, plus a videotape for parents, that show math lessons taught in actual classrooms;
- on-site visits to schools to help refine teaching strategies and assess student learning; and
- free online support, including grade-level lessons, book reviews, inservice information, and district feedback, all in our quarterly *Math Solutions Online Newsletter*.

For information about all of the products and services we have available, please visit our Web site at *www.mathsolutions.com*. You can also contact us to discuss math professional development needs by calling (800) 868-9092 or by sending an e-mail to *info@mathsolutions.com*.

We're always eager for your feedback and interested in learning about your particular needs. We look forward to hearing from you.

Math Solutions.
PUBLICATIONS

To the students and teachers of Project Challenge

Contents

Preface:
Talk in Action

What is the basis for the descriptions and recommendations you will find in this book? One source is the research and teaching literature that deals with classroom talk and student learning. In the back of the book we include a number of references for readers who want to learn more. But in addition, we have experience in the planned use of classroom discourse to support students' thinking and reasoning in mathematics. We have seen tremendous changes take place in classrooms and in students, over a period of four years in one low-income urban school district.

From 1998 through 2002 we implemented Project Challenge, an intervention project funded by the Jacob K. Javits Gifted and Talented Student Education Program of the U.S. Department of Education. The Javits program was specifically looking for projects that would increase the number of ethnic and linguistic minority students in programs for gifted and talented students. For many years it has been the case that programs for gifted and talented students served primarily white, affluent students. In many poor urban districts, where students are primarily nonwhite and where many are English-language learners, there have been few programs for gifted and talented students. When we started out, the goals of Project Challenge were to identify English-language learners, minority students, and economically disadvantaged elementary and middle school students who had potential talent in mathematics, and to provide them with a reform-based mathematics curriculum that focused on mathematical reasoning and communication. We hoped that by combining a solid curriculum, instruction based on mathematical understanding, and a heavy emphasis on talk and communication about mathematics, we would be able to help these students become robust learners of mathematics: learners able to think deeply and insightfully, learners who would not give up when a problem was difficult, and learners who would legitimately come to think of themselves as mathematically able.

From the beginning, obstacles to these goals appeared with regularity. First, the students in the schools we worked with were not high-performing students. The district had no programs at all for gifted or talented students. Some teachers and administrators suggested that there were very few gifted students in the system. About 85 percent of the district's students qualify for free or reduced-price lunch, and over 75 percent speak a language other than English at home. We began by evaluating the six hundred or so students in the fourth grade in September of 1998 to see if we could identify about one hundred to participate in the project starting later in the fall. On alternative assessments (created to reflect the local curriculum) very few of the students performed at a level that would indicate any special talent in mathematics. Of the approximately six hundred students we evaluated, less than a dozen stood out as obviously talented in mathematics.

But our assumption in designing this intervention was that many students had abilities and interests in mathematics that could be nurtured and developed, even if these did not show up at the time on standardized tests. We were looking for potential in mathematics, not demonstrations of accomplishment. Finally, using teacher recommendations, student work, and prior achievement in mathematics, we selected about one hundred students to begin participating in a daily mathematics curriculum, organized into four classes, each containing about twenty-five students. These students closely mirrored the demographic profile of all students in the district in terms of ethnicity and home language.

We worked with many teachers to combine solid curriculum materials (*Investigations in Number, Data, and Space* in fourth and fifth grades and *Connected Mathematics* in grades 5–7) with the strategic use of various forms of classroom talk. We instituted weekly quizzes as a way to reinforce the importance of studying and remembering the content introduced during each week. We gave each teacher daily "warm-up" problems in logic and spatial reasoning to work through with students every morning before classes began. In addition, we introduced major projects that students worked on at the end of the year, culminating in a mathematics fair. Other students and parents were invited to this fair.

From the beginning, we attempted to incorporate various forms of classroom talk into the mathematics work. During the first year, many of the fourth-grade students in our first cohort were reluctant to talk in class, or to speak loudly enough so that others could hear. Others were confused by the new forms of activity and participation, and still others resisted the whole process. But we persisted, working alongside committed teachers who worked hard to put these new forms of instruction into place. Gradually, we began to see real changes in the ways our students were thinking and talking. After about seven or eight months of our first year's efforts, we noticed that students' reasoning had become more complex, more sophisticated, and more recognizably mathematical. Students were better able to give clear explanations for their problem solutions, their use of language became more precise, and their communication skills improved noticeably.

As our first cohort of students moved through fifth grade, we started to see results that were more striking. Even students who had been nearly silent the entire first year of the program began to speak up, explain their thinking, respond to other students' contributions, and ask and answer questions that reflected a growing interest in mathematics as well as a growing ability to think mathematically. Other teachers who taught these students in their language arts and social studies classes began to comment on their striking ability to verbalize their thoughts and explanations. Parents who had previously seemed disconnected from the program began to communicate that they were happy with their children's growing interest in mathematics.

In addition, we got strong support for our efforts in the form of results on standardized tests. At the beginning of the program, we administered the Test of Mathematical Abilities—Second Edition (TOMA-2) to our first cohort of students. Only 4 percent were rated as superior or very superior (which indicates a "high probability of giftedness in mathematics") and 23 percent were rated as above average. The remaining 73 percent were rated as average or below average in their mathematical abilities. After two years in the program, however, we again tested those students who had remained in the program (approximately eighty). After two years, 41 percent were now superior or very superior, and 36 percent were above average. Only 23 percent of our first cohort were classified as having average ability in mathematics after two years in the program, and none were below average.

In order to examine student achievement growth over time, we also used data from the mathematics subtest of the California Achievement Test (CAT). After three months in the project, the students in our first cohort scored better on the CAT than 70 percent of a national sample. This score undoubtedly indicated that we had identified students who did have potential ability in mathematics. Two years later these same students took the CAT mathematics subtest again. This time, they scored better, on average, than 91 percent of a national sample. Furthermore, after three years in the program, 90 percent of the sixth graders in our first cohort placed in the top two categories on the Massachusetts Comprehensive Assessment System (MCAS) test in mathematics, a rate greater than that of nearby affluent suburbs.

The growth in achievement has continued for students who entered the program after the first year. We have analyzed the growth of the second cohort—roughly one hundred students who entered the program as fourth graders in the second year of Project Challenge. Like that of the first cohort of approximately one hundred, the achievement growth of the second group was significant; in two years that cohort went from having a mean total mathematics score at the 74th percentile to a ranking at the 91st percentile.

To what can we attribute these results? First, we credit the hard work of the teachers and students involved in the program. Second, we believe that a well-planned mathematics curriculum that emphasizes student understanding is a critical centerpiece to our story. The supporting activities—the projects, the weekly quizzes, the daily logic-problem warm-ups, and an emphasis on achievement—all played an important part in the high levels of performance we saw our students achieve. In addition, we believe that these results are due in part to the productive use of classroom discourse in these classes, something we have carefully scaffolded since the beginning of the project. There are a number of reasons that the classroom talk occurring between students and teachers in these classrooms was supportive of mathematical thinking and learning:

- Talk about mathematical concepts and procedures caused misconceptions to surface and helped the teachers recognize and address what students did and did not understand.
- Discourse formats, such as extended group discussion, played a part in helping students improve their ability to reason logically. When one student made a claim, the teacher would ask for evidence to support the claim. Examples or counterexamples to the claim provided fodder for reasoning. Over four years, this had a noticeable impact.
- Allowing students to talk about their thinking and problem solving gave them more to observe and listen to, and more chances to participate in mathematical thinking. This pushed them beyond their incomplete, shallow, or passive knowledge by making them aware of discrepencies between their own thinking and that of others.
- Classroom discussion provided motivation. Students became more motivated through taking an interest in their peers' claims and positions within a discussion.

In short, we believe that the ways we used talk in the classroom helped these students make their thinking public; it helped students to explicate and elaborate their reasoning; it allowed them to model, build on, and add to the development of complex ideas and in at least some cases it provided a socially grounded motivation to learn.

None of the participants would say that the work of Project Challenge has been easy. In some ways, our experiments with using classroom discourse to promote student learning have been the most challenging aspect of the program. But we believe that our results—the whole range of our results, from test scores to student testimonials—indicate that productive talk was a crucial part of the program. It enabled these low-income students, three-quarters of whom spoke a language other than English at home, to become mathematically articulate. They learned to express their mathematical thoughts to their peers and to their teacher. This was a formative experience for them, and it was a formative experience for us as well. Our experiences with Project Challenge are a large part of the reason that we decided to write this book, so that teachers who wish to support the learning of their students could build on what we have learned.

Acknowledgments

In 1998, the authors began to work together on Project Challenge, a program to enhance learning opportunities for urban students with potential talent in mathematics. Suzanne Chapin brought her experience in professional development and mathematics education, Cathy O'Connor brought her background in linguistics and the study of classroom discourse, and Nancy Anderson brought her training in math education and her willingness to try new approaches to mathematical communication in the classroom. This book grew out of our collaboration. Its contents are based on what we learned during Project Challenge, and on our years of work in our respective fields.

We are grateful to all the Project Challenge teachers who so willingly tried new methods and materials, even in the face of pressures from high-stakes testing. They were willing to think deeply about what it means to be talented in mathematics, and to spend many hours in demanding professional development activities. Our profound thanks go to Beth Brogna, Ali Brown, Patty Burge, Lauren Carilli, Roseanne Cataldo, Maureen DeFreitas, Janice Fields, Kathy Foulser, Laura Glavin, Monty Grob, Gina Lally, Mesook Lee, Claire Moran, Magaly Rodriguez, Alice Rourke, Rene Sacco, Sally Siriani, Alissa Stangle, Andrea Taddeo, Henry Utter, Tanya Walsh, and Carol Wolf, as well as other teachers, support staff, project staff, and district administrators who offered time and support of many kinds.

Marilyn Burns has had a tremendously positive impact on the form and contents of the volume; it has been a pleasure to work with her.

Many of the ideas and practices described in this book came from the work of individuals that Cathy O'Connor has had the opportunity to collaborate with over the past decade. She is very grateful for help and discussion over the years from Lynne Godfrey, Maggie Lampert, Sarah Michaels, Robert Moses, Pam Paternoster, Lauren Resnick, Vicki Bill, Matthew Robert, Marty Rutherford, and many others.

We are greatly indebted to our funders. The Spencer Foundation has supported Cathy O'Connor's work on language in mathematics classrooms in several ways over the past decade. Project Challenge itself was funded by the Jacob K. Javits Gifted and Talented Students Education Program (Grant No.

R206A980001). The opinions expressed in this book do not necessarily reflect the position, policy, or endorsement of the U.S. Department of Education or of the Spencer Foundation. And although we are grateful to all of the individuals and institutions cited, none of these individuals or institutions should be assumed to endorse the contents of this volume.

Finally, we would like to express our appreciation to the students of Project Challenge, and to their families. We have been deeply encouraged and inspired by their hard work and consistent effort over these four years.

1

Talk
in the
Mathematics Class

1

An Overview

The students in Mrs. Schuster's third grade are discussing a question she has set out for them to consider: "Does the order of the numbers in a multiplication sentence affect the answer? Explain why or why not." In order to explore this question, they are generating examples of multiplication sentences and testing what happens when they change the order of the factors. Students know many of the basic multiplication facts but have not yet learned an algorithm for multidigit multiplication.

One student has made a conjecture that the order of the factors does not make a difference—"the answer is the same no matter which number goes first." Students are agreeing with this conjecture by bringing up other examples that work, such as $3 \times 4 = 12$ and $4 \times 3 = 12$. Mrs. Schuster then asks if this conjecture works with larger numbers and suggests that they use calculators to check. Students are able to generate many examples to verify the conjecture, but explaining why the products are the same is not as straightforward as carrying out the multiplication.

1. Eddie: Well, I don't think it matters what order the numbers are in. You still get the same answer. But three times four and four times three seem like they could be talking about different things.

2. Mrs. S: Rebecca, do you agree or disagree with what Eddie is saying?

3. Rebecca: Well, I agree that it doesn't matter which number is first, because three times four equals twelve and that's the same thing as four times three. But I don't get what Eddie means about them saying different things.

4. Mrs. S: Eddie, would you explain what you mean?

5. Eddie: Well, I just think that like three times four can mean three groups of four things, like three bags of four apples. And four times three means four bags of three apples, and those don't seem like the same thing.

6. Tiffany: But you still have the same number of apples! So they do mean the same!

7. Mrs. S: OK, so we have two different ideas here to talk about. Eddie says that order does matter, because three times four and four times three can each be used to describe a different situation, like four bags of three apples or three bags of four apples. So the two number sentences mean different things. And Tiffany, are you saying that those two number sentences *can't* be used to describe two different situations?

8. Tiffany: No, I mean that even though the number of bags is different, the answer is the same.

9. Mrs. S: OK, so you're saying that order doesn't matter because the answer is the same?

10. Tiffany: Right.

11. Mrs. S: OK. We need to think about this. In Eddie's statement, order makes a difference in the situation you're describing. In Tiffany's statement, order doesn't make a difference in the answer we get. So when does order make a difference in multiplying two numbers together?

Mrs. Schuster is using classroom talk to deepen students' understanding of the commutative property. She knows that this mathematical idea may be clear enough for the operation of addition, but that it gets complicated when we introduce multiplication. She knows that in the case of addition, students can easily see that the number sentence 2 + 3 and the number sentence 3 + 2 can be used to describe the same situation. It doesn't really matter whether we mention the three pears or the two apples first. In the case of multiplication, however, if we focus on the particulars of the problem situation, the order of elements in the number sentences suddenly matters. As Eddie points out, two bags of five apples and five bags of two apples are very different.

Mrs. Schuster knows that this is one of many points in the early grades where students' mathematical reasoning and their appreciation of real-world problem situations can come into apparent conflict. Yet in the long run, students' ability to use mathematical expressions to model real-world situations will be central to their progress in mathematics and science. She knows that it is therefore worth time and effort to clarify things here in her third grade, and she has chosen to use classroom talk as a tool to support that aim.

For over a decade, the National Council of Teachers of Mathematics (NCTM) has been urging teachers to emphasize communication—talk and writing—as part of mathematics teaching and learning. Their arguments make sense: The mathematical thinking of many students is aided by hearing what their peers are thinking. Putting thoughts into words pushes students to clarify their thinking. Teachers can spot student misunderstandings much more easily when they are revealed by a discussion instead of remaining unspoken. And the previous classroom interchange exemplifies what we are aiming for: a respectful but engaged conversation in which students can clarify their own thinking and learn from others through talk.

But for many teachers, it has not been easy to implement new ways of using talk in mathematics class. Researchers have found that few American classrooms display consistent or even occasional use of student talk. Instead, most classroom talk consists of the teacher lecturing, asking students to recite, or posing simple questions with known answers. Of course, lecturing, recitation, and quizzing are useful instructional tools. They form the bedrock of most teachers' instructional practice and we would not want them to disappear. However, they have limitations, as do all forms of talk.

As teachers, we have many different academic goals, and many things we want to achieve in our classrooms. We need as large and diverse and powerful a set of instructional tools as we can find. The purpose of this book is to enable you to enhance and expand the array of instructional tools you know how to use. We will introduce you to a variety of discourse-based tools— ways of using language in teaching mathematics that will allow students to engage more fully in mathematical thinking and reasoning. These include conversational strategies and ways of structuring interaction in your classes that will help you achieve the goals you have for your students. Some of these goals may be social: you want your students to be able to listen to one another respectfully, to cooperate, and to build on one another's ideas. Some of these goals will be both social and cognitive: You want your students to be able to make mathematical conjectures, present evidence, voice agreement and disagreement with the claims of others, and support their own positions. And finally, some of the goals will center on your students' learning of core mathematical concepts and procedures. In this book, we aim to help you integrate all of these goals and support them through the skillful use of classroom talk.

When should students talk, and about what? If we simply ask students to talk, without thinking carefully about our purposes, we may end up with irrelevant, hard-to-manage discussion that serves no clear academic purpose. Sometimes this aimless talk may be pleasant; sometimes it may be unpleasant. But in either case it probably will not significantly advance student thinking and learning. Instead, for talk to be productive, we believe that it must be carefully integrated with the content of the mathematics lesson. Our goal is not to increase the *amount* of talk in our classrooms, but to increase the *amount of high quality* talk in our classrooms—the mathematically productive talk.

How can we tell when the talk in our classrooms has been productive, and not simply a waste of time? It seems clear that we can't simply rely on our feelings. Think back to the last time you had a conversation that you enjoyed. It may or may not have been intellectually significant. Obviously, the best conversations—in or out of school—are the ones that are fun and exciting, and also intellectually or personally important. But we cannot use fun and excitement as our only criteria for whether classroom talk has been productive. We have to find ways to recognize and appreciate which forms of talk are most mathematically productive for our students, and for a particular lesson or topic.

How Classroom Talk Promotes Student Learning

Classroom talk may support and promote student learning in mathematics both directly and indirectly. Classroom dialogue may provide direct access to ideas, relationships among those ideas, strategies, procedures, facts, mathematical history, and more. Through classroom discourse, all of these aspects of mathematical thinking can be discussed, dissected, and understood. Classroom dialogue also supports student learning indirectly, through the building of a social environment—a community—that encourages learning. Through classroom discourse of certain types, students are encouraged to treat one another as equal partners in thinking, conjecturing, exploring, and sharing ideas. Mutual respect is fostered when norms exist that set expectations for respectful and civil discourse.

These two results of talk, direct and indirect learning, are of equal importance. If we use talk to establish a supportive learning environment, but we do not succeed in creating productive talk about the actual content of mathematics, our students are not as likely to succeed in learning the mathematics we want them to know. On the other hand, if we fail to build a supportive learning environment—one in which students can talk about their mathematical thinking without fear of ridicule—then many students will not participate at all. Throughout this book we address both the social aspects and the content-focused aspects of productive classroom talk.

Cognitive Aspects of Student Talk in Mathematics Learning

We've all experienced learning about a concept by listening to a teacher talk about it. After we listen to the teacher we may feel that we understand the concept. However, when asked to put the concept into words, we may discover that our understanding is not as deep as we thought. We may become inarticulate, even speechless. We don't yet have the understanding necessary to put the idea into words. Yet unless we are put in a situation where we must talk or write clearly about the concept, we may never come to realize that our knowledge is insufficient.

How can we push learners beyond incomplete, shallow, or passive understanding? One way is to incorporate into lessons student talk about the concept that they are trying to understand. Asking students to talk about mathematical concepts, procedures, and problem solving helps them understand more deeply and with greater clarity. It can make clear to them what they do and do not understand, and what other students think about these same issues. Often the first step in setting out to learn something involves realizing that you don't understand it. And sometimes it is this first step that is most difficult to elicit from our students. Getting students to talk about mathematical ideas or procedures can bring to the surface their gaps in understanding. It's important to note that the students are not the only beneficiaries of hearing their own thinking made public. Such talk also allows teachers to hear students' misconceptions and thus identify what students do and don't understand.

There are other benefits as well. Certain forms of talk may promote specific kinds of reasoning. For example, discussion, either in small groups or with the whole class, can play a critical part in helping students improve their ability to reason logically. Many people think that logical abilities are something we are born with (or born without), and that teachers cannot do much to change them. In fact, many researchers claim that logical reasoning can be strongly affected by teaching. The basic components of logical reasoning can be very effectively taught in the context of a discussion. For example, in a discussion, when one student makes a claim, the teacher can ask for evidence to support the claim. The examples or counterexamples to the claim can then be discussed and taken apart by the group. Each student hears the reasoning of others and can make a contribution when ready to do so. In this way students gradually learn how to make and support arguments.

We all know that humans learn through observing, listening, and doing. Allowing students to talk about mathematical thinking and problem solving gives them more to observe, more to listen to, and more chances to participate in mathematical thinking. When we give students a text to read, we allow them time to read it more than once, to consider the details. Yet we often forget that when we are talking to the class, presenting new material or explaining, our words and ideas swiftly pass by. Students can't call them back and reflect on them to reconsider ideas, pose questions, or work out details. By carefully incorporating certain kinds of discourse in the mathematics classroom, however, we give students time and space to consider more deeply the content we expect them to learn and to revisit what has just been said.

Finally, talk gives students practice in reflecting on their own thinking processes. Expert thinkers are able to coordinate the ideas and understandings inside their heads with ideas and information outside, in the world. When engaged in thinking or solving problems, expert thinkers keep track of their moment-to-moment understanding or lack of understanding. When they realize that they don't understand something, they immediately address their confusion by asking a question, or stopping the process completely until they find a way to address what they don't understand. But this ability to expertly adapt and respond to one's own internal processing does not develop overnight. Students need a great deal of practice to become expert thinkers in this respect. And in the context of a lecture or recitation, they do not get any practice in this particular *self-regulative* aspect of thinking. Based on our experience, we have concluded that certain kinds of discourse practices support the development of expert thinkers.

Social Aspects of Student Talk in Mathematics Learning

In the world of adults, mathematical and scientific work are often carried out by groups of people working together. The ability to communicate clearly and precisely is essential. But this ability—like all the capacities previously mentioned—does not develop overnight. It takes many years of striving to make oneself clear to others. Finally, it takes motivation, and we all know adults who do not seem interested in communicating clearly with others.

As teachers, how can we encourage our students to do the hard work necessary to become clear communicators? In order to make the effort to communicate clearly, people need the motivation of knowing that others want to hear what they have to say. A number of researchers have observed that certain forms of classroom discourse seem to motivate students to make their thoughts clear. If students know that the teacher and their classmates will hold them accountable for making themselves clear, many of them will make great efforts to do the best they can to be clear and comprehensible.

Another benefit of classroom talk is to build students' confidence about their own ability to engage in intellectual discussion. Some students have not engaged in intellectual discussion before and may find it stressful to talk in front of their classmates. Students bring with them to school a great variety of experiences in using talk to explore intellectual topics. In some communities, for example, it is considered normal and desirable for children to engage in argument and discussion with adults. Such children may have more confidence in the value of their own ways of expressing their thoughts. In fact, it may be hard to stop them from taking the floor! In other communities, children are not supposed to assert themselves in this way—it might be considered rude, pushy, or obnoxious. In such communities, adults may be entitled to discuss their thoughts, while children are considered apprentices. There are many cultural variations: in some communities such behavior may be considered acceptable for boys, but not for girls. In any case, children who have been taught that they should take an observer's role in intellectual discussions may find it challenging or even upsetting to take an active role in a classroom discussion.

Nevertheless, to engage in serious mathematical and scientific work in high school, college, and beyond, a person must be able to assert him or herself in ways that are expected by members of those communities. In fact, some students leave the serious study of mathematics and science in high school or college because they find the intellectual discourse intimidating or uncomfortable. We have found that helping students learn to talk in the ways valued by scientists and mathematicians results in real changes in how students present their thoughts and ideas, and in how they feel about themselves as thinkers. We believe it will eventually help them do well in advanced high school and college courses, where the subject matter requires students to feel at home with scientific and logical argumentation.

When a teacher succeeds in setting up a classroom in which students feel obligated to listen to one another, to make their own contributions clear and comprehensible, and to provide evidence for their claims, that teacher has set in place a powerful context for student learning. Over time, students come to value their classmates' contributions and strive to make their own contributions of value to others. The class as a whole develops an understanding about values held by mathematicians and scientists all over the world: precision, clarity, intellectual honesty, effort, and thoroughness. But to accomplish this takes effort, planning, and many months of work.

CHAPTER

2

The Tools of Classroom Talk

As teachers, we elicit responses from our students in various ways—with questions, commands, hints, jokes, and so on. When students become familiar with our inventory of phrases and expressions, they usually know what we expect of them. Although we rarely stop to think about our most common conversational prompts, they are among our most important instructional tools. From our work in Project Challenge, we have found it useful to think carefully about these tools: it matters what you say and how you say it.

In this chapter we present a number of examples of talk in action in mathematics lessons and describe the tools that teachers use to implement classroom talk. The tools include strategies—what we call "talk moves"—that support mathematical thinking, talk formats that provide different ways to organize students for conversation, and ideas for creating a classroom where respect and equal access to participation are valued norms. Narrative examples, or cases, illustrate how the basic tools of talk look in action in four different classrooms.

Five Productive Talk Moves

In this section we introduce five talk moves that we return to repeatedly throughout the book. Each move is a suggested action that we have found to be effective for making progress toward achieving our instructional goal of supporting mathematical thinking and learning. For each, we describe the move, give a brief classroom example to illustrate it, and then explain the teacher action required. Each move serves various purposes, and we describe some of those purposes in this chapter. However, you will discover other purposes for the moves in later chapters, and you may even discover some new purposes as you implement these moves in your own classroom. (It's important to note that these five moves are not the only ones that teachers can use to support productive mathematical talk. However, we focus here on these five as they provide a solid base on which to begin.)

Revoicing. ("So you're saying that it's an odd number?")
When students talk about mathematics, it's often very difficult to understand what they say. Even if their reasoning is sound, it may not appear sound when they try to put their thoughts into words. Sometimes it's impossible to tell whether what they have said makes sense at all. And if you as the teacher have trouble understanding it, there's not much hope that the student's classmates will do any better. Yet given your goals of improving the mathematical thinking of all students, you cannot give up on an especially unclear student. If the only students whose contributions are taken seriously are those who are easy to understand, few students will ever improve. Deep thinking and powerful reasoning do not always correlate with clear verbal expression.

Therefore, teachers need a talk move that can help them deal with the inevitable lack of clarity of many student contributions. They need a tool that will allow them to interact with the student in a way that will continue to involve that student in clarifying his or her own reasoning. And they need a tool that will help other students continue to follow along in the face of the confusion. One such tool has been called "revoicing." In a revoicing move, the teacher essentially tries to repeat some or all of what the student has said, and then asks the student to respond and verify whether or not the teacher's revoicing is correct, as in the dialogue below.

Ms. Davies has given her third graders a series of numbers, and in a whole-group discussion has asked them to say whether the numbers are even or odd. They have established that if you can divide a number by two evenly, then it is an even number. Philipe has tackled the number 24. His contribution is less than completely clear.

1. Philipe: Well, if we could use three, then it could go into that, but three is odd. So then if it was . . . but . . . three is even. I mean odd. So if it's odd, then it's not even.

2. Ms. D: OK, let me see if I understand. So you're saying that twenty-four is an odd number?

3. Philipe: Yeah. Because three goes into it, because twenty-four divided by three is eight.

After hearing Philipe's confusing contribution, all Ms. Davies could grasp was that Philipe *might* be saying that 24 is odd. She hazards a guess in the form of a revoicing move: "So you're saying that twenty-four is an odd number?" By phrasing this guess as a question, she is essentially asking Philipe if her understanding is correct. By using this move, she gives him a chance to clarify. As it works out, he shows that he did intend to claim that 24 is an odd number, and he gives his reason. By opening this conversational space for Philipe to respond, Ms. Davies has learned that he has a basic misconception about even and odd numbers. She has gained a foothold in the discussion that she did not have after simply hearing Philipe's first contribution.

While revoicing is especially useful in situations such as that described with Philipe, it's also an effective move when you understand what a student has said but aren't sure that the other students in the class understand. Revoicing can make one student's idea available to others, give them time to hear it again, position a student's claim with respect to a previous student's claim in order to create the basis for an ongoing discussion, or focus on a change that has occurred in the discussion. Revoicing provides more "thinking space" and can help all students track what is going on mathematically.

Asking students to restate someone else's reasoning.
("Can you repeat what he just said in your own words?")
In the example above, the revoicing move was used by the teacher. However, the teacher can also extend the move to students, by asking one student to repeat or rephrase what another student has said, and then immediately following up with the first student. Ms. Davies used this move to continue the classroom conversation.

4. Ms. D: Can anyone repeat what Philipe just said in his or her own words? Miranda?

5. Miranda: Um, I think I can. I think he said that twenty-four is odd, because it can be divided by three.

6. Ms. D: Is that right, Philipe? Is that what you said?

7. Philipe: Yes.

This move has several potential benefits. First, it gives the rest of the class another rendition of the first student's contribution. It gives them more time to process Philipe's statement, and adds to the likelihood that they will follow the conversation and understand his point. It thereby supports the teacher's goal of giving all students full access to participation. This move is particularly valuable for students whose first language is not English. Second, this move provides evidence that the other students could and did hear what Philipe said. This is important: if students could not or did not hear what a speaker said, they cannot easily participate in further exchanges. Finally, it yet again clarifies the claim that Philipe is making and provides Philipe with evidence that his thinking is being taken seriously. Over time, as students come to realize that people are listening closely to what they say, they increasingly make efforts to make their contributions comprehensible.

Asking students to apply their own reasoning to someone else's reasoning. ("Do you agree or disagree and why?")
After a student has made a claim, and the teacher has made sure that students have heard it and have had time to process it, she can move on to elicit student reasoning about the claim. Ms. Davies employs this move to pursue the issue.

8. Ms. D: Miranda, do you agree or disagree with what Philipe said?

9. Miranda: Well, I sort of . . . like, I disagree?

10. Ms. D: Can you tell us why you disagree with what he said? What's your reasoning?

11. Miranda: Because I thought that we said yesterday that you could divide even numbers by two. And I think you can divide twenty-four by two. And it's twelve. So isn't that even?

By asking Miranda whether she agrees or disagrees with Philipe's claim and why, Ms. Davies is directing attention to Miranda's reasoning. Note that Ms. Davies has refrained from supporting one or the other position. At this point she is using talk moves to elicit respectful discussion of ideas. Later on, as students more fully understand the issues, Ms. Davies can make sure that they converge on the correct understanding of even numbers.

It's important to note that Ms. Davies does not simply ask whether Miranda agrees or disagrees but then follows up by asking her to explain why. As with the revoicing move, asking students to explain their reasoning is a key part of this move, and is critical in general to supporting students' mathematical learning. The point of this move is to cause students to make explicit their reasoning by applying their thinking to someone else's contribution. Therefore, she prompts Miranda to explain *why* she disagrees.

Prompting students for further participation.
("Would someone like to add on?")

At this point Ms. Davies increases participation in the discussion by asking for further commentary. First she uses the move of revoicing again as a way to clarify the two positions that have emerged, and to model how to talk respectfully to the originators of the two positions. Then she asks others to contribute, prompting them to either state agreement or disagreement, or to add other comments. This prompting for more input on previous statements will, over time, result in students showing more willingness to weigh in on what the group is considering.

12.	Ms. D:	So we have two different ideas here about the number twenty-four. Philipe, you're saying that twenty-four is odd because you can divide it by three?
13.	Philipe:	Uh-huh.
14.	Ms. D:	And Miranda, you're saying that it's even because you can divide it by two? Is that correct?
15.	Miranda:	Yes.
16.	Ms. D:	OK, so what about other people? Who would like to add to this discussion? Do you agree or disagree with Miranda's or Philipe's ideas? Tell us what you think, or add on other comments or insights.

Using wait time. ("Take your time . . . we'll wait . . .")

The final talk move we mention in this chapter is not actually speech at all, but silence! Many teachers are familiar with the important finding that after having asked a question, a teacher should wait at least ten seconds for students to think before calling on someone for an answer. Wait time also comes into play after a student has been called on. After a teacher has called on a particular student, that student should be given at least the same amount of time to organize his or her thoughts.

In the exchange above, after Ms. Davies has presented the class with a summary of Miranda's and Philipe's competing positions, and has asked for additional input, she waits . . . and waits . . . and waits. One or two students raise a hand immediately. Others look thoughtful, but don't volunteer. After five seconds, the students see that Ms. Davies is waiting for more responses. These students know that in their classroom it is not always the same super-fast two or three students who will answer all the questions. They know that Ms. Davies will wait until a number of them think through her question.

After fifteen or twenty seconds, slowly, other hands go up. After forty-five seconds, Ms. Davies finally calls on Eduardo. He is hesitant, and actually sits silent after she calls on him even though his hand has been raised. So again, Ms. Davies waits. Ten seconds go by. Finally, the student responds:

17. Eduardo: Yes, I agree with Miranda's idea, because the only way you told us to find out if something is even is to divide by two. And if we divide twenty-four by three, we can also divide it by four. And we can divide it by six, too. So I think we should stick with two only.

By waiting patiently, Ms. Davies has made it possible for Eduardo, a second-language learner, to make an important contribution that she and other students can build on in the ensuing discussion. But this move is not easy for her. Although the research is clear on the value of wait time, it is actually quite difficult to adopt consistently. We all tend to feel uncomfortable with silence, not wanting to put a student on the spot. Yet few students can speedily put together an answer to a complicated question about their own reasoning. So if we do not use wait time consistently and patiently, students give up and fail to participate, knowing that they cannot "beat the clock." In later chapters we again address this and related moves designed to give students the time they need to think and reason mathematically.

Three Productive Talk Formats

Along with thinking about talk moves that guide students' learning, it's also useful to consider the talk formats available to teachers. Talk formats are different ways that teachers configure classroom interaction for instruction. For example, Ms. Davies took advantage of all five talk moves and used the talk format of whole-class discussion, having her entire class participate together in mathematical thinking and reasoning. Every classroom teacher makes use of a variety of talk formats, and these formats are among the major tools that teachers use to accomplish their goals for student learning. Each format carries with it certain opportunities and certain limitations.

Each format has its own "rules for talk." Some of these rules are rarely discussed, but students know them, nevertheless. For example, in the traditional and familiar talk format that we might label *direct instruction* or, in the higher grades, *lecturing*, the rules go something like this: the teacher has the right to talk, and students must not talk unless the teacher calls out their name. *Quizzing* is another commonly used talk format in which the teacher asks questions for which he or she knows the answers and expects the students to know the answers as well. The rules are as follows: the teacher calls on a student and evaluates the answer given as to its correctness. "Jamie, how much is three times eight?" "Twenty-four?" "Good." In research on classroom talk this is called the IRE format, for *initiation* (by the teacher), *response* (by the student), and *evaluation* (by the teacher). Other talk formats include *sharing time, group recitation,* and *student presentations.*

While there are many academic purposes that may be served by using these formats for mathematics instruction, in this book we focus on three talk formats—whole-class discussion, small-group discussion, and partner talk. We have found these talk formats to be particularly helpful in maximizing opportunities for mathematical learning by all students.

Whole-class discussion.

The talk format that appears most prominently in this book is whole-class discussion. In this talk format, the teacher is in charge of the class, just as in direct instruction. However, in whole-class discussion, the teacher is not primarily engaged in delivering information or quizzing. Rather, he or she is attempting to get students to share their thinking, explain the steps in their reasoning, and build on one another's contributions. These whole-class discussions give students the chance to engage in sustained reasoning. The teacher facilitates and guides quite actively, but does not focus on providing answers directly. Instead, the focus is on the students' thinking.

It takes students a great deal of practice to become solid and confident mathematical thinkers, and this talk format provides a space for that practice. In whole-class discussion, the teacher often refrains from providing the correct answer. He or she does not reject incorrect reasoning, but instead attempts to get students to explore the steps in their reasoning, with the aim that they will gain practice in discovering where their thinking falls short. Invariably, these discussions reveal many examples of faulty reasoning, mistakes in computation, and misunderstandings. These flaws, however, are the raw material with which teachers can work to guide students' mathematical learning. And, in the process, students become more confident in their ability to stick with making sense of concepts, skills, and problems. They gradually lose some of the anxiety and avoidance behaviors that many students display when confronted with complex mathematical ideas.

The purpose of whole-class discussion is to provide students with practice in mathematical reasoning that will further their mathematical learning. To accomplish this, the focus is on the students' ideas, not on the correctness of their answers. This does not mean that we are advising teachers to de-emphasize correct answers and mathematical truth. In our view, the ultimate goal is for students to achieve mathematical power through precision, accuracy, insight, and reliable reasoning. However, we have found that it's important for students to have opportunities to practice their reasoning in discussions without an immediate focus on correct answers.

How can students' learning of mathematics be supported if teachers don't let them know when their thinking is misguided or an answer is incorrect? Aren't there times when it's better to tell students when their answer or idea is wrong? To answer these questions, it's important to think about what learning of mathematics involves. More specifically, when confronted with any new mathematical concept or skill, it's important to consider where the source of the knowledge is for the student.

Sometimes the source of mathematical knowledge lies outside a student and the only way that a student can have access to the knowledge is from an external source, such as a book, a television program, the teacher, or another student. For example, the mathematical symbols we use to represent ideas are socially agreed upon conventions, and the source of learning these symbols lies outside the student. There is no way for a student to "discover" the meaning of a plus sign—we show it to students and tell them what it means. The same is true for the operation signs for subtraction, multiplication, and division, for the relational symbols for equal, greater than, less than, even for the way we write the numerals. These symbols have no meanings that are inherent to them but rather are mathematical conventions that we all agree to use for ease of representing and communicating mathematical ideas. The same is true for the terminology we apply to mathematical ideas—*triangle, prime number, even, fraction*, and so on. When mathematical knowledge is linked to social conventions, direct instruction is appropriate for furthering students' learning.

When mathematical concepts and skills are not linked to social conventions, but rather, have their own internal logic, the source of knowledge is not external to the student. Instead, students learn by processing information, applying reasoning, hearing ideas from others, and connecting new thinking to what they already know, all for the goal of making sense for themselves of new concepts and skills. The source of the knowledge, of creating new understanding, lies within the student, and making sense is the key. We can tell a student, for example, that the order of the numbers in a multiplication problem doesn't alter the answer, that 2×5, for example, produces the same product as does 5×2. But this is an idea that students can figure out for themselves, from experimenting with problems, thinking about what happens to the products when factors are reversed, and then talking about their ideas, as the students in Mrs. Schuster's class did in the example presented in Chapter 1.

Dictating to students in direct instruction is not appropriate for teaching ideas for which the source of the knowledge is inside the student. In order for children to learn, understand , and remember, they need experiences interacting with the idea, thinking about it in relation to what they already know, uncovering its logic, and then applying their thinking to this new idea. Using talk in a whole-class discussion provides students the opportunity to make sense of new ideas. Such discussions may also reveal students' confusion, partial understandings, and misconceptions, important information for teachers to have when planning instruction. Explaining their reasoning is important for all students as it helps them to cement and even extend their thinking. Over the long run, we have seen that being asked "Why do you think that?" has profound effects on students' mathematical thinking and on their "habits of mind" in general.

Small-group discussion.

In this book we make a distinction between whole-class discussion and small-group discussion. In the small-group-discussion format, the teacher typically gives students a question to discuss among themselves, in groups of three to six. While the rules for whole-class talk formats are generally familiar to students, students need help becoming familiar and comfortable with the rules for small-group discussion, since multiple conversations occur. In this format, the teacher circulates as groups discuss and doesn't control the discussions, but observes and interjects. The teacher necessarily plays a diminished role and therefore cannot ensure that the talk will be productive. Students can spend time on off-task talk, and there is no guarantee that students will treat one another in an equitable manner. This format has many important functions in mathematics class. However, it figures less prominently in this book. Our focus here is on how teachers can actively create conditions for talk that will be reliably productive in terms of mathematical thinking and reasoning.

Partner talk.

Small-group discussion is distinct from what we call *partner talk*. In this talk format, the teacher asks a question and then gives students a short time, perhaps a minute or two at the most, to put their thoughts into words with their nearest neighbor. This format has several benefits: students who are keeping up with the lesson but are hesitant about voicing their thoughts will have a chance to practice their contribution with just one conversational partner. Students who have not understood completely can bring up their questions with the partner, and perhaps formulate a way to ask them to the class. For many students, particularly those who are learning English as a second language, this one- or two-minute aside is invaluable. They can emerge from the partner talk ready to participate in the whole-group discussion. When wait time doesn't increase the number of students willing to talk, changing the talk format to partner talk can help. A teacher can initiate partner talk by saying to the class, "Turn and talk about this with the person next to you." This results in a much noisier class, but the noise has benefits as more students think out loud. After a few moments, the teacher can stop the partner talk and return to the format of whole-class discussion.

Ground Rules for Respectful Talk and Equitable Participation

First and foremost, before any talk moves can be implemented, the teacher must establish ground rules for respectful and courteous talk. You will not be able to use successfully the moves described previously unless you have established a classroom culture in which students listen to one another with respect. If students are afraid that their ideas will be ridiculed, they will not talk freely, no matter what inducements you offer. They must feel that their classroom is a safe place to express their thoughts. Therefore, your first steps in creating the conditions for productive classroom talk must involve setting up some clear ground rules for interaction. It is very important to put this step first. Even one hostile or disrespectful interchange can put a serious damper on students' willingness to talk openly about their ideas and thoughts. It is imperative that you consistently maintain the ground rules for respectful and courteous talk, and that your students know that there will be no exceptions.

The ground rules must center on each student's obligation to treat one another with respect. No name-calling or derogatory noises or remarks are ever allowed. "I was just joking" cannot be an acceptable defense for a disrespectful remark, and students must know that you will hold them to a high standard. There must be clear consequences for violation of these rules. You may need to remind students of these rules every day until they become a routine part of your classroom culture. We recommend creating a poster or wall chart and prominently displaying it so that you can make reference to it when necessary.

As you establish the conditions for respectful and courteous talk, you will also need to set the conditions for full participation: all students must have the opportunity to engage in productive talk about mathematics. This means that you must make sure of three things: (1) that every student is listening to what others say, (2) that every student can hear what others say, and (3) that every student may participate by speaking out at some point.

As part of your ground rules for respectful and courteous talk, you no doubt will have put in place a rule that obligates students to listen attentively as others talk. This is respectful behavior, but just as important, it is pragmatic behavior. It enables students to participate in the ongoing talk. If they do not know what was just said, they cannot possibly build on it. While establishing these ground rules may sound difficult, many teachers have had success within the first few weeks or months of teaching this way. In Chapter 9 we introduce specific suggestions to help you put these norms in place.

Four Cases: What Docs Productive Talk Look Like?

The following narrative examples, or cases, show you how talk moves look in action in the classroom. These cases, or examples, are composites based on actual classes we have taught or observed. The examples in this chapter are from grades one, three, five, and six. Each case begins with a brief description of the mathematical ideas or problems that are central to the lesson, along with a description of what the class has done so far. We then present the interaction in the form of a script, tracking the teacher's and students' contributions to the conversation.

Case 1. ("I disagree with Juana's solution because four won't work.")

In Ms. Day's third-grade class, the students had been finding solutions for pairs of equations that are number sentences in which unknowns are indicated by squares and triangles. For each pair of equations, students must figure out one value for the square and one value for the triangle that makes both sentences true. For example, in this case, students had been considering the two number sentences shown below and have been asked to figure out what values of the square and triangle make both equations true.

$$10 - \square = \triangle$$
$$\square + \square + \triangle = 13$$

In order for both sentences to be true, the square must have a value of 3 and the triangle must have a value of 7.

A problem like this is useful for a number of reasons. First, it gives children practice with arithmetic as they try out different numbers to make both sentences true. Second, it provides children early exposure to two ideas that are central to algebraic thinking—finding a value for an unknown, and finding a solution that simultaneously solves two different equations. Third, the problem is accessible to almost all students because it can be solved using a guess-and-check strategy. Third graders have no way to manipulate these equations algebraically, so they have to start with the strategy of guessing two numbers that might work, and plugging them in to check whether they do work. Finally, because there are two number sentences for which the numbers must work, students must perform the logical operation of checking whether the numbers they choose work for both sentences.

Ms. Day knows that some of the students understand that they are finding a solution that works for both equations, while others do not. Although she has explained to them that the value they choose for the square and triangle must remain the same for both sentences, many of them do not seem to comprehend her explanation fully. She decides to use a session of classroom talk to help them.

First, Ms. Day gives the students five minutes to work on the problem individually. As they work, she circulates through the room looking over their shoulders. She notices that Juana has not grasped the connection between the two number sentences, while Jaleesa has already solved the problem. David seems to be wavering between treating each number sentence as an isolated problem and connecting the two as one system to be solved. Ms. Day refrains from giving students any assistance during this time. After the five minutes are up, she starts the whole-class discussion session with a statement:

1. Ms. D: I'd like someone to explain the solution you got, and I'll write it on the board. Then we can see who agrees, who disagrees, who has the same answer, or who has a different answer. Juana, what was your solution?

2. Juana: Umm, I think the square can be six, and then the triangle is four.

3. Ms. D: [Writes on the board:] $\square$ = 6, $\triangle$ = 4. OK, so tell us what your reasoning is.

4. Juana: Well, if you put them in the sentence, then ten minus six is four.

5. Ms. D: OK, so let's hear what people think. Did other people get the same answer, a different answer, or what do you think

about what Juana said? Jaleesa, your hand is up. Did you agree or disagree with Juana's solution? And tell us why.

6. Jaleesa: Well, I sort of disagree, because four doesn't work.

7. Ms. D: Hmm, so you think four doesn't work. But look, in this sentence here, it does work. Juana says the square is equal to six. Ten minus the square, which is six, equals the triangle, which is four. That works, right? So what doesn't work? I'm confused. Can someone else explain what Jaleesa is saying? How about you, David?

8. David: I think I know what Jaleesa is saying. She's saying that four doesn't work in the *second* sentence—square plus square plus triangle equals thirteen.

9. Ms. D: So, Jaleesa, is that what you were saying?

10. Jaleesa: Yes, because in the second sentence if you use four for the triangle then the two squares will have to equal up to nine and that can't work. Because in the first one they're six.

11. Ms. D: Wait, I'm not sure I'm following that. I'm a little confused here. You're going kind of fast. David, do you want to try to say what Jaleesa said in your own words?

12. David: OK, I think she means that the triangle number has to be the same number for the first sentence *and* the second sentence. And the square number has to be the same for both sentences too. So if you put four in for the triangle on the first sentence, then you have to put four in for the triangle on the second sentence. And that won't work.

13. Ms. D: That won't work? Is that what you meant, Jaleesa?

14. Jaleesa: Yes, because . . . can I show you on the board?

15. Ms. D: Sure. Come on up.

Notice that Ms. Day has used the talk move of revoicing in several different ways here. In Line 7 she asks David to revoice Jaleesa's position, and then she herself completes the revoicing move by asking Jaleesa, in Line 9, if he is correct in his summary of her position. In Line 11, she models confusion, and asks him to once again "put it into his own words." Then she again checks with Jaleesa. By the time Jaleesa comes to the board, her own position has become clearer to her and she is eager to share it.

16. Jaleesa: OK. [She writes on the board:]

$$\boxed{10} - \triangle\!\!\!/6 = 4$$

OK, this one works. But now we have to put the same numbers in the second sentence and it has to work too. [She writes:]

$$\boxed{6} + \boxed{6} + \boxed{4} = 13$$

But this one doesn't work. [She sits down.]

17. Ms. D: OK. Hmm. So Juana, what do you think about that? Do you agree or disagree with what Jaleesa said? And tell us why.

18. Juana: Well, I guess I didn't think that we had to put the same numbers in both sentences. I thought we could use different ones.

19. Ms. D: Yes, this kind of problem is harder than just filling in one sentence, isn't it? We have to fill in two at the same time! We have to make sure that both sentences are true. Let's do another one. This time you can spend three minutes working with the person next to you. [Ms. Day writes two different equations on the board:]

$$\square - \triangle = 15$$
$$\square + \triangle + \triangle = 21$$

Recognizing and understanding the teacher's moves

A great deal is going on in this series of exchanges. Let's focus on the teacher's purposes and her use of talk. While many teachers already use the instructional strategy of asking students to share their solution to a problem, our focus in this case is on Ms. Day's use of talk to bring the students to a common ground of understanding. She knew that not all students had understood the constraints of the problem, even though she had done her best to explain it. Her immediate purpose was to clarify one aspect of the math problem: the problem solver has to consider *both* sentences simultaneously in order to find a valid solution. She had observed that some students, like Jaleesa, understood this. Some students, like David, were wavering. And still others, like Juana, did not understand this constraint.

This situation, where different levels of understanding can be found side by side in the same class, is extremely common and is always a challenge. It is one reason that teachers sometimes shy away from carrying out a whole-class discussion. How can we have a discussion involving all students if only some of them understand the problem? But Ms. Day used the students' contributions in a systematic fashion to clarify a misconception that she suspected many students held, not just Juana.

So why did Ms. Day say what she did? Why did she call on the students she called on? Ms. Day first brought the misconception to the forefront by asking Juana to present her solution. She did not correct Juana, but asked the students in an open, neutral way whether anyone agreed or disagreed with the solution. She knew that Jaleesa would disagree, and would present some form of argument against Juana's claim. So she called on Jaleesa. Jaleesa did disagree, but did not provide a full explanation of why she disagreed with Juana's solution. Right after Jaleesa gave this partial explanation, Ms. Day expressed confusion.

Why does Ms. Day say in Line 11 that she is confused? Was she really confused? No, but she knew that other students were. Jaleesa's explanation was quick and Ms. Day knew that it would be difficult for some of the other students to follow. An explanation that cannot be understood is not worth much to the other students. In instances like these, the teacher must try to expand the time and space available for the class to understand what one student already knows. So here Ms. Day makes a skillful move: she brings a third student into the conversation, David, who is not entirely clear about the constraints of the problem. By asking him to revoice Jaleesa's explanation, she is hoping to draw him (and others) into Jaleesa's thinking and lead him to a fuller acceptance of the two-sentence constraint on the problem. Finally, after David helps construct a fuller explanation, Ms. Day returns to Juana, and allows her to revisit her original analysis. Then, by moving on to another, similar example, and allowing students to talk to one another as they solve it, Ms. Day is using talk in yet another way to solidify students' understanding.

Ms. Day's use of whole-class discussion

It takes students a great deal of practice to become solid and confident mathematical thinkers, and the talk format of whole-class discussion provides a space for that practice. Accordingly, within a class discussion, the teacher often refrains from providing the correct answer. The teacher does not reject incorrect reasoning, but instead attempts to get students to explore the steps in that reasoning, with the aim that they will gain practice in discovering where their reasoning falls short. In this case, Ms. Day did not correct Juana's misconception directly, but instead asked other students to react to what Juana had said. As we said earlier, whole-class discussions will reveal many examples of faulty reasoning, mistakes in computation, and misunderstandings. Ms. Day decided to use these as her raw material to help her students develop their problem-solving abilities.

When Ms. Day refrains from correcting the students in this part of the discussion, she is not losing sight of her ultimate goal: that her students achieve mathematical power through precision, accuracy, insight, and reliable reasoning. She knows, however, that her students need to practice their reasoning in complex problem solving without an immediate focus on the answer. After this discussion, Ms. Day will summarize and review the correct solutions, along with the generalizations that the group has made based on their discussion.

Case 2. ("This is a triangle because it just looks right.")
Ms. Sigler's first-grade students are learning about geometric figures. The students have been given a set of polygons to sort into two groups: triangles and other shapes. Within the set there are many different sizes and kinds of triangles, including scalene, equilateral, isosceles, and right triangles. The triangles are cut out of colored paper and are either red, green, or blue. Other shapes are also in the set—squares, rectangles, hexagons, and parallelograms. Students are working in groups of four. Ms. Sigler notices that one group of students has separated the equilateral triangles from all of the other triangles and grouped them alone. They have placed most of the other triangles in the "other" category.

  1. Ms. S: I see that you have separated the shapes. What is this group of shapes called? [Points to the set of equilateral triangles.]

  2. All: Triangles.

  3. Ms. S: I'd like each of you to explain your thinking to me. I'd like each of you to explain to me why all of the shapes in this group are triangles [points to the equilateral triangles] and all of these are not triangles [points to some triangles in the other group].

  4. Ollie: This [points to one equilateral triangle] just looks like a triangle.

  5. Ms. S: In what way?

  6. Ollie: It's short and fat and just looks right.

  7. Yoon So: Yeah. This one [points to a scalene triangle] is too skinny and pointy. It isn't a triangle.

  8. Ms. S: What do you think, Paul?

  9. Paul: Well, you know these are maybe triangles [indicates the group of equilateral triangles] because you know they just look like triangles.

 10. Ms. S: What does a triangle look like?

 11. Paul: Hummm. [Paul looks around the room and then points to a poster behind the door of geometric shapes. The shapes on

the poster are all regular polygons and the triangle on it is equilateral.] Like that one. See, triangles look like this [puts thumbs and forefingers together to make the shape of an equilateral triangle]. They're flat on the bottom.

12.	Ms. S:	Ollie, what did Paul just say?
13.	Ollie:	These are a triangle [uses his hands to make the same shape Paul made].
14.	Ms. S:	What else did he say?
15.	Ollie:	They have to sit on their bottoms—there aren't pointy parts on the bottom.
16.	Ms. S:	OK. Look at this. [She takes one of the large equilateral triangles from the triangle pile and turns it so a vertex is pointing downward.] Is this a triangle?
17.	Paul:	[Turns the triangle so it is sitting on a side.] Now it is.
18.	Ms. S:	Sim, you have been very quiet. What do you think? Is this a triangle? [Turns the equilateral triangle around so the point is again facing down.]
19.	Sim:	I don't think so. I don't know.
20.	Ms. S:	Why don't you think it's a triangle?
21.	Sim:	I don't know. [Long pause.] Maybe it is. Because I can turn it and it looks like a triangle.

Ms. Sigler has been asking each student in turn to justify their categorization of the equilateral triangles as the only "real" triangles. Ms. Sigler has seen that the children in this small group have a restricted idea of what a triangle is. This is quite typical for young children: their definitions for geometric shapes are based on their visual memory of their previous experiences with that shape. Equilateral triangles are typically used to illustrate the concept of "triangle." One teacher we know calls this the "Sesame Street" level of understanding geometric shapes.

Some readers might find this small-group interchange to be somewhat slow and laborious. Is the teacher really moving the children toward changing their understanding? Yes, but first she must assess what they believe, find out how they think about the question. And to do this, she is getting them to *externalize* their ideas by asking them each to speak in turn. Notice that with each new contribution, their low level of understanding gets a bit more obvious. Even though the teacher pushes them to justify their categorization of the triangles, they offer simplistic reasons like "it looks right." It doesn't seem that the talk is moving the group very far into new understandings, but at this stage Ms. Sigler does have a pretty clear picture of the level of this group's understanding. She sees that this classification task has not been an effective instructional activity up to this point.

The next day, Ms. Sigler brings out a large box of cardboard strips of different lengths, with holes at the ends, which can be fastened together by the use of brads. From the previous day's discussion she knows that the students are simply identifying the names of geometric shapes with a typical image. They are not considering the defining properties of a triangle, such as the fact that a triangle is any closed figure with three straight sides. She gives each child three strips from the box, and asks them to use the strips and the fasteners to create a triangle. In grouping the strips, she has made sure that all varieties of triangles—equilateral, isosceles, and scalene—will be produced by the students in the class.

After each child has made a triangle, Ms. Sigler tapes them all to the front board (see Figure 2–1). She then holds a large group discussion about the triangles.

1. Ms. S: Let's look at these. Does anybody notice anything about the shapes? Cecile?

2. Cecile: All of them are made from three strips.

3. Ms. S: Does anybody see a triangle that was made from more than three strips?

4. Students: No, no.
They're the same.
They all have three.

5. Ms. S: I notice that all of these triangles are not identical; they don't all look the same. How are they different? Pooja?

6. Pooja: Some of them are big and some are small.

7. Ms. S: What makes a triangle big or small? See these two triangles? [Mrs. Sigler takes one large triangle and one small triangle and places them next to each other on the board.] What did someone do to make them different?

8. Pooja: You use long strips to make the big one and short strips to make the small one.

9. Paul: Mine is the big one and I used the really long strips.

10. Ms. S: How many long strips did you use, Paul?

11. Paul: Three.

12. Ms. S: Who else made a big triangle? [Points to a couple of large

FIGURE 2–1   Triangles constructed using cardboard strips.

triangles on the board.] How many strips did you use?

13. Cristobal: I made that one over there. [Points to an isosceles triangle.] I used three strips.

14. Ms. S: Who made a small triangle?

15. Ben: I did! I used three strips, too!

16. Ali: Me, too. My triangle took three strips.

17. Ms. S: OK, so now let's use a word that people use to talk about some geometric shapes. We can use the word *side*. This triangle has three sides—one, two, three. [Ms. S points to each side as she counts.] How many sides does Ali's triangle have? [Here Ms. S points to Ali's triangle, a long and thin scalene triangle made with two longer strips and one short one.]

18. Ali: My triangle has three sides.

19. Marsha: But Ms. Sigler, I don't know if that's a triangle. It doesn't look like the triangles from yesterday.

20. Ms. S: That's an important question. Can somebody repeat for us what Marsha just said? Ali, can you repeat what Marsha just said?

21. Ali: She said that my triangle isn't really a triangle because it doesn't look like the ones we put in the triangle group yesterday.

22. Ms. S: Marsha, is that what you said?

23. Marsha: Yes, but I didn't mean that Ali's triangle wasn't a triangle. I just meant that it didn't match the ones from yesterday in our group.

24. Ms. S: OK, so Marsha has asked a really important question. Is this shape a triangle? And what about those triangles from yesterday? Remember yesterday, when we were sorting triangles? Some of you thought that a shape like this [points to

Ali's triangle] didn't belong in the same group with triangles that looked like this [points to an equilateral triangle on the board]. So we have a really important question here. Just what *is* a triangle?

Ms. Sigler has brought the discussion to a very important point: the children's attention is now focused on whether or not all of the shapes they have constructed are triangles. She now has several choices. She could tell them that Ali's shape is a triangle and ask them to figure out why. She could ask them what they think and see where the discussion leads. She could provide some direct instruction about the properties of triangles, starting with the fact that they have three sides and are closed figures and then asking the students to check whether all of the figures on the board meet those two conditions.

Ms. Sigler has succeeded in using classroom talk to bring these first graders to a point where they are ready to engage with the idea that triangles that are not equilateral triangles are also properly called triangles. What talk moves did Ms. Sigler use with these first graders? Notice that she asked many students to reiterate the idea that three strips are needed to make a triangle, even though everyone had agreed that all the shapes on the board had used three strips. Students need time to generalize important ideas; in this case they had to consider the fact that all of the different-looking shapes have three sides. Although this idea is less complex than those we describe in some other examples in this book, it's an important idea for these first graders. They deserve the time that it will take to make sure that everyone has made the same generalization.

The slow and gentle nature of the talk in this first-grade classroom is also reflected in other ways. Ms. Sigler lets these students spend time in their small groups, working with an activity while she circulates among the groups. Then she moves the activity to a whole-class format, making sure that all students have had a chance to think about and talk about the material that will be discussed in the large group.

Notice that although Ms. Sigler makes sure to give students time to consider the problem and to listen to one another, she does not shrink from difficult material. For example, Ms. Sigler does not hesitate to introduce correct mathematical terminology. She uses the term *geometric shapes* and she directs the students to use the word *side* when talking about their triangles. She could have spent even more time with this, particularly if she had had many English-language learners in the class.

Finally, it is important to note that even with these young children, Ms. Sigler allowed the students to consider her questions for quite some time without providing them with answers. She could have started the first day by simply telling the students that they were wrong in their categorizations, that all three-sided closed figures are triangles. In some situations one might want to proceed in this way, and we would not rule it out as an option. But Ms. Sigler chose the more indirect route, in the belief that letting students follow the ideas at their own pace and in their own way would more likely result in their being ready to face the question that Marsha brought up. Her ultimate aim is to use classroom talk to bring students to understand the criteria for what makes a shape a triangle, thereby moving them beyond their *Sesame Street* understanding of this geometric shape.

Case 3, Episode 1. ("So you drew a picture of the tarts?")

Ms. Stangle's fifth-grade class is focusing on a problem that is designed to give them experience with fractions:

> *Ms. Stangle wants to make peach tarts for her friends. She needs two-thirds of a peach for each tart and she has 10 peaches. What is the greatest number of tarts that she can make with 10 peaches?*

Ms. Stangle has the students work on the problem on their own for ten minutes. At the end of the ten minutes, she doesn't know what types of solutions students have come up with, because she had an unexpected visitor to the classroom and did not get a chance to circulate and look at their work. However, she expects that some students had difficulty setting up the problem, others had difficulty representing the facts accurately, and still others struggled with computation.

1. Ms. S: Who wants to present their solution? How about some hands here? OK, Marco.

2. Marco: Well, first I looked at them all and then I made lines on each one and then I counted.

3. Ms. S: Marco, I'm not really sure I follow you. It sounds like you drew a picture of the tarts and the peaches, is that right?

4. Marco: Well, yeah.

5. Ms. S: We can't really follow what you say about your solution unless we can see the picture in our minds. We have to be able to listen to you and really understand what you're describing. Would you like to tell us again about the details of what you drew?

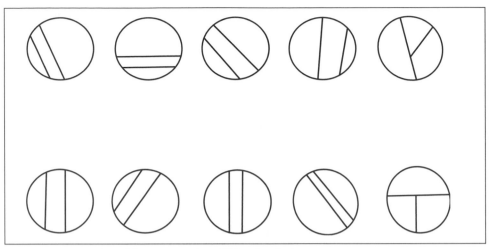

FIGURE 2–2 Ms. Stangle's representation of Marco's solution.

6. Marco: Um, OK. I drew the ten peaches and then I cut each one into three parts. Then I counted all the parts. So it was thirty parts. And the problem says that each tart needs two parts of a peach.

7. Ms. S: Hold on, I'm getting lost again. I thought the problem said . . . well, wait. So you're saying that I can take any two parts of a peach and that will be enough for a tart? Is that what you're saying?

8. Marco: Two of the three parts.

9. Ms. S: OK, so let me see if I can draw what you're describing. Here are my ten peaches [draws ten circles] and here I'm dividing each one into three parts [draws unequal partitions of each peach; see Figure 2–2]. Did anyone else have a picture like this?

10. Students: Nooo!
Wait!
Not like that!

11. Ms. S: No? How come [innocently looking surprised]? What's wrong with this? I've cut each peach into three parts.

12. Ginny: No, it has to be equal or it won't be thirds.

13. Ms. S: Oh, so the problem says it has to be thirds? Is that right?

14. Ginny: Yes.

15. Ms. S: OK, so Marco do you want to add to your statement of your solution?

16. Marco: OK. I drew ten peaches and I drew lines that cut them

into *equal* thirds! And then I drew ten tarts and I matched them up.

Recognizing and understanding the teacher's moves

You might wonder why Ms. Stangle didn't just ask Marco to draw a picture on the board. After all, it's good mathematical practice to have students present their graphic representations to the class. What is Ms. Stangle trying to do here? Why is she subjecting the students to this ordeal of clarification? Why is she being so cautious in making sure that their meaning is absolutely clear? She could not be as obtuse as all that—surely she knew that Marco knew he was counting thirds, not just random parts of a peach.

In our work we have found that one of the most effective ways to increase students' attention to precise language is to engage in just such episodes as the fragment previously presented. When the teacher sets a high criterion for clarity, when she herself "fails" to understand what the students are saying until they are utterly clear, she is modeling for them an attention to detail in language that will serve them in a variety of ways. Experiences like these will eventually lead students to use language more precisely, because it raises their level of awareness of the audience. They will also begin to similarly scrutinize the language of others. We have seen this kind of awareness lead to clear gains in reading comprehension, both in mathematics and in English language arts.

In this excerpt Ms. Stangle skillfully uses the technique of revoicing. She repeats what the student has said, clarifying, adding, or making more obvious some problematic feature of it. She then asks the student whether that is the correct interpretation. In the first few lines, she uses this conversational move in order to get Marco to clarify his first statement from Line 2. Like many students, Marco is not particularly skilled at anticipating what his audience will need. An outsider to the classroom would not understand him when he says, "Well, first I looked at them all and then I made lines on each one and then I counted." And although the other students have been working on the same problem, there is no guarantee that their solutions look the same. Therefore, Marco's description has to be clear enough for others to envision exactly what he has done, and to connect it to what they have done.

Ms. Stangle could have asked Marco to draw his picture on the board, and in fact she often has a student do just that. But in this excerpt, she skillfully uses classroom discourse to get Marco to reach a higher level of verbal precision. In Line 9, she takes his words literally and draws a picture that matches what he has said (although it does not match his intentions). As other students see the discrepancy, they understand the problem and want to correct it.

Case 3, Episode 2. ("Thirds of tarts or thirds of peaches?")

17. Ms. S: Can somebody repeat what Marco did for his solution so far? Cheryl?

18. Cheryl: I think he said he drew a picture of the ten tarts, and then he, like, drew a picture of the ten peaches. Then he cut the tarts into three pieces each. And he drew, like, lines to the peaches.

19. Ms. S: OK, so does everyone agree with Cheryl's rendition of what Marco said? Was that what Marco said? Does anyone want to weigh in here? Ginny?

20. Ginny: Well, it was almost the same, but Cheryl said that Marco drew ten tarts and cut them into three pieces each. And I think he said that he drew ten *peaches* and cut them into three pieces, three thirds, each.

21. Ms. S: So Marco, would you clarify? Which one did you do? Did you cut the tarts into thirds in your picture or did you cut the peaches into thirds?

22. Marco: Umm . . . I'm not sure now.

23. Ms. S: OK, who can help out? Did anyone else have a picture where they divided either the tarts or the peaches into thirds? Tyavanna?

24. Tyavanna: I drew ten peaches? And . . . um . . . like . . . um, I think that's what you have to do because you have to show the thirds of the peaches? 'Cause that's what you have to figure out to make the tarts. Not the other way around.

25. Ms. S: OK, can somebody repeat what Tyavanna just said? Kenny, can you repeat it in your own words?

26. Kenny: Well, I think she's saying that we have to draw pictures of the ten peaches so we can draw the thirds of each peach. She's saying we don't have to draw thirds of each tart. But I didn't draw the peaches at all.

27. Ms. S: OK, so you did it a different way? Will you tell us how you started out?

28. Kenny: I wrote the fraction *three-thirds* and I wrote it once for each peach. Then I added up all the three-thirds and I got thirty-thirds. So then I knew how many thirds I had to work with. Then I knew that each tart had to have two thirds, so I just divided two into thirty and I got fifteen. So I knew there could be fifteen tarts.

Recognizing and understanding the teacher's moves

Notice how at the beginning of episode two, in Line 17, Ms. Stangle asks Cheryl to repeat what Marco said. This move quickly puts students on notice that they must listen to their classmates' contributions and cannot simply sit and wait for their turn. They must actively engage in trying to understand what others are saying. In fact, Cheryl incorrectly repeats what Marco said, perhaps because she does not understand or perhaps because she has made a simple speech error. We do not know which is the reason for her error, and neither does Ms. Stangle. Nevertheless, Ms. Stangle brings other students into the process of clarifying and correcting. As part of this process, she asks Tyavanna to explain her understanding, and Tyavanna is able to shed some light on the situation.

Why does Ms. Stangle choose to ask Kenny to repeat what Tyavanna has said (Line 25)? Is it because she thinks he isn't listening and she wants to call him back? Or is it because she wants to make sure that all students have heard and understood what Tyavanna has just said? Ms. Stangle could have both intentions: her skillful use of this request for students to repeat could serve both functions simultaneously. But some readers may ask whether this set of moves—the questioning about details and the requests for repetition—isn't awfully time-consuming, and perhaps even annoying. How could one run every class this way? Who has the time? Doesn't this focus on precision drive people crazy?

Ms. Stangle does use these techniques with regularity, but there are many times during lessons when she does not require students to achieve the same degree of precision as in episode one. For example, when students encounter a new idea, and are trying to come to grips with it, their language typically becomes imprecise and even incoherent. A moment's reflection reveals that this is true of adults as well—when we are dealing with new concepts and unfamiliar ideas, any of us may sound quite inarticulate! As the cognitive demands on us increase, our ability to talk precisely may deteriorate precipitously. Knowing this, teachers like Ms. Stangle strike a delicate balance. She does not require absolute precision of students as they are working through new ideas. When they are engaged in the most demanding kinds of thinking, she is less stringent in her attention to clarity and precision. On the other hand, when students are more comfortable with the mathematical ideas, she can afford to emphasize the precision of their language. Her students encounter these demands for precision often, and thereby come to understand and accept the need for precision. They develop an appreciation for the effort we all must make to communicate clearly, in mathematics and elsewhere. And although at first students do not like to have to repeat what other students have just said, over time they become remarkably attentive and skilled at keeping track of where the conversation is going. It is in just such settings that teachers are able to eventually achieve real advances in mathematical understanding through talk.

Case 4. ("Discuss this with the person next to you.")
When we divide a whole number by a fraction, such as 2 divided by $\frac{1}{4}$, the quotient, 8, is larger than the dividend! For most students, this is a confusing new result that does not connect well with their previous experience of division. In lower grades, division problems typically yield answers that are *less* than the dividend. Also, this problem does not lend itself to being interpreted in the way students more often interpret division situations, as "sharing." How can you share two pies among one-fourth of a person? And what does an answer of 8 mean in terms of the most common situations associated with division, like sharing? In the face of this departure from the students' favorite meaning of division, many teachers resort to simple computational rules: to divide some number by a fraction, you simply "invert and multiply" or "multiply by the reciprocal of the fraction." But very few students understand why this works.

To help his sixth-grade students develop understanding of division by fractions, Mr. Harris plans several days of instruction. First he discusses with the students the fact that in this set of lessons they would encounter some new ideas about division. He writes on the board a simple division problem with whole numbers:

$$12 \div 4 = \underline{\quad}$$

He asks the students to give an example of what the problem might mean. Students respond with "sharing" interpretations. For example, one student says, "If you share twelve pies among four people, how many pies will each get?" Mr. Harris reminds the students of another way to interpret a division problem, as making equal groups rather than sharing. He counts out twelve sheets of paper and tells the students that they will use them to make booklets. "We need four sheets for each booklet," he says. "How many booklets can we make with these twelve sheets of paper?" The answer is obvious to the students, and Mr. Harris models it by putting the paper into piles, or groups, with four in each, having the students do the subtraction to figure out how

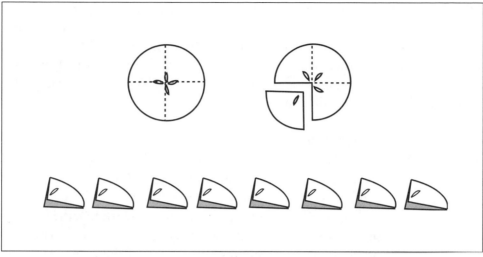

FIGURE 2–3 Mr. Harris's illustration, showing how one-fourth can be subtracted from two pies eight times.

many sheets of paper are left each time he makes a group of four. In this way, he reviews interpreting division as repeated subtraction.

Mr. Harris then writes another equation on the board:

$$2 \div \tfrac{1}{4} = \underline{\hspace{1cm}}$$

He presents the conundrum of dividing two pies among one-fourth of a person. The students all agree that this does not make much sense to them. Then he gives another interpretation of the problem, as dividing the two pies into equally sized groups with one-fourth of a pie in each group. By drawing pictures, he illustrates the process of successively subtracting one-fourth of a pie from two pies to arrive at eight groups, thus showing how the answer of 8 is derived. (See Figure 2–3.)

Finally, Mr. Harris writes on the blackboard the following table of number sentences, in which 2 is divided by some unit fraction.

$$2 \div \tfrac{1}{2} = ?$$
$$2 \div \tfrac{1}{3} = ?$$
$$2 \div \tfrac{1}{5} = ?$$
$$2 \div \tfrac{1}{6} = ?$$
$$2 \div \tfrac{1}{9} = ?$$
$$2 \div \tfrac{1}{20} = ?$$
$$2 \div \tfrac{1}{50} = ?$$

Mr. Harris calls on different students to read each number sentence aloud using this format: "How many times can we subtract $\frac{1}{5}$ from two?" For example, "How many times can we subtract one-fiftieth from two?" He then asks students to talk together in groups of four to solve the entire set of number sentences. He gives them twenty minutes to do this as he circulates around the room, checking in with different groups.

Mr. Harris's use of small-group discussion

Mr. Harris thinks that the students need time to think about the answers to the problems. If he asks them to do so individually, he knows that students who are having difficulty could be stranded without help. Therefore, Mr. Harris uses the small-group format and asks students to work together on the problems. This provides support for the students, giving them a chance to talk with one another about their thinking. It keeps all of them engaged with the problems. And it allows Mr. Harris to circulate and check on the students' understanding. When he notices that most groups have written answers for all of the problems, Mr. Harris asks the students for their attention. Then, calling on students to report their answers, he fills in the chart. As students report, he revoices their answers and then reinforces the subtraction idea: "So you found that two divided by one-sixth is twelve, because you can subtract one-sixth from two . . . *twelve* times. Is that right?" Finally the table looks like this:

$$2 \div \tfrac{1}{2} = 4$$
$$2 \div \tfrac{1}{3} = 6$$
$$2 \div \tfrac{1}{5} = 10$$
$$2 \div \tfrac{1}{6} = 12$$
$$2 \div \tfrac{1}{9} = 18$$
$$2 \div \tfrac{1}{20} = 40$$
$$2 \div \tfrac{1}{50} = 100$$

1. Mr. H: OK, so now we've filled in the chart. Does anyone see a pattern?

Mr. Harris waits for thirty seconds. He asks again: "What pattern do you see?" The students are staring at the board, perusing the table. No hands are raised. Mr. Harris again uses "wait time" with determination, but then begins to think that perhaps this situation calls for something more drastic. He decides that the students need to voice their questions and externalize their thinking with one another first, before they tackle talking about this complex problem in the context of the whole class.

2. Mr. H: Turn and talk to your partner about the table. Do you see a pattern that relates the quotient to the first two numbers? See if you can come up with an answer that you and your partner agree on.

The room explodes in talk. Students had ideas about the pattern, but they were hesitant about voicing these developing ideas in front of the whole class. Many students are reluctant to speak up when they are not absolutely sure of themselves. However, if they are given the opportunity to talk to one other person, a peer, in an environment where only that one other person will be paying attention to their initial attempts to articulate their thoughts, they gain confidence and clarity with respect to their thinking about new concepts.

Mr. Harris's use of partner talk

At this point, let's consider one of the benefits of Mr. Harris's use of talk. Although many of the students may have noticed a pattern in the numbers listed in the table, they are unable or unwilling to describe it aloud at the start. Partner talk or "turn and talk" is especially effective when students reach an impasse—the teacher gives students a short time, perhaps a minute or two at the most, to put their thoughts into words with their nearest neighbor. As noted, often students are reluctant to voice their partially formed mathematical ideas in front of a whole-class group. Mr. Harris also has students who are learning English as a second language who may be hesitant for both linguistic and mathematical reasons. All students can benefit from the two minutes of partner talk, particularly when faced with a knotty new problem. This talk practice is simple, but it can have a profound impact on ensuring equitable participation in the classroom. While a few students may always be ready at a moment's notice to give an answer to anything, the whole class suffers if the teacher is unable to create the conditions for equal access for all students.

After the two minutes, Mr. Harris continues:

3. Mr. H: So let's hear what you have decided about the pattern in the chart. Verette?

4. Verette: Me and my partner think the pattern is that the answer is twice as much as the bottom number.

5. Mr. H: Let's hear from others. George.

6. George: We think you take the denominator and multiply it by the first number, and then you get the quotient.

7. Mr. H: Is the pattern that Verette found the same as the pattern that George found? Paula?

8. Paula: I think they are the same, because Verette said the bottom number and George said the denominator, and those are the same thing, and you multiply them by the first number, which is two.

9. Mr. H: Does the pattern work for every single case? Let's check each example. If we take the first number, two, and multiply it by the denominator in the first example, two, what do we get? Four. It works. Let's try the next one. Marcia, can you talk us through that one? [Mr. Harris continues through the entire chart, having individual students talk through the calculation for each one.]

Recognizing and understanding the teacher's moves

Notice how Mr. Harris uses the contribution of different students in a sequential fashion to build understanding for the entire group. He does not simply announce the pattern at the start. Nor does he correct or clarify the contribution of the first student, Verette. Instead of evaluating Verette's formulation he asks for another formulation from a different student. The next student, George, presents the same generalization but in different terms. Still Mr. Harris does not evaluate, but instead moves on to ask whether these two are the same. The third student, Paula, gives yet a third formulation of the same generalization in slightly different words, combining George's and Verette's contributions.

Mr. Harris's moves here are not necessarily the best or only way to handle this conversation. He could certainly have homed in on Verette's contribution and elicited more detail, as he has done many other times. But we offer this example as a way of showing how a skillful teacher can use the contributions of students to accomplish several goals at once. First, Mr. Harris is giving the students practice in putting their mathematical reasoning into words. Second, he is letting students who need more processing time hear several different versions of the target generalization. And third, he is modeling for students the practice of listening to one another, and conveying their obligation to try to make sense of one another's words.

As the lesson goes on, Mr. Harris gives the students another set of examples, in which the dividend for each problem is 3, not 2, and the divisor is still a unit fraction with a numerator of 1. He again asks them to look at the examples and find a pattern. And he again uses partner talk to give students time to see that once more the quotient equals the dividend times the denominator (e.g., $3 \div \frac{1}{5} = 15$).

All in all, Mr. Harris invokes partner talk nine times during the entire lesson. And the rewards are great. With a step-by-step, careful, and systematic approach, Mr. Harris gives plenty of time for students to process the current question with their partner, and he uses students' subsequent contributions to solidify everyone's understanding. This leaves the students ready to work the next day on generalizing still further, beyond division by unit fractions (e.g., $2 \div \frac{2}{5}$ or $3 \div \frac{2}{5}$). The computations in problems like these are more difficult: repeated subtraction of $\frac{2}{5}$ from 2 is not as straightforward as repeated subtraction of $\frac{1}{5}$ from 2. And while the answer to $2 \div \frac{2}{5}$ is a whole number, 5, as were all the answers in the earlier tables, the answer to $3 \div \frac{2}{5}$ isn't a whole number. If you subtract $\frac{2}{5}$ from 3 seven times, you are left with $\frac{1}{5}$, which isn't enough to subtract another $\frac{2}{5}$. It's only half of what's needed. The answer to $3 \div \frac{2}{5}$ is $7\frac{1}{2}$, which means that you can subtract $\frac{2}{5}$ from 3 seven and a half times. This is complex for students to grasp. Nevertheless, by continuing slowly and carefully, alternating among partner talk, small-group discussion, and whole-class discussion, and building on students' contributions, Mr. Harris was able eventually to lead students to adopt the strategy of multiplying the dividend by the reciprocal of the divisor. But in their case it would not simply be a computational trick, it would be undergirded by a real understanding of the mathematical relationships. In Mr. Harris's view, what the students accomplished would not have been possible without the extensive use of the talk moves and strategies we have been describing.

Integrating Talk and Content

Each of these teachers had taken the time to set up classroom norms for respectful and courteous discourse. They had also made it possible for all students to have equal access to participation. Their students are obligated to listen quietly and to speak up when they make a contribution. They are not allowed to express disrespect, and they follow standard turn-taking procedures.

These teachers rely on three talk formats: whole-class discussion, small-group discussion, and partner talk, using whole-class discussion and partner talk most often to get students to focus on mathematical reasoning, both their own and that of their classmates. Each of these teachers uses other talk formats as well, but in these lessons we paid special attention to these two because they facilitate the kind of mathematical thinking we are interested in supporting. Within the context of these talk formats, each teacher made skillful use of the talk moves introduced in this section.

But the talk formats and talk moves together still do not add up to a full and coherent lesson. As the teacher, you must integrate the tools of talk with the mathematical content, adjusting and refining both to the particulars of your own unique teaching situation. To help you, we suggest a three-part cycle that you will engage in again and again as you incorporate productive talk into your mathematics class.

1. Planning and projecting: creating a roadmap.

Your first step is to plan carefully for a specific lesson. You need to spend time identifying the important mathematical ideas and concepts you'll be talking about, as well as potential misconceptions or difficulties that students might have. You also need to plan which talk formats you will use, and how you will incorporate the specific talk moves we've introduced.

2. Improvising and responding: in the midst of the lesson.

As we all know, if you are actively engaging with students, even the most carefully planned lesson involves improvisation. You cannot be sure that things will go as you planned. And when you make extensive use of student talk, you introduce an element of uncertainty. Therefore, part of the cycle of introducing productive talk into your mathematics class necessarily involves improvisation and responding in the moment. And although you may not remember everything that happens in the lesson, you will aim to keep track of how your plans actually did or did not unfold as you expected.

3. Summarizing and solidifying: So where are we now?

During a talk-intensive lesson there will be moments when you and your students will feel overwhelmed: too much will have been said, and you will feel that you are losing focus. At these times, it's important to step back and review what has been said so far, and what the most significant points have been. Furthermore, after every such lesson, you will want to spend some time reflecting on what important mathematical ideas, conjectures, claims, and arguments have emerged during the class. When you return the next day, it will be important for you to present to the students a review of the most important aspects of the previous day's discourse. Talk-intensive lessons can be difficult to summarize, but as the teacher you will want to make sure that you take a few moments to review, clarify, and solidify the important points that have been made. This will also help you as you return to the "planning and projecting" part of the cycle.

PART
2

The Mathematics
What Do We Talk About?

3

Mathematical Concepts

Mathematical knowledge is sometimes classified into two categories: conceptual knowledge and procedural knowledge. Conceptual knowledge consists of well-defined concepts, more informal mathematical ideas, and relationships among ideas, concepts, and skills. For example, conceptual knowledge of division includes knowledge of the relationships between division and multiplication and division and subtraction. It involves information about the different representations for division, the uses of remainders, and how remainders are affected by the size of the divisor. It includes an understanding of mathematical properties such as associativity and commutativity, and knowledge of which properties hold true for division. When students have conceptual knowledge of division, they can talk or write about these relationships and can give examples of problems and tasks that could be solved using division. Carefully guided classroom talk is an especially effective method for developing concepts and building connections among mathematical ideas.

Procedural knowledge, on the other hand, involves knowledge of facts, symbols, rules, and procedures. In the case of division, students with procedural knowledge may have memorized the basic division facts, know the symbols used to represent division, and can perform short and long division computations. It's possible to have procedural knowledge of a topic and to have little or no conceptual knowledge. However, without knowledge of the important concepts and ideas, it's impossible to truly understand that topic. For example, when students lack conceptual knowledge of division, they may have difficulty applying division to problem-solving situations, noticing when an answer given to a computation is unreasonable, or knowing what to do if they get stuck when doing long division. They exhibit fragile understanding of division.

Conceptual understanding is sometimes described in terms of how information is represented and structured in the mind of the student. When teachers indicate that students have conceptual understanding, they usually are referring to the fact that the students have an integrated and functional grasp of a number of mathematical ideas. Their knowledge is "organized into a coherent whole which enables the students to learn new ideas by connecting them to what they already know" (National Research Council 2001, 118). The role of connections in understanding is considered central by the vast majority of psychologists and educators. When students are able to connect ideas and concepts to procedures and representations, learning is especially robust. Thus, one of the things we want to talk about in mathematics class is how concepts and relationships among concepts connect to what students already know. We believe that talk can be used to assist students in organizing what they already know into larger and more powerful conceptual structures—the "big ideas" of mathematics.

Exploring a Mathematical Concept

In a second-grade classroom, the teacher, Mrs. Hollinger, asked students to work individually and use base ten blocks to show the number 37 in more than one way. About half of the students represented 37 with three "ten" blocks and seven "one" blocks, whereas the other half used thirty-seven one blocks. One of the students used one ten block and twenty-seven one blocks. Another student used two ten blocks and seventeen one blocks. Mrs. Hollinger wanted her students to understand that all of these groupings showed the quantity 37. Whereas she could *tell* her students that the four combinations of blocks were equivalent, she thought that if she asked students to talk about the different combinations possible they would gain insight into grouping by tens and ones. She hoped that they would conclude that three tens and seven ones uses the fewest blocks, is the most efficient grouping, and connects directly to the numeral that represents the quantity.

First, Mrs. Hollinger initiated small-group discussions, organizing students into groups of three to share what they had done individually and then to work together to generate other combinations. She asked groups to try to show the quantity 37 in four different ways. After groups had time to work, she called the class to attention. She asked a student to bring one combination of blocks to the front of the room and place them so that everyone in the class could see them. Then she asked other students to display different combinations, continuing until all four grouping combinations were displayed—three tens and seven ones, two tens and seventeen ones, one ten and twenty-seven ones, and thirty-seven ones. Mrs. Hollinger then asked the class, "How can we be sure that each of these four different combinations of base ten blocks equals thirty-seven?" Mrs. Hollinger was not sure that all students agreed that the different groupings were equivalent, so she asked students to count the value of each pile of blocks displayed. Two students counted by tens and ones, and the other two counted just by ones, but all four verified that each combination of blocks equaled 37.

After students had counted all of the piles, one student stated, "The piles look different but they are the same amount." Another student added, "The three tens and seven ones pile uses the smallest number of blocks." Mrs. Hollinger then chose students to explain to the class how they decided on their combination of blocks.

1. Mrs. H: Liana, can you explain one way you used blocks to show thirty-seven?

2. Liana: I used three tens and seven ones since you can count like ten, twenty, thirty. Then I had to use ones to get to thirty-seven.

3. Mrs. H: How is your combination the same or different from one of the others?

4. Liana: I used tens and took a tens block for each ten. The thirty-seven ones doesn't use any tens blocks.

5. Mrs. H: So you used all the tens you could, right? [Liana nods.] Pete, can you explain another way, a different way?

6. Pete: I counted out thirty-seven ones. Then I took one ten and put away ten ones. So I counted the rest. I have one ten and twenty-seven ones.

7. Mrs. H: Could you have divided the other twenty-seven ones into groups of ten the way Liana did?

8. Pete: Mine is sort of like Liana's but I have lots of ones left. I could have made more tens but I didn't.

9. Mrs. H: OK, so Liana used three tens, and Pete used one ten. What can we say about the different number of tens and the number of ones we can use to show thirty-seven? Crystal?

10. Crystal: You can have one, two, or three tens.

11. Luis: Can't you also have zero tens?

12. Mrs. H: Does anyone agree or disagree with Luis's idea?

13. Students: Agree.
I agree.
Yes!

14. Crystal: Yes, you can have zero tens. Like the one that uses thirty-seven ones blocks.

15. Mrs. H: So let me ask you this. If we can use zero, one, two, or three

tens to show thirty-seven, why do you think we usually
show thirty-seven using three tens and seven ones? Talk to
your partner for a minute and then be ready to share your
ideas with the class.

After two minutes of partner talk, the discussion in Mrs. Hollinger's class
continued for another twenty minutes as students shared their ideas about how
grouping by tens is related to the symbols we use to represent the quantities.

The concept of grouping by tens is important to place value, as is the concept that we use the most efficient grouping by tens to represent quantities
numerically. In addition, the fact that we can represent the same quantity using
a different number of tens is a key concept in making sense of the standard subtraction algorithm. Mrs. Hollinger realized that talking about these concepts
furthered students' conceptual understanding. Also, listening to students gave
her a better grasp of what individual students did and did not know.

What talk formats are featured in this lesson? Mrs. Hollinger primarily
uses whole-class discussion, but uses small-group discussion one time and
periodically moves the class to partner talk. Mrs. Hollinger finds partner talk
an effective method for getting every student involved in the talk, and her second graders are at the beginning stages of being proficient at talking productively in pairs. What talk moves does Mrs. Hollinger use? First, she asks many
students to explain the grouping methods they used. Occasionally she revoices their explanations, to make sure that everyone heard and to emphasize the
number of tens that they used. It's important as well to ask students to
describe how their methods differ from those already described. Finally, Mrs.
Hollinger uses a variation of the "do you agree or disagree and why?" talk
move in order to get students to apply their own reasoning to others' contributions by reflecting on a grouping method different from their own.

Uncovering Misconceptions and Errors

Classroom talk not only helps students develop conceptual understanding, it
is also effective for revealing and clarifying students' partial understandings
and misconceptions. In the process of making sense of experiences, students
often generalize ideas in incomplete ways. For example, as seen in Chapter 2,
if young students' experiences with triangles only involve viewing pictures of
equilateral triangles oriented along a base, their generalization of the concept
"triangle" may be very limited—they might conclude that scalene triangles are
not triangles or that a triangle that is resting on a vertex is not a triangle. Talk
is a powerful tool for revealing students' partial understanding of a concept or
their misconceptions about that concept.

Mr. Lyman used talk to learn about his fifth-grade students' generalizations (and misconceptions). One topic that Mr. Lyman felt was not too difficult for his students was decimal addition and subtraction. Yet he noticed that when he didn't list the numbers vertically, one under the other with the decimal points lined up, many students made errors. Because of comments by a few students, he began to suspect that their understanding of decimals was procedural and not very complete. One day, when students were working in small groups on decimal word problems, he noticed that one group of four students incorrectly solved the computation 25 − 17.7 by setting up the exercise with the 2 and 5 underneath the two 7s:

$$\begin{array}{r} 17.7 \\ -\ 25 \\ \hline \end{array}$$

Mr. Lyman decided to probe the understanding of the students in the small group.

1. Mr. L: I noticed that you have been adding and subtracting decimal numbers to solve these word problems. How are decimals the same or different from whole numbers? How is adding and subtracting decimals the same or different from adding and subtracting whole numbers? Take a minute to think about what you know about decimal numbers and how we add and subtract them. Then I'll talk with your group about this.

After giving them a minute to think, Mr. Lyman listened carefully to his students' ideas. At first he allowed them to make their points without much commentary from him, but then he began to ask clarification questions as alternative understandings emerged.

2. Sarah: Decimals are like regular numbers, you just line them up and add them.

3. Corey: Yeah, it's easy because we all know how to add and subtract.

4. Kei: Decimals are numbers with a dot in them.

5. Mr. L: Sarah, what do you mean by "like regular numbers"?

6. Sarah: You know, like the numbers we use to count with—tens, hundreds, thousands.

7. Mr. L: So decimals are exactly the same as the counting numbers?

8. Sarah: Yes.

9. Mr. L: What do other people think? Are decimals the same or different from our regular counting numbers?

10. Kei: They are the same. You just line everything up on the right side and then add or subtract.

11. Mr. L: Could you give us an example, Kei?

12. Kei: Sure. Eight point two plus seven point nine. [Kei records and solves the addition problem correctly.] I lined up the two and the nine on the right and then just added. You bring the decimal point straight down.

13. Bob: I think you have to line up the decimal points.

14. Mr. L: What do you mean, Bob?

15. Bob: Well, if the problem was eight point twenty-five plus seven point nine, you don't line up the five and the nine.

16. Mr. L Bob, would you please say those numbers again but read them so we hear the place values?

17. Bob Sure. Let's add eight and twenty-five-hundredths and seven and nine-tenths. I think we should line up the decimal points, not the last two numbers.

18. Mr. L: Would you all discuss what Bob just said? What do you think of his idea?

Mr. Lyman has already learned a lot using the small-group format for this short discussion. First, three of the students in the group did not think there was a difference between whole numbers and decimal numbers. He now doubts that many students in his class think of a decimal number as the sum of a whole number and a part of a whole. He now suspects that many students' conceptions of decimals are unrelated to quantity and that they instead think that a decimal is a number with a "dot" in it. When adding decimals, they do not consider the size of the numbers or the place values of the digits. By discussing their ideas in a small-group format, Mr. Lyman was able to hear from each student and learn about their superficial understanding. Sometimes talking with a small group can clarify and extend concepts for students, but in this case, Mr. Lyman realized that small-group talk was not enough and additional instruction would be necessary. Mr. Lyman used productive talk to get mathematical ideas and concepts visibly out on the table. Both he and the students benefited from this interaction; Mr. Lyman learned that students held some misconceptions and the students had an opportunity to grapple with the alternative approach suggested by Bob.

CHAPTER

4

Computational Procedures

Acomputational procedure is a series of steps or actions that we use when operating on numbers. For example, when we add, subtract, multiply, and divide we use some sort of procedure. Some procedures are algorithms. An algorithm, in terms of arithmetic procedures encountered in grades one through eight, is a generalized set of steps used to solve any problem of a particular class. Algorithms are efficient, produce accurate results, and can be used to solve many similar tasks using the same process. The regularity of the steps, known by memory by most people, allows the solver to focus his or her energies on more complex or important aspects of a mathematics problem.

It's useful for students to invent their own procedures when learning concepts and skills. Sometimes these "invented procedures" are identical with widely used algorithms. For example, the partial-sums method for solving multidigit addition problems is one that many students discover on their own: when solving 37 + 49, they first add the tens (30 + 40 = 70), then add the ones (7 + 9 = 16), and then add the partial sums (70 + 16 = 86). However, other times students' invented procedures are not algorithms; they produce a correct answer for that one particular problem, but are not generalizable and do not work for similar problems.

Why Talk About Computational Procedures?

When we teach computational procedures, our goal should be student understanding as well as skill. Discussions about students' invented procedures can help teachers achieve this goal. Mrs. Parker's first-grade class has been exploring pairs of numbers that add to the sums of 5 and 10. She wanted her students to apply what they learned about these number pairs to solve a problem.

After reading aloud to her class *Rooster's Off to See the World*, by Eric Carle, Mrs. Parker asked her students to work in pairs to find out how many animals went along for the trip. (On the trip, Rooster is joined by two cats, three frogs, four turtles, and five fish.) After approximately ten minutes, Mrs. Parker asked the students to explain how many animals were on the trip and how they figured this out.

1. Caitlin: I drew a picture of all of the animals and I counted starting with one and got to fifteen.

2. Mrs. P: So, Caitlin counted her pictures to solve the problem. Who solved it a different way?

3. Ross: I used the blocks. I took one block for the rooster, two more for the cats, three more for the frogs, four more for the turtles, and five more for the fish. When I had all of the blocks I counted them. There were fifteen.

4. Mrs. P: So Ross, it sounds like your strategy is similar to Caitlin's. You both counted animals. Is that right?

5. Ross: Yes, it's similar because I counted the animals. But I used blocks. So it's different too.

6. Mrs. P: So your approach was similar to Caitlin's, since you counted the animals, starting with one and going all the way to fifteen. But instead of a picture, you used blocks to help you count. Did anyone solve the problem a different way?

7. Amelia: I wrote down that there were one, two, three, four, and five animals on the trip. I put the rooster and the two cats together to get three. Then plus the three frogs makes six. Then I remember that six plus four more is ten. I know ten plus five is fifteen.

8. Mrs. P: Amelia, can you tell us again what you added and I'll write the number sentences on the board? [Mrs. Parker writes the equations as Amelia offers them.]

9. Amelia: One plus two is three:

   1 + 2 = 3

   Three plus three is six:

   3 + 3 = 6

   Six plus four is ten:

   6 + 4 = 10

   Ten plus five is fifteen:

   10 + 5 = 15

10. Mrs. P: So Amelia, can you explain to us why you were adding these numbers?

11. Amelia: Because we want to put them all together and see how many are on the trip.

12. Mrs. P: Billy, can you explain in your own words where the one and the two come from in Amelia's number sentence "one plus two equals three"?

13. Billy: From the rooster and two cats.

14. Mrs. P: Why did Amelia add three plus three? Where did those numbers come from? Hoai?

15. Hoai: From the one plus two and three more frogs.

16. Mrs. P: So Hoai, you're saying that the rooster plus two cats makes three, then three more frogs make six animals in all? [She points to the numbers in the number sentence as she says this. Hoai nods.] That makes sense to me. Who can tell me where Amelia got the numbers for the last two sentences?

17. Pete: There are six so far, then four more come, the turtles, so that's ten. Then five fish come, and that's fifteen.

18. Mrs. P: So let's look at Amelia's method. Amelia solved the problem by adding two numbers at a time. She started by adding one plus two and then took that answer, which was the total number of animals so far, and used it to keep adding. Could Amelia have started with a different pair of numbers? Vanessa?

19. Vanessa: Yes, we played that game and one of the pairs was four plus one is five. So that's five. Then there's another five and that's ten. And then there's three plus two which is another five. That's fifteen.

20. Mrs. P: Vanessa, you said a lot. Let's back it up a little. What do you mean by "that game"?

21. Vanessa: The game where we looked for numbers that add to five. One of them was four plus one and another was two plus three.

22. Mrs. P: Who else remembers that game? Do you agree that four plus one and two plus three is five? [Students nod.] Who can explain why Vanessa thinks that this will help us solve the problem?

23. Kevin: The rooster and four turtles make five, the five fish is another five. The two cats and the three frogs make five. That's five, ten, fifteen animals.

24. Mrs. P: So Vanessa had a slightly different approach than Amelia.

> Vanessa has explained to us how to solve the problem by
> finding numbers that add to five. This is a useful strategy,
> since fives are easy to count by: five, ten, fifteen.

By focusing the discussion on the procedures that students use, and asking them questions about the meaning of their procedures, Mrs. Parker is supporting her students' mathematical thinking skills. She is showing them that their own procedures are of great value and use in their learning of mathematics. Because Mrs. Parker is interested in helping students use strategies other than counting, she focuses most of the discussion time on exploring the strategies that use addition.

Notice how Mrs. Parker uses revoicing both to summarize students' contributions and to compare their different solution methods. Mrs. Parker knows that her first graders will benefit from hearing each solution method a second time. Furthermore, when she asks them to consider whether their solution strategies are the same or different from others, she is giving them practice in paying attention to the different dimensions of a solution method: the operations used, the groupings of numbers, the form of representation, and so on. Finally, in order to keep the focus on the mathematical goal of using addition, she asks further questions about each computational procedure. In Line 14, for example, she asks, "Why did Amelia add three plus three? Where did those numbers come from?"

Lessons that use talk can serve multiple purposes. Students can practice computational skills and also can deepen their understanding of the operation by talking about what they are doing and why. Mrs. DeFreitas's fifth-grade students have been exploring different ways to solve multidigit multiplication problems. Some students use repeated addition, some use partial products, and some use the standard multiplication algorithm. As they apply strategies for multiplying, they also must justify their steps, thus reinforcing the idea that mathematics makes sense. In the following example, one student in Mrs. DeFreitas's class uses a particularly efficient mental procedure to solve the problem 19×12, based on the distributive property. Mrs. DeFreitas asks this student to explain his method to the class.

1. Kim Lee: I wanted to solve nineteen times twelve. This looked hard to me. So instead I first did twenty times twelve because that's easier, it's two times twelve which is twenty-four with a zero—two hundred forty. Then I did two hundred forty minus twelve, which is two hundred twenty-eight.

2. Mrs. D: Kim Lee, I want your classmates to really understand your pro-

cedure because I think they will want to use it themselves. Can you talk us through it again, this time a little more slowly?

3. Kim Lee: OK. Nineteen times twelve would be tough for me. Nineteen is close to twenty and twenty times twelve is easier because we know a shortcut for multiplying numbers that end in zero.

4. Mrs. D: Let me stop you for a minute. What's one way to interpret nineteen times twelve? Fran?

5. Fran: Nineteen groups of twelve.

6. Mrs. D: Then, twenty times twelve means twenty groups of twelve. Keep going, Kim Lee.

7. Kim Lee: Yeah, so once I figured out that twenty times twelve was two hundred forty, I subtracted twelve.

8. Mrs. D: Who thinks they can explain why Kim Lee subtracted twelve? Talk to the person next to you for a moment about this. [Partners talk for about one minute.] Go ahead, Felicita.

9. Felicita: The number *two hundred forty* is from twenty groups of twelve. We only want nineteen groups of twelve so we have to get rid of one group of twelve.

10. Mrs. D: Is that why you subtracted, Kim Lee? [He nods.] Kim, as you talk us through your procedure tell me what number sentences to write. [Mrs. DeFreitas writes Kim Lee's equations as he states them.]

11. Kim Lee: OK, it's nineteen groups of twelve, which is close to twenty groups of twelve, so write *twenty times twelve*.

    20×12

    But now I take away one group of twelve, since I only want nineteen groups, so write minus twelve.

    $20 \times 12 - 12$

    The answer is two hundred twenty-eight.

12. Mrs. D: We can use parentheses to show what operation we do first. [She writes on the board:]

    $(20 \times 12) - 12 = 228$
    $19 \times 12 = (20 \times 12) - 12$

    In both equations we write equal signs because both sides of the equal sign equal two hundred twenty-eight.

13. Mrs. D: Let's try Kim Lee's procedure for eighteen times thirteen. Work with the person next to you. [Partners work on solving this problem.]

One reason that Mrs. DeFreitas asks everyone to try Kim Lee's procedure is because she suspects that students are confused about which number to round, what to round it to, and how much to subtract. While students work, she circulates among them, noting who is applying Kim Lee's method correctly and who is not. She notices that Jonathan's answer is correct while Sierra and Beatriz and Felicita have made different types of errors. She plans on using their errors in the discussion to help students better understand Kim Lee's method.

14. Mrs. D: OK, now that you've had a chance to try Kim Lee's procedure, who would like to explain to us what you did? Beatriz?

15. Beatriz: Me and Felicita did twenty times thirteen to get two hundred sixty, because thirteen times two is twenty-six and then add a zero.

16. Mrs. D: What do you mean "add a zero"?

17. Beatriz: It's not thirteen times two, it's thirteen times twenty, so you need to put a zero down.

18. Mrs. D: Why?

19. Felicita: It's like the two is really a twenty but you pretend it's a two since that's easier and then put the zero back when you're done.

20. Mrs. D: Who can explain why they rounded eighteen to twenty?

21. Richard: Kim Lee's method works with friendly numbers, like ones that end in zero. So you look for a close number that ends in zero. Eighteen is close to twenty.

22. Mrs. D: Is that why you did it? [The girls nod.] Who thinks they can predict what we have to do next?

23. Jonathan: I think we do two hundred sixty minus twenty-six. The twenty times thirteen means twenty groups of thirteen but we only really want eighteen groups, so we need to take away two groups of thirteen, which is twenty-six.

24. Mrs. D: Does anyone else have a different prediction?

25. Sierra: I think it is two hundred sixty minus eighteen, because you have to take away eighteen.

26. Mrs. D: Does anyone else have a prediction? Okay, Felicita and Beatriz, tell us what you did.

27. Beatriz: We subtracted thirteen, because that's what Kim Lee did in his problem. The answer is two hundred forty-seven.

Mrs. DeFreitas realizes that the discussion may be confusing many in her class. She decides that she needs to slow everything down even further and summarize the main points students have made. Since there are a number of suggestions for what to subtract from 260, she decides to recap them and then recommence the discussion.

28. Mrs. D: OK. So we have several different predictions here, and several different answers have been mentioned. So let's take stock here. What do we agree on? So far, to solve eighteen times thirteen we all agree that you can multiply twenty times thirteen, which equals two hundred sixty. This is part of Kim Lee's method to work first with friendly numbers. But it is not clear what number should be subtracted from two hundred sixty. We have three predictions. The first prediction, I'll call it A, suggests that we should subtract twenty-six, the second prediction, called B, is that we should subtract eighteen, and prediction C is that we should subtract thirteen. I am going to write the number sentences on the board while everyone talks to their partner about the three predictions. Which of the predictions do you agree with and why? [Mrs. DeFreitas writes the following on the board and gives students about two and a half minutes to discuss them.]

$$18 \times 13 = ? \quad \text{Step 1: Multiply } 20 \times 13 \quad 20 \times 13 = 260$$

$$\text{Step 2: Predictions}$$

$$A: (20 \times 13) - 26$$

$$B: (20 \times 13) - 18$$

$$C: (20 \times 13) - 13$$

29. Mrs. D: OK, which prediction did you and your partner decide upon? Lindsey?

30. Lindsey: We got rid of prediction B because it's eighteen groups of thirteen changed to twenty groups of thirteen.

31. Mrs. D: Would you elaborate a bit more for us? I agree it is twenty groups of thirteen but why is that important?

32. Lindsey: Since it's groups of thirteen we think you subtract groups of thirteen, not a group of eighteen.

33. Kim Lee: I agree with Lindsey. I would subtract twenty-six, since twenty times thirteen is over by two groups. You need to take away those two groups of thirteen, which is twenty-six. The answer should be two hundred thirty-four. I checked with the calculator and that's right.

34. Mrs. D: Peter, would you please explain in your own words what Lindsey and Kim Lee said?

35. Peter: They said that prediction B is wrong because twenty is too many groups of thirteen, so you have to subtract groups of thirteen, not eighteen.

36. Mrs. D: OK, let's look at the third prediction. Can someone explain why you think prediction C is either right or wrong?

37. Jonathan: It only takes away one group of thirteen, not two, like Kim Lee said.

38. Mrs. D: Beatriz, what do you think of what Jonathan and Kim Lee both said?

39. Beatriz: I think I get it. You don't always take away the number. You have to think about how much you rounded up and then take that many groups. We rounded up two so we have to subtract two groups.

Mrs. DeFreitas's class then used Kim Lee's procedure to multiply other numbers. They discussed the reasoning behind each step, especially how much to subtract and why. As they became more comfortable with the method, they discussed different number sentences they could write. Mrs. DeFreitas chose not to formally introduce the distributive property at this time because the class was still grappling with making sense of the idea of rounding up and subtracting. However, she would return to the topic and focus exclusively on the distributive property in a future lesson.

Did you notice how Mrs. DeFreitas asked more than one student to suggest what number should be subtracted from 20×13? Jonathan gave a correct answer, but Mrs. DeFreitas knew that not everyone in her class could immediately make sense of his reasoning. Thus, she called on two students she suspected might have incorrect predictions. This allowed the class time to really think about which number to subtract and to discuss their reasoning. Discussing a variety of possible answers to a calculation can help students make sense of the numbers used. Furthermore, recall that Mrs. DeFreitas did not identify any prediction with a particular student's name but instead labeled the predictions in an impersonal way with letters. Sometimes teachers want to focus the discussion on the mathematics, rather than on the person that gave the response, so that incorrect responses are not associated with individuals. Other times teachers want to identify a procedure or conjecture with a particular student's name as a way to recognize that student's contributions.

It's important that students understand the algorithms they learn to use, rather than just applying them in a rote fashion. When students are learning a computational procedure, understanding why it works will help them commit it to memory. One of the best ways to assist students in understanding and remembering procedures is to talk with them about the procedures. Talking about the math we are doing slows down and clarifies processes so that more students can understand them. Additionally, many students are motivated to compare their own ways of solving a problem with those of other students, which teaches them new computational procedures and strengthens their understanding of the workings of procedures they are more familiar with. Furthermore, by listening to students talk, teachers can gain insights into their understanding of procedures as well as into their misconceptions and mistaken ideas about computation.

Aiding Understanding, Memory, and Self-Monitoring

In the following example, we illustrate one of the many ways that teachers can use talk to gain insight into their students' current level of understanding of computational procedures. In the same example, we will see the teacher simultaneously supporting students' abilities to monitor their own use of computational procedures. Ms. Webster wants to review a procedure for regrouping tens when subtracting with her third-grade students and has decided to use the format of whole-class discussion. On the board, she writes the problem:

$$81 - 43$$

Then she allows time for everyone to complete the calculation individually.

1. Ms. W:	What is this problem asking me to find? Juan?
2. Juan:	You need to find the answer between eighty-one and forty-three.
3. Ms. W.	We can call the answer in a subtraction problem the "difference."
4. Ms. W:	Jane, did you have a comment?
5. Jane:	You could also say, "What's eighty-one take away forty-three"?
6. Ms. W:	Yes, we can. Now I want to estimate the answer before I solve it. How can I do this? Marge?
7. Marge:	Well, eighty-one is close to eighty and forty-three is close to forty. Eighty minus forty is forty so your answer will be close to that.
8. Ms. W:	OK, so to estimate my answer, Marge says I can work with friendly numbers that are close to eighty-one and forty-

three. Now what about when I want to find the actual answer? What should I do first?

9. Lou: You need to see what's one take away three but you can't do that. So you cross out the eight and write seven above it. Then you write a one next to the one since it's eleven now. [Mrs. Webster writes this equation on the board.]

$$\begin{array}{r} ^7\cancel{8}{}^1 1 \\ -\ 4\ 3 \end{array}$$

10. Ms. W: Lou, can you explain your procedure to us? Why should I cross out the eight and write seven?

11. Lou: Since the one wasn't big enough to take away three you had to get some more. The eight has some more.

12. Ms. W: OK, I want to make sure I'm following you. Remember, we've been talking about what these two-digit numbers like eighty-one really stand for. Lou, can you tell or show me what eighty-one looks like with the base ten blocks?

13. Lou: It's eight tens and one one.

14. Ms. W: So in this problem [points to the 81] you said I should cross out the eight in eighty-one and write seven above it and the one in eighty-one becomes eleven. Can you either explain to me or show me why this makes sense?

15. Lou: Well, you need to take away three ones, but you only have one in eighty-one. So you take this ten [picks up a ten from the base ten blocks on the teacher's desk] and trade it for ten ones. Those go over to your other one and now you have enough to take away.

16. Ms. W: Who else can explain to me why I cross out the eight and write a seven?

17. Lara: Lou traded one ten for ten ones so now you only have seven tens left.

18. Ms. W: Who can explain to me why the one one became eleven ones? Wally?

19. Wally: Your ten new ones got added to the other old one to get eleven.

20. Ms. W: So let's review. First Marge helped me estimate the answer. Then what did we do next?

Ms. Webster continued questioning her students until the computation was complete and the answer checked. Other questions she then asked included,

"How do I know when I'm done?" and "How do I check my answer?" The dialogue shows that Ms. Webster asks questions that focus on the meaning of the actions in a computational procedure. When Lou offered an answer that did not indicate much understanding, she spoke with Lou for a while to see what he did and did not know. Ms. Webster involved other students in this dialogue as well. She did this because in her years of teaching she has encountered many students who struggle in the same way Lou does. Since this lesson was mainly a review, Ms. Webster used this question-and-answer session to model for students the questions one can ask oneself when working through computations.

In addition to increasing students' ability to monitor their own understanding of any procedure, Ms. Webster's question-and-answer whole-class discussion accomplishes other goals. Some of the questions she asks serve to link students' informal procedures to the traditional regrouping algorithm. For example, she asks for other ways to solve the problem and then asks students to compare and contrast the steps of each method. Linking students' own procedures to standard algorithms validates students' invented methods and encourages them to use algorithms that are most efficient and effective. Ms. Webster also gives attention to the meaning of vocabulary that the students use. Later in the lesson, she questions what students mean by *borrow* and, once they've clarified, asks them to repeat their statements using more accurate terms such as *regroup* or *trade*.

Deepening Students' Understanding of Number and Operations

Talking about computational procedures can do more than clarify students' understanding of the ins and outs of those procedures. It may actually promote a more profound understanding of the numbers and mathematical operations at the center of those procedures. In other words, at the same time that talk is building facility with procedures, it may deepen conceptual knowledge as well.

Recall Mr. Lyman's fifth-grade class as described in Chapter 3. In the small-group discussion about 25 – 17.7, Mr. Lyman realized that some students did not have a strong conceptual grasp of decimals and were also making computational errors when subtracting. He concluded that the whole class needed to revisit subtraction of decimals to deepen their conceptual understanding and to reinforce correct procedures. He decided to have students make up a problem that fit the computation and helped them to consider what might be a reasonable answer.

1. Mr. L: We just reviewed that it's important to line up digits so that
we are subtracting ones away from ones, tens away from

tens, and so on. Now let's look at yesterday's problem. It was twenty-five minus seventeen and seven-tenths. Who can tell me a story for this problem? Alexa?

2. Alexa: I was in a race that was twenty-five miles. I ran seventeen-point-seven miles so far. How many miles do I have left to go?

3. Mr. L: Alexa, would you restate your problem again but remember to use place values to say the numbers so we can think about their size.

4. Alexa: OK. I ran a race that was twenty-five miles long. By noon I had run seventeen and seven-tenths miles. How many miles do I have left to run?

5. Mr. L: Work with your partner for a few moments to see if you can solve this problem. [After two to three minutes, Mr. Lyman asks Kyle and Ben to explain their solution strategy.]

6. Kyle: This is what we did. Three more tenths gives her eighteen miles. Then she has seven more to go. So she has seven-point-three miles left.

7. Mr. L: And what is another way to say seven-point-three miles?

8. Ben: Seven miles and three tenths of a mile.

9. Mr. L: Can you write a number sentence for your solution? [Ben writes the following number sentence:]

17.7 + 7.3 = 25.0

10. Mr. L: So, to find the difference, it looks like you added three more tenths to get another whole, which gave eighteen whole miles in all with seven more miles to go to finish the race. Is that what you did? [Kyle and Ben nod.] That's one way to solve this problem. Let's think now about how to solve it with subtraction. Yesterday, most of you thought that to solve twenty-five minus seventeen and seven-tenths, we should write it like this. [He writes the problem vertically, purposefully misaligning the numbers.]

17.7
– 25
———

Talk to your partner about this for a few moments.

    Mr. Lyman spoke with the math curriculum specialist in his school to learn more about the kinds of difficulties students have when subtracting decimals. He learned that students often set up these problems incorrectly when one number has more digits after the decimal point than does the other, or when one of the numbers in the problem does not explicitly show the decimal point. Some students do not understand that a whole number such as 25 can be written with or without a decimal point. Mr. Lyman called on Bob after students had time to reflect on how the problem was set up.

11. Bob: The problem is written wrong. The seventeen-point-seven—oh, I mean the seventeen and seven-tenths—should be under the twenty-five. The problem is twenty-five minus seventeen and seven-tenths.

12. Mr. L: What do some other people think about this? Do you agree or disagree with what Bob just said? Aipana?

13. Aipana: I agree, like in the other problems, the number that's being taken away goes underneath.

14. Mr. L: So, how do you think it should be written? Who would like to write it on the board? [Two students come up and write the two problems shown here.]

$$\begin{array}{r} 25 \\ -17.7 \\ \hline \end{array}$$

$$\begin{array}{r} 25 \\ -17.7 \\ \hline \end{array}$$

15. Mr. L: So we have two different versions of the problem written here. What is the difference between them? Ken?

16. Ken: Well, in one, the twenty-five is all the way to the right, and the seventeen and seven-tenths is lined up under it. In the second one, the twenty-five is above the seventeen, and the point-seven sticks out to the right. But I'm confused. Twenty-five doesn't have a decimal point. So she lined it up as though it did. Shouldn't the twenty-five be to the right?

17. Mr. L: That's a question for us to consider. The number twenty-five doesn't have a decimal point as it's written here, but could it? Talk at your table about this for a minute.

Mr. Lyman goes over to a small group of three students and overhears the following interaction.

18. Corey: No, it can't. That's why the first problem is right.

19. Silvia: I disagree. I think the decimal point goes right after the five, since the five is five ones.

20. Jennifer: If the decimal point went right after the five it would be there and it isn't, so there just shouldn't be one.

After the partner talk, Mr. Lyman asks for student reactions. He calls on Sarah.

21. Sarah: If there could be a decimal point there, then why don't books always put it in? Shouldn't they tell us where it goes?

22. Mr. L: Sometimes you have a choice whether or not to show the decimal point. If there are tenths or hundredths or thousandths you have to show the decimal point so we know the value of the digits, but if there are no decimal parts in the number you can decide whether or not to record the decimal point. When might it be important to write the decimal point in the number *twenty-five* and where would it go? Kyle?

23. Kyle: You can write the twenty-five as twenty-five-point-zero— that shows there are no tenths.

24. Mr. L: Do you agree, Corey?

25. Corey: Oh, yeah. Then you can do the problem.

26. Mr. L: You said "then you can do the problem." What do you mean? Can you explain that a bit more?

27. Corey: Now that we have twenty-five-point-zero, we want to take away seven-tenths from nothing, so we need to borrow a one.

28. Mr. L: OK, let's look at this. [Goes to the board and adds the decimal point and zero to the second example.]

$$25.0$$
$$-\,17.7$$

But if I regroup a one, aren't we now taking tenths away from ones?

29. Jen: No, that one becomes ten-tenths. That makes it OK. Ten-tenths minus seven-tenths is three-tenths. Like in the story problem, you took three-tenths of a mile to complete one mile.

This discussion ended with students explaining how to complete the regrouping procedure. Then, Mr. Lyman made the following comment.

30. Mr. L: Let's review what we just talked about. When we look at numbers we need to think about the digits and their values,

meaning what place they are in. This goes for whole numbers and decimal numbers. Decimal numbers are numbers that include parts of wholes. For example, seventeen and seven-tenths means seventeen whole miles with seven more tenths of a mile and twenty-five means twenty-five whole miles and zero tenths. When we add and subtract, we need to add and subtract things that are alike. These are the kind of things you need to think about as you add and subtract decimal numbers.

Students often forget and mix up the many rules for adding, subtracting, multiplying, and dividing with decimals. When students make sense of these rules, namely when the steps are meaningful, they can more easily remember them. Furthermore, they can "re-invent" what to do based upon their understanding, determine when an answer is reasonable, and apply computational procedures to new situations (Burns 2000). Does this mean that it's best to try to develop students' conceptual understanding of number and mathematical operations before exploring the computational procedures related to them? Unfortunately, students' progression through conceptual and procedural understanding is not always linear. Furthermore, robust understanding comes when procedures and concepts are connected. The most effective way to build robust understanding and strong procedural abilities involves consistently moving from concepts to procedures and back to concepts. Carefully planned classroom talk can provide an excellent vehicle for this back-and-forth process. Discussing the concepts on which procedures are based as well as the reasons behind the steps in any procedure can serve to strengthen students' understanding of both.

CHAPTER
5

Solution Methods and Problem-Solving Strategies

Problem-solving strategies are a good topic for discussions in mathematics classes. To most educators, a "problem" in mathematics is a puzzling yet intriguing situation for which there is no immediate, apparent solution. In other words, when faced with a problem, a student can't immediately call upon a procedure or an algorithm to find the answer. In solving a problem, the solver makes a plan for reaching the solution and then carries out the plan. The procedures by which the solver accomplishes this are referred to as solution methods. Talk about solution methods and problem-solving strategies can reveal shallow understanding or holes in previously learned concepts, as well as misconceptions and overgeneralizations that may impede current and future learning. Once these issues are revealed, teachers can make instructional decisions, both immediate and long term, based on students' needs.

George Polya (1945), perhaps the most influential figure in the history of mathematical problem solving, outlined a four-step problem-solving method: (1) understand the problem; (2) make a plan for solving the problem; (3) carry out the plan; and (4) look back and reflect on the answer in terms of the initial question. While Polya's method may at first appear to be a lockstep approach to solving problems, it really describes a process of mathematical thinking and acting wherein the solver moves back and forth among the four steps until a solution is reached.

While a plan can draw from many possible strategies, commonly used problem-solving strategies include guessing and checking, looking for a pattern, using an algorithm, making a list or table, modeling the situation, making a drawing, and solving a simpler problem. If taught in isolation, problem-solving strategies like these may appear to be merely tricks or shortcuts rather than powerful tools for mathematical thinking. Therefore, rather than focus classroom talk on discussing particular problem-solving strategies in isolation, we think it's most effective to incorporate discussion of problem-solving strategies in the context of the content of the mathematics curriculum.

When students discuss problems that focus on the content of their curriculum, they use a variety of problem-solving strategies. Mr. Evans's first-grade students are discussing a problem about the various ways in which ten friends can divide themselves up into two groups. The focus of the lesson is on the mathematics—what are two addends that sum to 10—but problem-solving strategies are also discussed.

1. Mr. Evans: Who would like to tell us how they solved this problem? Robin?

2. Robin: There are five ways. You can see from my picture. This one shows one friend and then the other nine. This one has two friends together and then eight together. Then I have three friends and seven in the other group, then four and six, and five and five. [See Figure 5–1 on page 68.]

3. Mr. E: Tell us how you found the different ways to group the friends.

4. Robin: I started by taking out just one person. Then I took out two and I kept going.

5. Mr. E: I'm not sure what you mean by "taking out." Can you tell us more about that?

6. Robin: There's first ten. So if you take one away, then there's nine and one person standing by themselves. Then take another one from the nine and there's two in that group and eight left in the other.

7. Mr. E: How did you know when you had found all of the different ways to divide the ten friends into two groups?

8. Robin: I just think I'm done.

9. Mr. E: So, Robin, you used a picture to solve the problem. Raise your hand if you also drew a picture. [Many students raise their hands.] Drawing a picture is one strategy for solving math problems. Did anyone use a different strategy? Anthony?

10. Anthony: I started like Robin did, but I wrote numbers. I wrote nine and one, then eight and two, seven and three, and I saw a

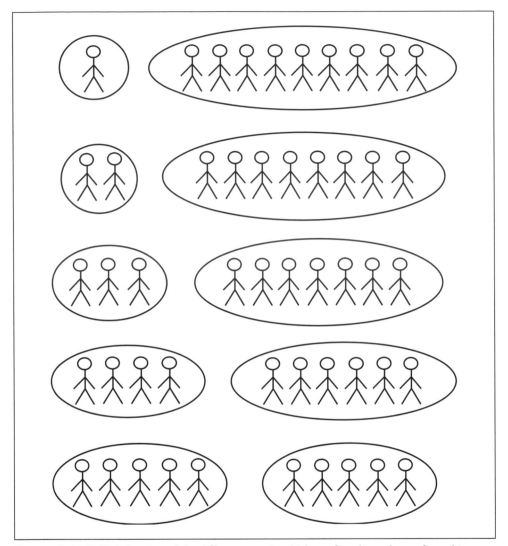

FIGURE 5–1   Robin's drawing of the different ways in which ten friends can be configured into two groups.

pattern. I realized that one number was going down and the other was going up.

11. Mr. E: Who thinks they can explain what Anthony means when he says that one number is going down and the other is going up? Nina?

12. Nina: He means like in the picture, every time another person gets taken out, the other group gets one more and the other group is one less.

13. Mr. E: Anthony, is that what you mean? [Anthony nods.] So how does your pattern help you figure out how many different ways there are to divide ten friends into two groups?

14. Anthony: The next one would be six and four, since the three goes up and the seven goes down. Then five and five and then four and six, three and seven, two and eight, one and nine, and zero and ten.

15. Mr. E: Raise your hand if you also saw this pattern. [Several students raise their hands.] Looking for a pattern is another strategy for solving math problems. Like Anthony did, once you find a pattern, you can often use that to get more information that helps solve the problem.

As this discussion continues, Mr. Evans asks other students who used these two strategies to share their methods. One purpose of this discussion is to introduce all students to these two strategies, which they might not have considered before. He also assigns the names "draw a picture" and "look for a pattern" to Robin's and Anthony's strategies so that he can promote common understandings in the classroom. In the future, when a student says, "I drew a picture" or "I looked for a pattern," the class already has common ground on which to build the discussion of their classmate's explanation. You might wonder why Mr. Evans does not pursue Robin's statement "I just think I'm done" in response to his question about knowing when she had all of the pairs. Or why doesn't he pursue the fact that Anthony formed a pair with zero and ten? Later in the class period, Mr. Evans returns to these ideas and asks everyone to consider them, but for now he is concentrating on the problem-solving strategies.

Talking Through the Givens of a Mathematics Problem

Research on problem solving has revealed that good problem solvers spend a lot of time on Step 1 of Polya's method (understanding the problem and all the relevant relationships), while novices rush to try a plan without really thinking through the plan's effectiveness. Good problem solvers ask themselves key questions about the given and unknown information in the problem. They constantly monitor their own progress in solving the problem, reevaluating choices and sequences, as well as finding and correcting errors and oversights along the way. Talk can be used to help all students spend more time on Step 1. Ms. Dunbar, a fourth-grade teacher, wrote the following mathematics problem on the board:

Mrs. Smith has to order pencils for all of the fourth-grade classrooms in the Miller School. Pencils come in packages of 48 pencils each. Mrs. Smith ordered 25 packages. Each of the six fourth grades will get the same number of pencils. How many pencils will each receive?

She told the class that before they would solve the problem, they were first going to make sure that everyone understood the information in it and what the question was. She then initiated a discussion.

1. Ms. D: Who can tell us what this problem is about? Missy?

2. Missy: This problem is about pencils.

3. Mrs. D: What else? Mohammed?

4. Mohammed: We have to figure out how many pencils there are altogether. You add all the numbers.

5. Ms. D: I'm not ready yet to figure out what to do to solve the problem. I want to understand all the facts and ideas in the problem first. Can you give me a fact, Mohammed?

6. Mohammed: Mrs. Smith has to order pencils for all of the fourth grades in the school.

7. Ms. D: Yes, that is a fact. Who can give me another fact? Ellen?

8. Ellen: There are forty-eight pencils in one package of pencils.

9. Ms. D: Where did you get that information, Ellen? Would you please show us? [Ellen goes to the board and underlines the sentence *Pencils come in packages of 48 pencils each.*] Now everyone read the problem again to yourself and see if you can find any other facts.

Ms. Dunbar goes on to elicit other relevant facts from the students. She writes them on the board. She realizes that some of the relationships in the problem may be difficult to understand, so she asks students to talk together as a group about the given information before proceeding to consider a solution method.

Talking Through a Method for Solution

Having now engaged the class in a common and accurate interpretation of the problem, Ms. Dunbar asks students to work in pairs to solve the problem. Ms. Dunbar notes that Sam and Amanda are able to solve the problem while Missy and Mel are stuck. She notices that many students use multiplication and division, but a few use repeated addition. Some students make computational errors when dividing. Ms. Dunbar decides to use a whole-class discussion of the problem to address these issues.

10. Ms. D: Sam and Amanda, could you please explain the method you used to solve the problem?

11. Amanda: Sure. First we wanted to find out how many pencils Mrs. Smith ordered. We did twenty-five times forty-eight and got one thousand two hundred.

12. Ms. D: What made you decide to multiply twenty-five by forty-eight?

13. Sam: Because there are forty-eight pencils in each package and twenty-five packages in all.

14. Ms. D: Missy and Mel, can you explain why your classmates multiplied twenty-five times forty-eight?

15. Missy: It's a faster way to add forty-eight plus forty-eight plus forty-eight, twenty-five times.

16. Mel: Yeah, they wanted to know how many pencils in all so if there's forty-eight in one package and you have twenty-five packages, you need to multiply.

17. Ms. D: So now that they know there are one thousand two hundred pencils, who can predict what Sam and Amanda did next? Raphael?

18. Raphael: I bet they divided one thousand two hundred by six to get two hundred, because we're splitting the pencils equally among six classes.

19. Ms. D: Is that what you did? [Sam and Amanda nod.] Alex, why do you think Sam and Amanda decided to use division?

20. Alex: Divide means sharing, and that's what we want to do with the pencils. We want to take all those pencils and split or share them between the classes.

21. Ms. D: Is that how you knew? [Sam and Amanda nod.] Missy, can you repeat what Alex said in your own words?

22. Missy: He said that they divided since we are sharing the pencils equally.

23. Ms. D: Sam and Amanda, how did you two figure out the answer to one thousand two hundred divided by six?

24. Sam: It's two hundred. We just divided.

25. Ms. D: OK, but how else can we be sure that two hundred is the correct answer? Why doesn't everyone talk to their partners

about this. [Partners talk for about two minutes.] Carla, I heard you and your partner describing your method. Would you share it with us?

26. Carla: If I were Mrs. Smith, I'd put all one thousand two hundred pencils into groups of one hundred 'cause that's easy to count. There would be twelve groups. Then, each class would get two of those groups and that's two hundred pencils.

Ms. Dunbar asked students who were confused to revoice and explain other students' explanations of their effective methods. She also asked students to predict what came next in solving the problem. When she did this, she checked back with the original speakers to see whether the prediction was accurate. As a result, many students who had not solved the problem or who had made mistakes were able to make progress in their understanding of the problem and one solution method.

Talking about methods of solution and problem-solving strategies can also enable students to gain insights into mathematical relationships. For example, as the discussion continued, one pair of students in Ms. Dunbar's class solved the pencil problem by dividing forty-eight by six (to find the number of pencils each class gets from one package) and then multiplying the answer, eight, by twenty-five, for a total of two hundred pencils. Students were surprised that the problem could be solved by dividing first and then multiplying; Sam and Amanda's method involved multiplying first, then dividing. The class discussed both methods, and then wrote number sentences to represent both of them—for example, $(48 \times 25) \div 6$ and $(48 \div 6) \times 25$. In the process they learned something about the order of operations, that when multiplying and dividing, it doesn't matter which operation you perform first.

Discussing methods of solution and problem-solving strategies also helps students learn more sophisticated problem-solving methods. Mrs. Steinfeld, a sixth-grade teacher, presented her students with a drawing of a large jar filled with six red and twenty blue marbles (see Figure 5–2). She asked the students to figure out how many more marbles she should put in the jar, and what color they should be, so that there will be three times as many blue marbles as red ones. In the class discussion, many students revealed that they had used a drawing to find the answer, circling groups of three blue and one red to decide how many to add. Mrs. Steinfeld then called on Bora, who remarked, "I noticed that there were twenty-six marbles altogether. You said there had to be three times as many blue marbles as red ones so that means three blue for every one red or four marbles together. So I have to have a total number of

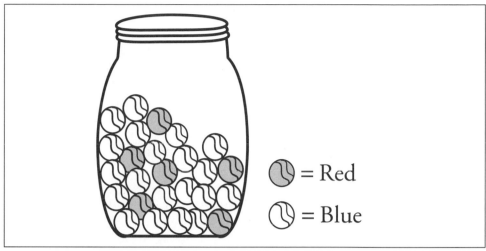

= Red

= Blue

FIGURE 5–2   Jar of red and blue marbles.

marbles that is divisible by four. Twenty-eight is divisible by four, so I need to add two marbles. Add one more blue and one more red marble, because if I have twenty-one blue and seven red, it works."

Mrs. Steinfeld then called on several of Bora's classmates to explain Bora's method as a way to assess their understanding of her explanation. Bora had to talk about her reasoning a few times before Mrs. Steinfeld felt that most students understood it. Mrs. Steinfeld also asked others to explain why Bora's method was both reasonable and efficient. Finally, Mrs. Steinfeld presented the class with two similar problems and encouraged them to use Bora's method. These "marble" problems were also then discussed. Notice that Mrs. Steinfeld didn't assume that simply hearing a more sophisticated method would lead to implementation by others. She required students to explain Bora's solution method and then to apply the method to new problems.

Increasing Students' Self-Monitoring of Thinking

As students talk about solving problems, they become more aware of their own understanding and can better monitor their own strategies and solutions. Monitoring your understanding of a topic calls for reflecting on what you do and do not understand. This kind of self-monitoring is sometimes referred to as a "metacognitive" ability. We have found that the process of explaining one's thinking aloud assists students in clarifying their own ideas and can help them correct their own mistakes, especially when teachers and classmates ask probing questions. The goal is for students eventually to monitor their own comprehension and ask themselves questions that will help them modify and refine their thinking.

Mr. Cooper, a third-grade teacher, wrote the following problem on the board:

> *The juice machine only takes quarters, dimes, and nickels.*
> *List all possible coin combinations you can use to buy a can*
> *of juice that costs 35¢.*

He gave the students time to work on the problem individually, and then he initiated a discussion.

1. Mr. C: Jaire, could you tell us how you solved this problem?

2. Jaire: I have a list here on my paper. I know that a quarter and a dime is thirty-five cents, then three dimes and a nickel is thirty-five cents, then you can also get it with seven nickels. [Mr. Cooper writes the following list on the board as Jaire talks.]

> *25¢ + 10¢ = 35¢*
> *10¢ + 10¢ + 10¢ + 5¢ = 35¢*
> *5¢ + 5¢ + 5¢ + 5¢ + 5¢ + 5¢ + 5¢ = 35¢*

3. Mr. C: We've talked a lot about how important it is to look back at your work when you think you have found a solution. How did you check your work?

4. Jaire: I checked my addition and each one added to thirty-five cents. So I knew I got it right.

5. Mr. C: Jaire has a list of some different coin combinations. He has checked to make sure that each one adds to thirty-five cents. Who would like to respond to Jaire's work? Rebecca?

6. Rebecca: Well, I think you might want to check if you had all of the combinations. I have three that aren't on your list.

7. Mr. C: Rebecca, can you give some advice to Jaire on what he can do to find these other combinations?

8. Rebecca: Well, I set my list up so that I wrote all of the ones that used a quarter first, then I wrote all of the ones that used dimes next. That way I wouldn't skip any.

9. Mr. C: Does anyone else have advice for Jaire? Louie?

10. Louie: Well, it's still a list and it kind of goes in order like Rebecca's, but I started with the way to use the least amount of coins, which was one quarter and one dime. Then I kept the quarter and changed the dime to two nickels. I kept doing that, changing from only a few coins to more.

11. Mr. C: How many people think they have every single possible combination? OK, I can see that most people think they might have missed a few. Let's see if we can make our lists more complete. Jaire, would you see if you can find some more coin combinations using one of the suggestions your classmates have offered?

12. Jaire: Okay, I'll try the one that starts with a quarter.

Instead of using the discussion to reveal to Jaire the missing coin combinations, Mr. Cooper used it to support thoughtful reflection about the overall process. He knew that many students, like Jaire, probably had missed some combinations through lack of a systematic strategy. Therefore, he took the time to have two students talk through their systematic approaches for finding all the combinations. As a result, Jaire and others will likely complete the list of possible combinations while learning how to reflect on the implementation of a strategy to maximize its effectiveness.

We believe that students improve their ability to choose and reflect on an appropriate strategy when they discuss the methods and strategies of a problem. Mrs. Lombardo consistently asks her fourth-grade students these questions:

- Why did you choose this strategy?
- Did you consider any others? Which ones?
- Why did you consider those?
- When have we used this strategy before?
- Why does it make sense to use the same strategy on these problems?
- Can you think of other problems where using this strategy would be appropriate?

On their own, students do not always see the mathematical connections among problems. When asked to consider such connections, however, students can do this well. The implications for learning can be profound. Generalizing about a specific problem-solving method enables students to figure out whether this method is appropriate when presented with a new problem. Having the chance to generalize problem-solving methods and strategies and discuss connections among problems helps students avoid using a method or strategy when it is not appropriate. When students are taught to use a strategy without discussing why and when to use it, they may be less successful in applying that strategy in sensible ways when confronted with new problems.

Assessing Student Learning

Months after a unit on subtraction in her second-grade class, Mrs. Rice wrote on the board:

There are 12 girls and 9 boys present today. How many more girls are there than boys?

After giving pairs of students time to solve the problem using partner talk, Mrs. Rice began a whole-class discussion.

1. Mrs. R: Who can tell us how they solved this problem?

2. Janice: We used these little teddy bears. [See Figure 5–3.] We put twelve red ones in a line for the girls. Then we put nine blue ones in another line for the boys. We saw that the line for the girls had three more. So there are three more girls than boys.

3. Mrs. R: Who solved the problem a different way? Darryl?

4. Darryl: We made a picture of twelve girls and nine boys. We crossed them out one boy, one girl until there were three girls and no more boys to cross out.

5. Mrs. R: Did anyone use subtraction to solve the problem? [No hands.] Did anyone try to use twelve minus nine to solve the problem?

6. Kirsten: That wouldn't work.

7. Mrs. R: Why not?

8. Kirsten: 'Cause twelve minus nine means twelve take away nine. We are not taking anything away.

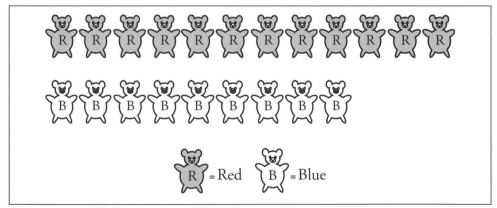

FIGURE 5–3   Janice and partner's illustration of problem, using teddy-bear counters.

9. Mrs. R: OK, so you're saying that this problem doesn't tell you to take the boys away from the girls? [Kirsten nods.] What do some other people think? Could you use subtraction here? Matthew?

10. Matthew: I don't think so. There's nothing being taken away here. It's not like the boys are leaving or something.

When students talk about how they solve word problems, teachers have an opportunity to assess students' understanding of content applied to situations. For example, Mrs. Rice realized that her students could solve this problem by modeling, but they had not generalized that comparisons can be solved using subtraction. Based on this discussion, Mrs. Rice decided to include more problems involving comparisons in her lessons. She also noted that by discussing the problems, it was likely that students would learn from each other more efficient solution strategies.

CHAPTER

6

Mathematical Reasoning

Reasoning stands at the center of mathematics learning. Many mathematics educators consider the NCTM standard concerning reasoning and proof to be its most important. Susan Jo Russell, coauthor of the *Investigations in Number, Data, and Space* curriculum, makes a number of points explaining why instruction must focus on reasoning.

> Mathematics is a discipline that deals with abstract entities, and reasoning is the tool for understanding abstractions. . . . First, mathematical reasoning is essentially about the development, justification, and use of mathematical generalizations. In the classroom where mathematical reasoning is at the center of activity, the solution of an individual problem is closely linked to the generalizations behind that solution. Second, mathematical reasoning leads to an interconnected web of mathematical knowledge within a mathematical domain. Third, the development of such a web of mathematical understanding is the foundation of what I call "mathematical memory," what we often refer to as mathematical "sense," which provides the basis for insight into mathematical problems. Fourth, an emphasis on mathematical reasoning in the classroom, as in the discipline of mathematics, necessarily incorporates the study of flawed or incorrect reasoning as an avenue toward deeper development of mathematical knowledge. (Russell 1999, 1–2)

Why Talk About Reasoning?

Reasoning is an integral part of doing mathematics. We reason when we examine patterns and detect regularities, generalize relationships, make conjectures, and evaluate or construct an argument. These activities are fundamental to making sense of content. Therefore, it seems natural to talk about mathematical reasoning in mathematics class.

Beyond these basic reasoning activities, however, there are more specialized types of reasoning that we want students to encounter, and teachers can use classroom talk to present these to students as well. For example, spatial reasoning and algebraic reasoning both have an important place in mathematics and are used to solve many types of problems. Spatial reasoning forms the cornerstone of all work with visual images such as geometric shapes, graphs, and tables. Students need to be able to perform a variety of operations on images, such as rotating shapes, translating between two-dimensional shapes and three-dimensional solids, and visualizing graphical data. Reasoning that involves topics such as variables, equations, and functions is often referred to as algebraic reasoning. Algebra is essential for success in mathematics and, therefore, all students should be provided with opportunities to reason algebraically. Each type of reasoning has characteristics or components that are specific to its type, and productive classroom talk is an especially effective way for teachers to help students master the complexities of logical thinking in all areas.

In addition, there are many general reasoning tools and skills that well-educated students should have available for use in mathematics, the sciences, social studies, and the humanities. For example, it's important for students to gain experience using the processes of deduction and induction. These forms of reasoning play a role in many content areas. Deduction involves reasoning logically from general statements or premises to conclusions about particular cases. Induction involves examining specific cases, identifying relationships among the cases, and generalizing the relationship. Productive classroom talk can enhance or improve a person's ability to reason both deductively and inductively.

For example, the use of negations and logical connectives (e.g., "and," "or," "if, then," and "if and only if") in deductive statements can be especially confusing. Discussing the interpretation of a negation or the inferences that can and cannot be made from particular statements helps students become skillful in drawing defensible conclusions. Likewise, talk can help students develop their inductive reasoning ability. In many problems that require students to find generalizations that hold for many different examples, it's sometimes hard for students to recognize patterns when the examples are presented in different representational formats. Students may have trouble seeing the commonalities among examples presented in words, symbols, tables, pictures, and graphs. Extended discussion can help students come to see that relationships among mathematical entities can be expressed in more than one form. Talk also provides ways to explore the limitations of inductive reasoning—sometimes a pattern does not generalize in a way that was expected and students need models for how to reassess the situation.

Mrs. Wolf regularly asks her fourth-grade students to talk about their reasoning when solving matrix logic problems. She finds that students at first do not know what type of conclusions they can reasonably make from given statements. She knows that her students have improved in their ability to make inferences and she thinks that talking about many problems in a very purposeful way has been a key ingredient in their success.

In this lesson, Mrs. Wolf wrote on the board a problem that is typical of the problems she uses to teach students to reason deductively:

Art, Bill, and Deborah play first base, second base, and third base on their school's baseball team, but not necessarily in that order. Art and the third baseman went with Deborah to the movies yesterday. Art does not play first base. Who's on first?

She did not give the students time to work on the problem on their own, but instead asked them to read the problem three times before initiating a class discussion.

1. Mrs. W: This logic problem requires us to reason from the statements that are given in the problem. Who can read us one of the statements and then tell us what conclusion you made from that statement? Jason?

2. Jason: I know that Art is not the first baseman because it says that Art does not play first base.

3. Mrs. W: I noticed that the statement you used to draw that conclusion is not the first statement in the problem. In most logic problems it's OK to take statements out of order. What else can we conclude? Zach?

4. Zach: I think Art plays second base. It says that Art and the third baseman went with Deborah to the movies, so Art is a different person from the third baseman.

5. Mrs. W: OK, so Zach thinks that Art plays second base. Do people agree, disagree, have questions? Yuree.

6. Yuree: I don't understand why you think that Art plays second base.

7. Zach: We know that Art doesn't play first from what Jason said. Then this other sentence says that Art went with the third

	Art	Bill	Deborah
1st base	X		
2nd base	✔		
3rd base	X		

FIGURE 6-1 Caroline's matrix.

baseman to the movies, so that just leaves second base, because Art and the third baseman are two different people. So Art can't play third base. Do you see what I'm saying?

8. Mrs. W: Caroline? Do you want to add on to this?

9. Caroline: Well, I have this method that I learned last year in Ms. Kinne's class that might help. [As she is talking, Caroline draws a matrix (see Figure 6–1) on the blackboard.] I make a box and put the names on one side and the positions on the other. I put an X in a box when I know that person can't be that position. So using Jason's information I know Art doesn't play first base, and using Zach's information I know Art doesn't play third base. That only leaves second base free under Art's name.

10. Mrs. W: Yuree, can you put this into your own words? How do we know that Art doesn't play third base?

11. Yuree: Art and the third base player went to the movies together so they have to be different people. I get it now, all that's left is second base!

12. Mrs. W: Yes, that supports that conclusion. Now, Caroline is using what we call a matrix. A matrix is a useful way to keep track of all the statements and our conclusions or deductions. Everyone should copy the matrix into their math notebook and then we will fill it in together.

This discussion continued with the class coming to the conclusion that Deborah was the first-base player. Then Mrs. Wolf asked students in pairs to take turns and explain to each other why that deduction was logical—namely to again justify the conclusion based on the statements. Since most of her students were not particularly adept at using deduction, Mrs. Wolf required everyone to practice explaining how they used the premises to reach the conclusions.

Notice how Mrs. Wolfe used a variety of talk moves to make sense of the logic statements. In Line 5 she asked students if they agreed or disagreed with Zach. When Yuree indicated that she was confused by Zach's statement, Mrs. Wolfe had Zach repeat it. Then in Line 8, Mrs. Wolfe asked Caroline to add her own ideas to Zach's comments. Finally, in Line 10, she went back and asked Yuree to revoice the previous statements. While it appears that this interaction was geared toward helping Yuree make sense of the logic, it actually benefited everyone in the class by providing students with multiple opportunities to understand what inferences might be made from the statement.

Reasoning About Algebra

It's generally assumed that all students will study algebra in middle school or high school. Algebra is considered a pivotal course in a student's education because students must make sense of algebra if they are to be successful in many other mathematics courses. Lack of success in algebra sometimes translates into lack of opportunity for future schooling and careers. Algebraic reasoning is an important topic for elementary students because the experiences students have in grades one through six can help prepare them for success in a formal algebra course. Activities and discussions that revolve around patterns, equality, properties, generalizations, and symbolism are the precursors to the formal study of algebra. When we have students talk about these topics and how they make sense of problems, we help them develop an understanding of algebra.

Mrs. Malloy is currently teaching sixth grade but has also taught algebra to eighth-grade students. She knows that her students often have difficulty making sense of the concept of equivalence. She remembers that many of her eighth-grade students could solve equations for unknowns by memorizing rules, but they didn't understand what they were doing or why they were doing it. Mrs. Malloy's goal this year is for her sixth graders to solve problems that involve unknowns in ways that make sense to them, by reasoning rather than following rules. She wants them to realize that in some situations there is only one value for a specific unknown, but in other situations a variable can represent a set of numbers. She also wants to help students gain a deeper understanding of equality so that they don't interpret the equal sign as a "do an operation" cue.

Mrs. Malloy has been using balance-scale problems as a means for reasoning about variables and equality. At the time of the following discussion, students have learned that in order for a scale to balance, the objects in each pan must weigh the same amount. They have had experience drawing balance scales to represent equivalent quantities. Mrs. Malloy wrote the following problem on the board and gave the students about five minutes to solve it on their own.

> *Three apples weigh the same as one orange and two plums.*
> *One orange weighs the same as four plums. How many plums*
> *equal the weight of one apple?*

1. Mrs. M: Andrea, would you share with us your solution process?

2. Andrea: First, I drew two scales to show the information. [See Figure 6–2.] On the first scale, three apples weigh the same as an orange and two plums. Then on the second scale I put an orange on one side and four plums on the other.

3. Mrs. M: I'm going to interrupt you for a minute, Andrea. Did anyone show the relationships between the weights of the fruit in a different way? Amira?

4. Amira: I drew pictures of the fruit and used equal signs. [See Figure 6–3.]

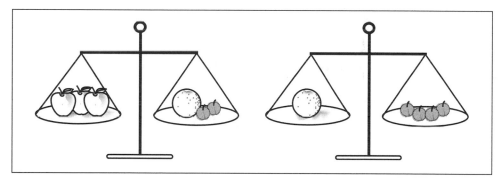

FIGURE 6–2 Andrea's balance-scale illustration.

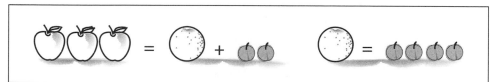

FIGURE 6–3 Amira's representation of the balance problem.

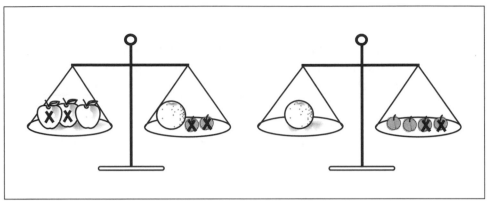

FIGURE 6–4 Andrea's attempt to solve the problem using her illustration.

5. Mrs. M: Are both of these representations OK? Does a balance scale and an equal sign show the same relationships between the weight of the fruit? Talk to your partner about these questions. [A minute elapses]. OK, Vicky?

6. Vicky: Yes, I think both are the same. When a balance scale is level or balanced it shows that the objects weigh the same. We can show that they weigh the same with an equal sign, too.

7. Mrs. M: OK, so an equal sign means that both sides of the equal sign are the same weight? An equal sign implies balance?

8. Students: Yes.
Right.
Uh, huh.

9. Mrs. M: OK, Andrea, go ahead. Please continue with your solution.

10. Andrea: On the first scale I took two apples away from one side and two plums away from the other side. I also took two plums away from the second scale. So we now have one apple and three plums left so one apple is equal to three plums. [See Figure 6–4.]

Mrs. Malloy knows that Andrea's answer isn't correct, and she isn't sure how Andrea arrived at this incorrect solution. In addition, Mrs. Malloy is unsure if she should correct Andrea or not, but decides not to pursue her thinking at this point. Instead, Mrs. Malloy elicits other solutions from other students as a way to keep the discussion moving.

11. Mrs. M: So here is one solution. Andrea is saying that one apple is equal to three plums. Does anyone else have a different solution? Ben?

FIGURE 6–5   Ben's representation of the balance problem.

12. Ben: Since one orange equals four plums, I can use this informa-
              tion to say that three apples equal six plums.

13. Mrs. M: Where did the six plums come from?

14. Ben: Three apples weigh the same as one orange and two plums.
              But one orange equals four plums, so the three apples equal
              six plums. [See Figure 6–5.]

15. Mrs. M: Then what?

16. Ben: I just divided each side of the balance scale by three and
              then I know that one apple equals two plums.

17. Mrs. M: OK, so we have two different solutions here. One is that
              three plums equal one apple and another is that two plums
              weigh the same as one apple. Which is correct? Discuss
              these two solutions with your partner. [After three minutes,
              Mrs. Malloy resumes the discussion by calling on the part-
              ner team of Nick and Elizabeth.]

18. Elizabeth: Nick and I think that two plums equal the weight of one
              apple because you can't just cross off apples and plums—
              maybe they don't weigh the same amount.

19. Brian: I agree with Elizabeth. You can't do what Andrea suggests
              because we don't know if the objects weigh the same.

20. Carlos: My partner and I think that Ben's method makes sense. We
              think one apple equals the weight of two plums. Because
              you trade the orange for four plums so that makes six
              plums.

21. Mrs. M: A number of you are using a technique in algebra called
              "substitution," where you substitute one value for another.
              Since one orange weighs the same as four plums, we can

substitute the value of one orange by crossing it out and writing four plums. Talk to your partner about this. Does this make sense?

Students in Mrs. Malloy's class are starting to reason algebraically. Some of them are realizing they can use substitution to find the number of plums that equal the weight of three apples. Others do not yet realize that they can't remove unlike objects from both sides of the equal sign or balance scale. Talk, however, makes students' reasoning visible and helps Mrs. Malloy assist everyone in interpreting and solving problems. As the students share their insights and misconceptions, she is able to make instructional decisions to further their learning. In addition, talk helps students sort through multiple interpretations of algebraic situations and settle on common ground.

When Andrea presents her solution strategy in Line 10, a teacher or other listener might have an immediate sense of confusion. How did Andrea get there? Could that method possibly be right? Should we take the time to work through her reasoning? Here the teacher chooses to focus on Andrea's solution rather than her reasoning, first eliciting another solution path from Ben and then letting students talk about the two possible answers. She could also have chosen to go into more detail with Andrea's reasoning, asking her to spell out her thinking in more detail. When using classroom talk to deepen mathematical reasoning, teachers frequently encounter puzzling or incoherent contributions from students. We return to this issue in Chapter 12.

One of the most important and difficult parts of trying to improve students' abilities to reason mathematically is to help them extend their knowledge about reasoning to new problems. When students encounter a new strategy or tool that helps them reason through a particular problem, they can seem to understand it well. However, often their understanding is limited to the context of that particular problem, and their teacher watches in frustration as students fail to see how to apply or extend the strategy to solve a slightly different problem. We have found that talking about the reasoning involved in a problem helps students generalize problem types and solution methods and apply them to new situations. To help them in this process, it's important to encourage students to look beyond the specific details of problems to the underlying mathematical relationships, talk about the similarities and differences among problems, and reflect aloud on how what they learned from other problems can be used in the solution process.

7

Mathematical Terminology, Symbols, and Definitions

If students are to become competent mathematical thinkers, able to work with and communicate about mathematical ideas, they must become familiar with mathematical words and symbols, such as *multiply*, *perimeter*, =, *square unit*, *prime number*, and so on. In our work, we have learned that simply providing students with definitions for mathematical terms doesn't result in students gaining a deep understanding of those terms. Understanding a term entails understanding the concept or action that term refers to, and the relationships that exist between that concept and related concepts and ideas.

Carefully guided talk—multiple opportunities to discuss aspects of the meaning of words and symbols—can help students develop understanding and also provide them needed practice in using terminology precisely and effectively. As we guide students in talking—clarifying and discussing the complexities associated with the appropriate words, phrases, and symbols—we are helping them clarify their own thoughts and understandings.

It's important in every subject to discuss the meanings of new terms, but this is particularly true in mathematics. Consider first how we learn the meaning of words that name ordinary objects, such as *chair*. Most of this learning takes place as we encounter examples, gradually learning which things other human beings label as chairs, and making inferences about what kinds of objects the label *chair* might refer to. Now consider how we learn the meaning of a word like *rectangle*. First we encounter examples of rectangles and learn to recognize and label them. But our work is not over. To really understand what the term means in mathematics, we must know that it names a closed figure with two sets of parallel sides, and four internal ninety-degree angles. In other words, understanding the concept *rectangle* means understanding a formal definition. This second step is difficult for students. If we ask elementary students to identify a rectangle, most of them will pick out the shape of a typical rectangle. When asked to provide a definition of rectangle, however, very few will list all of the criteria that define what a rectangle is. Only by explicitly talking about the formal definition of a rectangle can we get at the real nature of the mathematical concept.

One of the challenges of mathematical language arises from the fact that some mathematics terminology also has everyday meanings. For example, the word *difference* can be interpreted mathematically as meaning the value we get when one number is subtracted from another number. But *difference* has non-mathematical meanings as well; for example, dissimilarity, disagreement in opinion, and distinction. Students must be aware of the various meanings of words in order to decide which meaning makes most sense in a specific context. Talk can help develop students' awareness of the meanings of mathematical terms, symbols, and definitions.

In general, words and symbols used in mathematics tend to have stricter or more precisely stated definitions than everyday words. If someone says, "Bring me a chair, I need to sit down," you are unlikely to be considered a failure if you bring them a stool or a bench. But if you are asked to construct a rectangle, you will fail unless it meets the criteria listed above. Mathematical terms carry "high stakes" definitions: there is less room for interpretation. As your students go on in school they will encounter such precisely stated "technical terms" in a wide range of content areas. The precise use of technical terms is difficult for many students, because it departs from their ordinary ways of using language. Talk about the exact meanings of mathematical terms can help them make the transition. Their discussions of definitions in your classroom may be their first encounter with the very important academic practice of using technical terms.

Sorting Out Different Word Senses

Why is it important to talk about definitions of words, phrases, and symbols? One aspect of being an educated person is having a broad vocabulary and being able to choose words that exactly express what you are trying to say. And one of our jobs as teachers is to help students learn to use correct vocabulary to express themselves clearly and articulately. In the past, many teachers felt that it was not necessary to worry about language arts issues in mathematics class. Yet it is clear that if we want students to use specific words and phrases correctly, they must have opportunities to discuss word meanings and to practice correct word usage.

For example, in studying the concept of similarity, Ms. Lee, a sixth-grade teacher, had reviewed with her class the definition presented in the textbook: Two figures are similar if and only if the corresponding angles have the same measure and corresponding sides are in proportion. The next day during the mathematics lesson, Ms. Lee noticed some confusion and posed the following question, "What does the term *similar* mean in geometry?" One student replied, "Similar means that the shapes are like each other." Not sure what the student meant by the phrase "are like each other," Ms. Lee responded, "Could you give us an example?" The student's response indicated her partial understanding: "Two rectangles are similar because they are both rectangles. They have similar characteristics like ninety-degree angles and parallel sides."

Notice that this student is using a nonmathematical definition of similar—having characteristics of likeness—rather than the mathematical definition—having corresponding angles with the same measure and corresponding sides in proportion. However, the student isn't completely incorrect, as angle measurement is important when considering similarity. This is a case where the mathematical meaning of a word is more restrictive and precisely stated than its everyday meaning, and yet they overlap, creating confusion.

To push the student's thinking, Ms. Lee drew two rectangles on the board, one long and narrow and one a square (see Figure 7–1). (She chose a square to remind students that a square is a rectangle with the special characteristic that its sides are all the same length.) Then she redirected the question to the entire class: Are these rectangles similar?

As students contributed to the discussion, some agreeing and others disagreeing that they were similar, the class as a whole was required to reflect on the mathematical meaning of *similar*. Guided by Ms. Lee, the term was linked to many examples, some of which did fit the mathematical definition and some of which did not. The students discussed each one in turn.

The discussion then returned to the task of determining a definition of the word *similar*. One student stated, "I think similar figures have the same shape but are different sizes." Another student added, "And to have the same shape

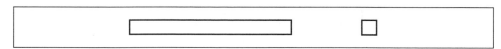

FIGURE 7–1 Ms. Lee's representation of the concept of "rectangle."

they have to have the same angle measures." In order to further assist students in understanding the mathematical use of *similar*, Ms. Lee directly addressed the confusion with everyday language by suggesting, "Let's compare the meaning of *similar* in everyday life with its meaning in math." She organized student responses on the blackboard into two columns, mathematical meaning and nonmathematical meaning, and asked a number of students to summarize the class responses. This type of careful consideration of vocabulary not only helped students heighten their awareness of the differences between technical terms and everyday language, but also helped them broaden their understanding of the concept of similarity.

Another reason for talking about mathematical definitions is that errors can be caused by a student's shallow understanding of the mathematical meaning of a word, and an overreliance on its everyday meaning. For example, in a second-grade classroom the teacher asked her students to write down the numerical expressions for different times of day. For the time "quarter past ten," a number of students wrote *10:25*. At first, the teacher thought that the students did not know how to tell time. Yet when asked about the definition of *quarter*, one student replied "twenty-five of something." When the teacher probed further, asking other students for meanings of the word *quarter*, several gave the definition "a piece of money that is twenty-five cents." Since a quarter has a value of twenty-five cents, the students had assumed that a quarter past ten was twenty-five minutes past ten. Their error was due, in part, to the fact that they had an incomplete understanding of the meaning of *quarter*. A student who has a thorough understanding of the word knows that it refers to a fractional part of a whole, and that the quantity it names depends upon the quantity that makes up the whole. A quarter of 100 is 25, but a quarter of 60 is 15. These students, like others you may have encountered, thought it referred to a specific quantity rather than a fraction of a whole. Getting students to understand this meaning is not easy; it takes time. Discussion of the meaning of *quarter* in the case of money versus time can move students closer to this understanding.

Extending Students' Knowledge Through Talk About Words

A further reason to talk about definitions of words and phrases is to extend students' knowledge. In Ms. Lee's classroom, the discussion about the word *similar* led to another discussion about the meaning of the word *congruent*. Logical relationships between the two words were introduced—If two shapes are congruent, are they also similar? And if two shapes are similar, are they also congruent? What started out as a short explanation of the word *similar* resulted in students learning more than was presented in the textbook. Definitions can play an important part in extending students' general knowledge when discussions about definitions require students to think about networks of underlying concepts.

Sometimes teachers must also monitor students' understanding of non-mathematical terms. When students do not know the meanings of words and phrases in a problem, they may have difficulty making sense of the content under discussion. For example, in Case 3 in Chapter 2, where the fifth-grade class was working on a problem about the number of peach tarts that could be made using a set number of peaches, as the dialogue progressed from where we left off, it became clear that a few students did not know what a peach tart was. They mistakenly confused it with the popular breakfast food Pop-Tarts. This confusion, though minor, made it difficult for them to follow other students' explanations of their solution processes. The students wondered why their classmates were representing the peach tarts with round circles, since Pop-Tarts are rectangular. Unfortunately, students often focus on irrelevant features of problems, in part because they are trying to make sense of those features they find confusing. By discussing vocabulary and phrases, and by providing background information, teachers can help students understand the context of a problem (which will improve problem solving), and they can also extend students' overall knowledge of the world.

Building and Monitoring Common Understandings

Whenever talk is used as an instructional tool in the classroom, it's important for students and the teacher to be in agreement on definitions. They must work at maintaining what is sometimes referred to as "shared meaning," so that everyone can follow a discussion as it develops. Central to the use of mathematical discourse is the premise that students and teacher will work toward common understandings that are satisfactory to all. The greatest value of this practice becomes apparent after a short time: when all students and the teacher have explicitly agreed upon facts, definitions, and procedures, this shared understanding becomes part of the ongoing discourse and helps move the whole class forward. Time invested in building a solid common ground of understanding pays off in multiple ways.

What do shared understandings look like in practice? In one elementary school, after third graders were asked to sort into two groups a variety of solid figures—pyramids, cones, cylinders, rectangular prisms, triangular prisms, spheres, and cubes—a class discussion was held regarding the sorting characteristics. Here are a few student responses:

- My group sorted them [solids] by looking at how all of these are flat [points to flat faces of prisms, cubes, and pyramids] and all of these are curved [points to curved surfaces of cones, cylinders, and spheres].
- We used the flat sides too, but we sorted them by a flat base or not a flat base.
- I separated the blocks by the roundness or flatness of the faces.

Students used a variety of words to describe the same idea—*side, face, base, flat surface*—but because they were able to point to a physical feature on the actual blocks, everyone was able to make sense of each individual student's contributions. If there had been confusion about the different terms for the side of a prism, the teacher would have needed to shift the discussion in order to clarify the meaning of each word. Note that this discussion was not intended as a discussion of vocabulary. Students were describing the basis for their sorting of shapes. The teacher intended to address solid-geometry vocabulary after the students were familiar with the solids and their characteristics. Nevertheless, the teacher had to carefully attend to the words that students used, in order to make sure that everyone was following the meaning of the discussion. She also had to monitor whether all students had access to what those words referred to. In this case, she had to ascertain whether all students could see what the speaker was pointing to when using a word like *side* or *face*. When the discussion is not about common physical objects, this monitoring process can get more challenging, but becomes even more important.

In some cases, teachers have to briefly stop a discussion in order to make sure that everyone agrees on the meaning of a word or phrase. During the geometry discussion above, one boy kept calling a cube a square, which confused other students. His teacher responded: "A cube is a solid figure, like a box, whereas a square is a flat shape—the faces of the cube are squares. It's easy to call the solid a square, but let's try not to, because it's confusing. If you say *square* we'll know you're talking about a two-dimensional shape such as the faces of some of these blocks, and if you say *cube* we'll know you mean a solid boxlike shape where all the faces are squares." In this case, the teacher established common understanding of the difference between a cube and a square and encouraged students to use the correct word as a way to ensure continued shared understanding.

Discussing the Meanings of Symbols

Mathematics sometimes is referred to as a language, partially because of its symbolic notation. Symbols enable us to express ideas unambiguously and to form precise statements about quantitative relationships. But symbols can be misunderstood and used incorrectly, especially by young learners, just as words can. As a result, we also need to talk about the meanings and uses of a variety of symbols. For example, researchers have shown that many students do not see the equal sign (=) as a statement of equivalence (Kieran and Chalouh 1993; Wagner and Parker 1993). Instead they interpret this symbol as a signal to "write the answer." When students rely on this interpretation of the equal sign, they might respond to the following equation, $12 + 8 = \_ + 12$, by replacing the blank with 20 instead of 8. Further evidence of this misunderstanding of the meaning of the equal sign is seen in the misreading of a chain of partial calculations that are connected by the equal sign (Stacey and MacGregor 1997). For example, the expression $1 + 6 = 7 \times 4 = 28 \div 2 = 14$ may be conceived by a student as a "running record" of thinking, with the incorrect implication that $1 + 6 = 7 \times 4$ and that $7 \times 4 = 28 \div 2$.

Just as words take on different meanings in different contexts, so do symbols. For example, a fraction bar can be interpreted in a number of ways. It can indicate a fraction ($\frac{2}{3}$—two parts out of three parts); a division ($\frac{2}{3}$—two divided by three); or a ratio ($\frac{2}{3}$—two items compared to three items). We need to find out what preconceived notions students have about symbols and orchestrate discussions that build on students' current understanding as we introduce them to new interpretations as well. One very useful practice we recommend is to call students' attention to the multiple meanings of a symbol or word. When we introduce a new meaning for a symbol, we explicitly ask students first to put into words their understandings of that symbol. We ask them to remember a previous lesson in which it was used in the way they are familiar with. Only after they have discussed and solidified their current understandings do we introduce the new meaning. Over time, we have seen real improvement in students' ability to monitor their own use of symbols and words. Their written and spoken expression becomes more precise, and they are more mindful of how they formulate their ideas in words.

8

Forms of Representation

Representations are tools that help us record and work with our mathematical ideas, communicate our thoughts to others, and clarify our own understanding. Students in the elementary and middle grades use a variety of forms of representation to record and communicate their thinking: symbols, drawings and pictures, tables and charts, physical materials, graphs, models, and oral and written language. The NCTM *Principles and Standards for School Mathematics* states: "Representing ideas and connecting the representations to mathematics lies at the heart of understanding mathematics" (NCTM 2000, 136). Some representations are conventions that are well known and accepted throughout the mathematics community, such as the addition, subtraction, multiplication, and division symbols we use to represent arithmetic operations; the greater than, less than, and equal signs we use to represent relationships among quantities; and the notations we use to graph a linear function. Students should be able to understand these and connect them to other conventional representations. For example, division can also be represented with fractional notation, and a graph can also be represented with its corresponding linear equation.

As students try to make sense of problems, concepts, and procedures, they may create other representations that are more idiosyncratic and not standard. It may not be essential that everyone in the class discuss or experience these. For example, Doug, a second grader, adds a column of two-digit numbers by first looking at the tens column and recording one X on his paper for each group of ten. He then counts the number of Xs and records that numeral in the tens column. He next makes check marks for the ones and counts them before recording the numeral. Sometimes he has to adjust the numeral he writes in the tens column if there are enough ones to make another ten.

Doug's use of Xs and check marks is a nonstandard way to keep track of the number of tens and ones.

$$23 \quad X, X, X, X, X, X$$
$$14 \quad \checkmark\,\checkmark\,\checkmark\,\checkmark\,\checkmark\,\checkmark\,\checkmark\,\checkmark$$
$$+\ \ 31$$
$$\overline{68}$$

While this notation is helpful to Doug, it creates an unnecessary extra step for other students. Also, students who have performed additions using base ten blocks (a line for a ten and a dot for a one) might find Doug's representation confusing. Thus, teachers must consider which representations are worth sharing with the whole class.

Whatever type of representation is used, however, it's important for teachers to maintain a consistent focus on the meaning of the representation. Our goal is for students to be able to understand and explain the mathematical meaning of each part of their symbolic, graphic, or language-based representation. Furthermore, we want them to be able to understand and explain the connections among different representations. In first grade, this might involve a student being able to explain that each dot in a diagram stands for one piece of candy that the children in a math problem got from their parents, or that the number 4 stands for the four dots, which indicates four pieces of candy. In the sixth grade this might involve students being able to explain that a ratio of two portions of lemon juice to one portion of sugar in a lemonade concentrate can be symbolized as 2:1, 2 to 1, or $\frac{2}{1}$, and can be shown on a bar graph by one bar that is twice as high as the other.

Why Talk About Representations?

As teachers, we sometimes take it for granted that students will understand various forms of representation in the same ways that we do. A set of base ten blocks looks to many students just like any set of differently sized blocks; it does not automatically convey the structure of the base ten system. Classroom talk can help them transform their understanding of that representation and its potential. Furthermore, even when students understand what the blocks are meant to indicate, it takes a long time for them to learn to interpret symbols, graphic objects, and the linguistic expressions that describe them. Here, too, talk can be used productively to get students to ask questions about what these forms of representation mean, and how their meanings are connected.

Ms. Sanchez regularly uses discussion in her fourth grade to find out how her students think about the representations they use. In one class she gave each student a "one-half" piece from a commercial product of fraction pieces. She asked her students to find different ways to exactly cover the area of the one-half piece using other fractional pieces from the set, using the same-size pieces for each different way they could find. (In other words, she asked them to find a way to exactly cover the one-half piece using only one type of fractional piece, not mixing fraction types.) This activity gave the students experience with an area model for fractions. The students were familiar with these manipulative materials and had used them before.

Once the students found which pieces they could use to cover the one-half piece, Ms. Sanchez asked them to write down the fraction corresponding to each different way that was equivalent to one-half. For this set of manipulative materials, students could cover the area of the one-half piece using five different-size pieces—fourths, sixths, eighths, tenths, and twelfths. She knew that their solutions could be represented by the equivalent fractions $\frac{2}{4}$, $\frac{3}{6}$, $\frac{4}{8}$, $\frac{5}{10}$, and $\frac{6}{12}$. In this activity, Ms. Sanchez wanted the students to connect the concrete manipulative representations of the fractions with the symbols they used to write the quantities. As students develop understanding of fractions, they make these connections automatically. At this early stage in Ms. Sanchez's class, however, students need practice in making these connections.

In this discussion, Ms. Sanchez had another purpose as well. She wanted to reinforce the important mathematical concept of equivalence of fractions, that fractions with different names, such as one-half, two-fourths, three-sixths, and so on, have the same value. She also wanted to reinforce the equivalence among all the different graphic representations of the area covered by the one-half piece. Her students had worked with fractions equivalent to one-half a month earlier, but had not related these to an area model of fractions. Ms. Sanchez thought that using the manipulative pieces would reinforce their understanding of equivalent fractions.

Ms. Sanchez drew two columns on the chalkboard and labeled one *fraction pieces* and the other *name*. She drew a picture of one-half of a rectangle in the "fraction pieces" column and wrote $\frac{1}{2}$ under the "name" column. She then proceeded to collect many contributions from students. She also used a magnetic board to display the actual fractional pieces that they were discussing.

Many of the students' responses surprised Ms. Sanchez because their answers didn't match her expectations. Students suggested that she write a whole number in the "name" column. For example, Eduardo stated, "You

Fraction Pieces   Name

Fraction Pieces	Name
	$\dfrac{1}{2}$
	3
	4
	$\dfrac{2}{4}$
$\dfrac{4}{8}$	$\dfrac{1}{8}$

FIGURE 8–1 Ms. Sanchez's chart showing equivalence of fractions.

should put a three on the name side. I covered my half with three pieces."
Anna said, "We put a four on the name side and a picture of the four pieces
that covered the half on the fraction pieces side." Other students' responses
were closer to what Ms. Sanchez had expected. For example, Angela said, "Put
a picture of two-fourths in the first column and write a two over a four in the
second column." But then Larry said, "I put the number four-eighths in the
first column, because it says 'fraction pieces' and there were four of the one-
eighth pieces on my picture, and then in the 'name' column I would write
one-eighth because the name of the piece I used was the one-eighth piece. Is
that wrong?" (See Figure 8–1.)

Ms. Sanchez realized that the chart was not as clear as she had thought it
would be. She decided to start a whole-class discussion about the disparity of
answers.

1. Ms. S: I notice that we have many different types of numbers in the "name" category. Are all of these numbers equal to one-half? Let's go around the room and have everyone tell us what he or she put in the name column. Carlos, do you want to start?

2. Carlos: Something is wrong, 'cause three is not the same as one-half.

3. Eduardo: But three of the pieces cover the half.

4. Carlos: Yes, but, like, think of three pies. Three pies are not the same amount as one-half a pie.

5. Eduardo: I don't get what you're saying. Ms. Sanchez said to put the name of what you put over the one-half piece. I'm just saying I put three pieces over it.

6. Carlos: But that's not the name, that's the number.

As you can see, Carlos and Eduardo were confused by the chart. At this point Ms. Sanchez realized that her label *name*, while seemingly straightforward, had been interpreted in several different ways by other students as well. Another student spoke up.

7. Sandra: I'm confused by what Larry said, because his one-eighth doesn't equal one-half either.

8. Ms. S: Larry, do you want to explain that for us again so we can understand your reasoning?

9. Larry: Well, I just thought by "fraction pieces" you meant how many pieces and what fraction we used. So I used four of the one-eighth pieces, so I put four-eighths. And then in the name column I thought you wanted us to tell you the name of the fraction piece that we worked with. Like Angela used fourths and I used eighths.

10. Ms. S: I can see that the way I've labeled this chart hasn't been too clear. So let's go back to the drawing board and see if I can communicate more clearly. Good mathematicians always worry about being clear communicators, and that should include all of us. In this first column, I've drawn a picture of the one-half piece. Here, I wanted us to remind ourselves of the pieces we used by drawing a picture of those pieces in the same shape as the ones we used. I want you to draw a picture that corresponds to what you put on top of the one-half piece. What should we call this column? I think "fraction pieces" was not clear enough. What do you think? Sandra?

11. Sandra: How about "picture of fractions"?

12. Ms. S: OK, what do other people think? Do people agree or disagree with Sandra's suggestion? Larry?

13. Larry: Well, couldn't that still mean what type of fraction we used? So I could just put a picture of the one-eighth piece. So if you want us to put a picture of all the pieces that we used to cover the one-half, you could label it "picture of pieces used to cover one-half piece."

Ms. Sanchez sees some dubious looks. She asks whether people agree or disagree and a few students say, "It's too long for the chart" and "It won't fit." She decides to make a point about how people come to agreements about conventions. Making such agreements is an appropriate topic, she decides, for a mathematics class.

14. Ms. S: OK, we have two suggestions. One is Larry's, which is "picture of pieces used to cover one-half piece." [She writes on the board: *picture of pieces used to cover $\frac{1}{2}$ piece*.] One is Sandra's, which is "pictures of fractions." Now, we don't have too much time, so I'm going to take a position here and see what you think about it. Larry says Sandra's might not be exact enough for everyone to understand. But some people think that Larry's is too long, even though it does tell us exactly what to put in that column. I'm going to suggest that we all agree that Larry's label does communicate what we want to put in this column, and that we can get around the length problem by abbreviating it a bit. Abbreviating means shortening. I think we could shorten it like this. [She writes on the board: *Picture: covers $\frac{1}{2}$*.] This is the same length as Sandra's, but we will all know what it means. We have an agreement about our label. We agree that it will stand for something longer, but we will know what it means. It means "draw a picture of the pieces you used to cover the one-half piece." Is everyone OK with this? [Students look thoughtful and nod. No one objects.]

15. Ms. S: OK. Now that we have that settled, we have to figure out what to label the next column, because my label of *name* didn't communicate clearly enough. What I want us to put in this column is a number, the total fraction that you used to cover up the one-half piece. So Larry told us he covered up the one-half with four-eighths. So he would write the name of the fraction four-eighths. Does anyone have a suggestion for how we should label this column?

This time a number of people had ideas, because they understood more clearly what Ms. Sanchez wanted them to do. They finally agreed on the label *Fraction: covers $\frac{1}{2}$*. This label clarified the contents and in addition made a connection with the first column, the pictorial representation.

During the discussion, one student asked whether he should write the number corresponding to his fraction or the words that named the fraction: $\frac{2}{4}$ or "two-fourths"? The teacher and students then discussed the fact that you could write $\frac{2}{4}$ as a symbol or write out "two-fourths," and both named the picture with two $\frac{1}{4}$ pieces covering the one-half piece. Finally, the students and Ms. Sanchez were able to line up the different fractions and discuss the ways in which they were equivalent to one-half and to one another.

Was it worth it for Ms. Sanchez to spend so much time on the issue of how to name the columns in her table? It might seem trivial, and it may seem that students should have understood what she wanted from the beginning. But in our view, Ms. Sanchez did something very intelligent. She saw that her own unintentional lack of clarity provided an opportunity to model for students the very habits that she wanted them to adopt. She knew that if she wanted her students to strive for clarity in their talk and writing, she would have to show them that she herself would strive for clarity as well. Instead of feeling embarrassment or annoyance when her chart was not understood, she seized the opportunity to model the process of trying to communicate clearly. By eliciting her students' help in coming up with labels that would be more transparent, she drew them into the activity of striving for clear communication. Gradually, through more and more episodes such as this, Ms. Sanchez's students came to see the struggle for clarity as part of their everyday work. They developed a much stronger sense of the audience, and what they had to do to be understood.

Even young children can benefit from discussions about the conventional meanings of various representations, particularly of symbols. Young children are just learning about using symbols as a form of representation. They often know less about the symbols used to represent a computational procedure than the actions associated with the procedure. They may know, for example, that Julie has eight candies in all if she had five and her friend gave her three more, but they may not know that this situation can be represented with symbols as 5 + 3 = 8. This should not be surprising—there is no intrinsic quality of symbols that signals their meaning. They are social conventions that children become familiar with over time and with much experience. Discussion, however, can help link young children's understanding of a computational procedure and the symbols used to represent it.

Mr. Dunbar presented the problem to his first-grade class:

> *Julie has five candies. Her friend gives her three more candies.*
> *How many candies does Julie have in all?*

He gave the children the chance to work on the problem individually and encouraged them to record their calculations in any way that made sense to them.

1. Mr. D: How did you figure out how many candies Julie had in all?

2. Tim: I started with five beans and got three more and then counted six, seven, and eight. She has eight.

3. Mr. D: I noticed that Geri wrote "five plus three equals eight" to solve the problem. Does anyone see any connection between Tim's actions with the beans and Geri's number sentence?

4. Meli: The five in what she wrote is the five beans that Robbie started with. The little t means to add three beans. Robbie did that. They both have the same answer.

5. Mr. D: Does anyone know what we call the little t? Does it always tell us to add three?

6. Sierra: It's called a plus sign. It means to do something to the numbers.

The purpose of this discussion was to help students start to link actions with real objects and with the number sentence that symbolizes them. Due to the complexity and variety of mathematical symbols, students will not likely make this connection on their own. Yet making this connection is crucial to success with computation. Mr. Dunbar uses discussion to clarify both the identification and meaning of the addition symbol. He does this by asking another student to react to her classmate's suggested name and meaning. By having students offer both ideas and clarifications, Mr. Dunbar is allowing them to develop their own shared, accurate interpretation of the symbols they'll use in future computations.

Implementing Talk
in the
Classroom

CHAPTER
9

Getting Started

Talk is productive in math class when it is used to strengthen students' mathematical thinking and reasoning. In order for this to take place, student talk must be respectful, engaged, and focused on mathematics. Only when both the social and the mathematical aspects of communication are in place do we find that classroom talk offers maximum support for learning. In this chapter, we first introduce five principles for you to keep in mind as you make plans to incorporate talk into your mathematics teaching. Following these are five approaches that we have found helpful as you and your students start to talk during math lessons. Finally, we introduce some practical suggestions for tracking your own progress in making talk an integral part of your math instruction.

Principles of Productive Talk

The following five principles deal with the major issues you will encounter as you start to build this kind of productive talk in your classroom. You will recognize some of these topics from the discussion of ground rules for respectful talk and equitable participation in Chapter 2. Here they have been formulated into principles so that you may more easily incorporate them into your mathematics teaching practice.

Principle 1. Establish and maintain a respectful, supportive environment.

It's common knowledge that learning takes place most easily within an atmosphere of respect and support. We have all had the positive experience of learning in a supportive environment, and have seen what it can do for us. Conversely, we have all experienced the feeling of being silenced or shut down, of not wanting to speak up because we are afraid of ridicule or criticism.

Neither students nor teachers will engage in productive talk about mathematics if they are afraid that they will be laughed at, "dissed," or somehow made to feel stupid. Therefore, it's important to emphasize the positive and forestall the negative. A big part of the preparation for using talk in mathematics involves putting in place classroom norms that will ensure a safe and supportive place for people to talk about their thinking.

As we discussed in Chapter 2, setting the ground rules for a respectful classroom culture must come first. It's helpful to emphasize to students that each of them has a right to be heard and have their ideas considered with respect. Along with this right comes an obligation: the obligation to listen to others just as they themselves will be listened to. We think it's important to emphasize the positive aspects of respectful discourse—the good thinking and learning that can emerge in a civil and supportive environment, and the pleasure of thinking together with one's classmates. It's important, however, to make clear to students that this respectful discourse is not optional, and that there are sanctions for failing to maintain the norms of respect that you set up.

As your students become more adept at talking about mathematics, you will be able to discuss with them further ramifications of respectful discourse in mathematics. For example, in your classroom, students will have a right to have their ideas taken seriously. This means, however, that they are obligated to try very hard to make their thinking available to others and communicate their thoughts as clearly as they can. To some extent, this happens naturally. As students have their ideas taken seriously, they begin to try harder to get those ideas across. They don't give up as easily, and they begin to pursue the consequences of their own ideas and those of others. Although this may happen naturally over time, it is nevertheless important to remind students from the start that they should try to communicate their mathematical thinking as clearly and explicitly as possible.

Principle 2. Focus talk on the mathematics.

As you establish norms for respectful discourse, you should simultaneously make sure that classroom talk is focused on the mathematical content and reasoning that is relevant to the lesson. Be sure to tell students that the role of talk in math class is to help them understand the mathematics they are studying, and that a thorough and solid understanding for everyone is the goal. To make sure that you and the students maintain this focus, you need to prepare lessons carefully, considering ahead of time how the mathematical topics and procedures might play out in the classroom talk. Using the categories of mathematics and ideas introduced in Part II, you can decide how to focus the talk in mathematically fruitful directions. In this way, a focus on talk can strengthen not just your students' understanding, but your own as well.

Principle 3. Provide for equitable participation in classroom talk.
All students can benefit from the kinds of discourse practices we are describing, not just those who are actively speaking, but also those who are listening. Yet it's important to think carefully about equitable participation. This has two aspects: how to make it possible for all students to participate actively in the talk from time to time, and how to make certain that all students are listening actively all of the time. If a student rarely has an opportunity to talk, that student does not have full access to participation. If a student can participate in the talk but is not listened to seriously, again, there is a problem with equitable participation. Finally, if a student does not listen, that student does not have access to participation.

One of the core obligations of teaching is to provide equal access to learning for all students. However, in every class there are challenges to achieving this goal. Some students are eager to discuss mathematics and feel confident doing so. Others, however, may seem diffident, reluctant to participate, even resentful of being asked to talk out loud. Still others may seem not to understand, or may understand so well that you fear they will be bored as others talk. Dealing with the variety of personalities, knowledge, and attitudes that one finds in any classroom is always a challenge. While this challenge will not disappear when you use talk in your classroom, carefully orchestrated talk may help. It may allow you to bring more students into the excitement of thinking mathematically, students who may not have participated as enthusiastically in the more traditional forms of instruction. Patterns of participation may change in ways that surprise and delight you. Many teachers have reported to us that as they began to focus on giving all students opportunities to talk about their ideas, they were pleasantly surprised by what they learned about their students' thinking.

The traditional method of calling on students (whether or not they have raised their hands) gives the teacher maximum control of who talks in the conversation. Some teachers augment this with a variety of methods of assigning turns. For example, some teachers institute a "gender rule" for taking turns, in which boys and girls alternate. In a class where girls don't participate as actively as boys, or vice versa, this rule supports girls (or boys) by making every other turn in the talk an opening for them. Some teachers allow a student to nominate the next speaker after he or she has finished speaking. This can be useful when there are one or two students who tend to monopolize the floor. Some teachers institute a reward system whereby students receive points for volunteering a question or an explanation. (There should be a limit to the number of points that can be gained this way, as otherwise the monopolizers will be encouraged.) Each classroom and school has its own set of norms for taking turns, but we encourage you to think creatively about this important aspect of setting up the conditions for equal participation in productive talk.

Principle 4. Explain your expectations about new forms of talk.

Preparatory discussion is essential whenever you introduce a new form of instruction so that students understand your expectations. To this end, explain clearly how you want students to participate in talking. Students often find it helpful to hear your reasons for asking them to engage in this new form of talk. Help them understand what the talk will accomplish and how it might improve their mathematics learning. We suggest that you do this every time you introduce a new form of talk, and follow up with numerous refreshers at later dates as necessary.

It's likely that there will be some students in your class for whom discussion of their ideas with adults is comfortable and familiar. But for other students, this form of activity will be completely new. Some students are from social or cultural backgrounds in which it's not typical for children to engage in talk on intellectual topics with adults. These children may be more used to listening attentively to what adults say, or to learning through careful observation. These students may need to hear that this type of talk is expected in school. Furthermore, some immigrant students may come from countries where students are never allowed to talk in school and the very idea may be confusing and even upsetting. For several reasons, then, it makes sense to first discuss what you are expecting students to do, and to make explicit why you think talk is a good idea. You may have to repeat this reasoning more than a few times, as students gradually get used to this new way of interacting.

Principle 5. Try one challenging new thing at a time.

Creating the conditions for productive talk is a complex task that involves coordination of several different things at once. Therefore, to keep things manageable, try one challenging new thing at a time. When introducing a new talk format or move, make sure that the mathematical concepts or procedures you are talking about are familiar to all of the students in the class.

Conversely, when you are introducing challenging new mathematical content, make sure that the talk routines you are using are familiar and can be used comfortably by all the students in the class. As the examples in the following section will illustrate, you may wish to introduce the key talk moves described in Chapter 2 only one or two at a time.

It's important to give yourself and the students adequate time to use these new tools. Consider the first time you tried to type a document using a new word processor, or the first time you tried to take a train in another country where the language was not your first language. Skills and abilities that you usually take for granted can easily grind to a halt as you try to add on the challenging new behavior or skill. Not surprisingly, the same thing may happen as you begin to incorporate talk into your mathematics teaching. Some teachers report that they feel like they are juggling plates, or that they go blank at unexpected moments because of the new demands of trying to orchestrate student talk while thinking about mathematics. If this is true for teachers, imagine how much more challenging it is for students!

Therefore, it's important to think through how you plan to introduce the new talk format or routine. You want everyone to be able to participate in the still-unfamiliar talk, so everyone should already understand the mathematics to a great extent. Introducing one new thing at a time will support participation by all students, as discussed in Principle 3. And of course, you should introduce your expectations explicitly, as stated in Principle 4. If students must figure out the rules of the talk at the same time as they are being asked to think about mathematics, their performance will not be optimal and participation is likely to be uneven.

First Steps

Some of the practices and moves we describe here will now be familiar to you. Nevertheless, as you start the work of instituting productive talk in your mathematics class, they may serve your purposes in new ways. The following suggestions present several different ways to begin teaching mathematics in a talk-intensive fashion.

1. Practicing two talk moves on your own.

Two of the talk moves we have introduced, revoicing and wait time, are moves that are primarily used by the teacher. But just as you should "try one new thing at a time" with your students, you should allow yourself to ease gradually into using these moves. Even before you begin the process of introducing your students to talk in math class, you may want to spend several lessons trying out these two moves without fanfare, using them yourself to get the feel of how they can help you support student understanding.

You might set up a lesson in which students must present their solutions for a particular problem. It can be a problem that is new to them. You are not going to present them with any new talk moves that they must execute, so they can focus on the mathematics. You will be using revoicing and wait time to help them.

When a student presents his or her solution method, try out a simple revoicing move. Imagine that a student has said: "I just drew a picture and then I drew lines for the things." Respond to the student: "So you're saying that you drew a picture and then you drew lines for things?" Let the student respond to your question. By this time, you will be able to formulate a further question: "So can you explain what you mean when you say you drew lines for things?" This is a good point of entry to a deeper discussion of the student's meaning. Using this very simple tool of revoicing, you're on your way to getting students to respond more thoughtfully, carefully, and clearly than they might otherwise. You are letting them know that you welcome their elaboration of their reasoning.

Try to use this move with several different students during the lesson. Practice it for several days until you feel completely comfortable using it. Remember that it's important not just to repeat what the student said and then move on; rather, you must repeat or rephrase, but then ask the student whether that is the correct interpretation of what he or she was trying to say. You can do this with a rising intonation—"So you're saying you think it's thirteen?" Or you can make it a statement followed by an explicit question— "So you're saying you think it's thirteen. Is that what you said?"

After practicing sticking closely to what the student has said, you may want to use the revoicing move to help the student expand his or her reasoning. Consider again this student response from Case 3, episode 2 in Chapter 2. Recall that the students are trying to clarify their representation of the peach tarts problem.

24. Tyavanna: I drew ten peaches? And . . . um . . . like . . . um, I think that's what you have to do because you have to show the thirds of the peaches? 'Cause that's what you have to figure out to make the tarts. Not the other way around.

At this point the teacher might have chosen to revoice Tyavanna's contribution by expanding and clarifying it, then asking her if this expanded version was in agreement with her intention:

Ms. S: So Tyavanna, you're telling us that if we want to know how many tarts we can make, we have to use the fact that each tart takes two-thirds of a peach. And so we have to figure out how many sets of two-thirds we have in our ten peaches? And so that means we have to draw the ten peaches and figure out how many thirds there are in those? Is that what you're saying?

Tyavanna: Yes, because if we drew the tarts instead, that wouldn't tell us anything about the peaches. We don't even know how many tarts to draw, because we don't know how many we can make.

In this case, Ms. Stangle's use of revoicing to clarify and expand Tyavanna's answer actually motivated Tyavanna to clarify even further. By the end of this interchange, the entire class could follow Tyavanna's logical reasoning about her choice of what to represent in her problem solution.

During the same lesson, or perhaps at a later time in another lesson, practice using wait time. Many of us think we are very good at waiting for students to answer. But if you actually time yourself, you may find that your average wait is only about three seconds. How can you time yourself if you are in the midst of teaching? Some teachers discreetly hit a stopwatch and look at it later. Others make an audiotape of their class and listen to it later. Still others ask a colleague to help them by observing and timing. Most people are surprised with the results, but self-knowledge is the first step when we are trying to change something.

Try to use wait time in your class in two ways. First, when you ask a question of the whole class, don't wait for just a few seconds and then call on the one or two students who have their hands up. Decide how long you will wait. Twenty seconds is a good place to start. Then make your students see that you are willing to wait. (It may take ten or fifteen repetitions of your determined waiting before they will actually believe that you are willing to wait for them to think through the problem and come up with an answer.) Second, use wait time when you finally call upon an individual. When you run across a student who needs extra time, surprise the student by giving him thirty or forty seconds. Although it may seem excruciatingly awkward, it can take students that long to formulate an answer to a complex question, particularly if they are English-language learners. If the student seems embarrassed, you can support his or her effort by saying: "These are complicated questions. It can take a long time to put something into words. That's OK. In this class we'll always wait for you to put your thinking into words."

Many teachers have the habit of leaving students alone if they seem reluctant to answer questions. When a student doesn't answer after ten seconds or so, most of us move on to someone else. None of us likes to be viewed as "mean" or as teachers that put students on the spot. Nevertheless, in Project Challenge we have found that many students respond very well if we tell them, "OK, I'll come back to you in a few minutes." Then, after calling on one or two other students, we return to the student who could not answer previously. The additional time, plus the support of hearing the other students talk, often allows the reluctant student to put together an answer. This practice, along with the determined use of wait time, lets students know that you expect them to keep trying, that you expect them to be able to participate eventually, even if they are stymied at the moment. It sends a message about your expectations for them, a message they will eventually hear.

2. Introducing students to talk-centered instruction.

After you have gotten a bit of practice using the two moves described, begin to explicitly introduce your students to talk-intensive work in mathematics. How should you introduce your students to talk? As the first principle suggests, your earliest moves should be about establishing the norms—the ground rules—for respectful and courteous discourse. In some classrooms these may already be in place. In other classrooms, teachers may need to introduce these separately, as the first step in the process. In addition, you need to introduce the actual talk moves that will require students to talk in new ways: the requests to repeat what another student has said, the requests that students provide a reason for their thinking, and the questions about agreement and disagreement.

In our view, the most effective way to introduce these norms is to tie them to your goal of supporting students' mathematical thinking, reasoning, and problem solving. This means that first you will introduce students to the idea that talking about mathematics can help them become better mathematical thinkers. Then you can discuss the conditions that have to be in place for this kind of talk to succeed. Finally you can introduce the specific talk moves, explaining to students why each is worth doing.

For young children (grades one and two)
The following outline is a suggested way of introducing talk moves to your students in a whole-class discussion. Of course, you can adapt these to the needs and backgrounds of your students.

- Thinking together about math can help us all understand math better.
- Each person's thinking is different and unique, and we can all learn from one another.
- We can think together by talking together about our thinking.
- What does it take for us to understand another person's thinking?
      We have to be able to hear what he or she says.
      We have to listen carefully and try to understand.
      We have to ask questions when we don't understand.
      We have to take turns so everybody who wants a chance gets one.

With young children, it's a good idea to start with the talk move of asking a student to repeat what another student has said in his or her own words. Tell students before you begin that you will be asking them to repeat what they have heard. You can explain to students that this will help everyone to make sure that they have heard what the speaker has said, and that they have understood it. It's a good idea to ask several students in a row to repeat what the same speaker has said. This lets them know that each student's listening and speaking are important. It lets children know that they are responsible for listening carefully to every speaker.

It's also a good idea to ask young children to support their own reasoning from early on. When a student provides an answer, begin with a gentle follow-up: "So can you tell us about your reasoning?" Or: "Can you tell us why you think that's the answer?" This will soon lead even young children to begin talking about their reasoning. You can use the technique of "revoicing" to make sure that other children can hear and begin to understand what the speaker is saying.

As previous sections have indicated, one very useful talk move is asking students whether they agree or disagree with another student's idea or claim. Teachers of very young children may want to introduce this aspect of the practice only after the children are comfortable talking about their own thinking and listening to others. However, this move is certainly possible for very young children.

For grades three through six
Here is a more elaborate outline of an introduction to productive classroom talk, more suitable for older students. However, keep in mind that students in this age range vary greatly in their ability to take in complex explanations for instructional practices. Rely on your own judgment in using and sequencing

these suggestions. Remember to be explicit in your explanations and leave time for discussion and clarification of this important first step.

- Thinking together about math can help us all understand math better. Difficult problems often call for more than one person to solve them. Furthermore, we can all learn new ways of thinking about mathematics from listening to how others think. And finally, talking through our thinking can help us clarify our own thoughts. If we try to communicate clearly, our thinking may get better as a result of our efforts.
- Thinking usually seems to go on inside one person's head. However, we can share our thinking by talking together about our ideas.
- What does it take for us to understand another person's thinking?

> We have to be able to hear the speaker. Everyone has a right to be heard.

> Everyone has an obligation to listen and to try to understand what the speaker is saying.

> We are obligated to ask questions when we don't understand.

> The speaker has an obligation to try hard to be clear.

> Everyone has a right to participate. How can we make sure that everyone has a chance to participate? [Here you might discuss your current methods of taking turns and ask your students to make suggestions.]

> What might keep people from participating? [Here a discussion of how people feel when others make fun of their thinking is a good idea. From this discussion you can derive your classroom's norms for courteous and respectful discourse, including agreements about what sanctions will be brought to bear on those who violate the norms.]

Some teachers have used such a discussion as an occasion to create a wall chart codifying the norms of respectful discourse and full participation. You can integrate your own concerns in this discussion, and of course the wall chart can be reviewed and changed as time goes on. Some teachers may want to introduce Principles 1, 2, and 3 to their students as a way to set up the classroom norms.

With older students, when asking students to explain their own reasoning, use the move of asking students to repeat what someone else said. Introducing the "agree or disagree" move may best be introduced a bit later, depending upon your students' facility with this kind of interaction. When you introduce this move, it may be a good idea to emphasize the connection between Principle 2 (Our talk is about mathematics) and Principle 1 (respectful discourse). For example, when you ask students to agree or disagree with what another student said, it's helpful to emphasize that the agreement or disagreement is about mathematics, not about the speaker him or herself. In the social world of the classroom, people can be very sensitive to the interpersonal implications of agreeing or disagreeing with a position someone has taken. On the playground, disagreements may ignite an actual conflict or dispute. In mathematics, a disagreement is a way of moving forward, of getting closer to a mathematical understanding. But we should not assume that students will take to this norm with ease. In fact, we should expect, anticipate, and deal preemptively with the possibilities for hurt feelings and conflicts.

A detailed introduction

The following introduction, written by an experienced teacher, describes how she introduces her older students to many of the norms and moves we've described. This introduction would probably be overwhelming for younger students, and many teachers might want to break it into smaller sections, introducing different parts at different times. Nevertheless, we include it here to give you an idea of the kinds of issues that should be explicitly addressed, either all at once or over time.

> You may be used to the kind of math class where the teacher asks the questions, you give the answers, and then the teacher tells you if you're right or wrong. If you're right, your turn is over. If you're wrong, the teacher then explains to you what the right answer is. This math class is going to be different. Although I'll still ask you questions, when you give me an answer, I'm going to ask you why you think what you think.
>
> But me asking you to explain your reasoning will probably not be the biggest difference between this class and others you've had in the past. In fact, a lot of you may be used to this. Here's what I think will be really different for you: When you give your answer and the reasoning behind it, I am usually not going to tell you whether you're right or not. Instead, I am going to ask your classmates to respond

to your comment. I may ask them to restate the comment in their own words. Or, I may ask them to state whether they agree or disagree with your comment and explain why. In this class, when you speak, you're speaking to everyone in the room, not just me. When you're not speaking, you need to be listening.

By now, you may have two questions. Why am I making you do this? And how are you going to learn how to do this? I'll talk about the why part first. There are lots of reasons why I want you to learn math this way. The most important one is that I truly believe you'll learn more math more deeply this way. When I ask you to explain your reasoning or why you agree or disagree with a classmate's idea, you may at first say to yourself, "Oh, that's easy to explain." But when you try to put the right words together, you may find that there are some things you're still confused about. When you know what's confusing you, you can then get the help you need. The second reason is that one of the goals I have for you is to become better at communicating mathematically. You live in a world where being able to communicate what you know is just as important as knowing it. One day, you'll each have a career where you'll be asked to solve problems. Maybe they'll be math or science problems, maybe they'll be other kinds of problems. You'll also be asked to present your solutions in a way so that others understand them and believe that they make sense. This class is going to prepare you to do just that.

Now onto the how part. Well, the first thing you need to do is talk. I know it can be scary to speak in public, but trust me, the first few times are the hardest. If you're nervous, make your first few comments only one or two sentences in length just to get over the jitters. Next, you need to talk loudly enough for others to hear. Pretend as though every time you talk you are talking to someone seated on the opposite side of the room. Thirdly, the content of each comment must be mathematical. Use mathematics vocabulary. Talk us through what you think, reason by reason. Talk us through your actions step by step. Explain to us the mathematical sense behind your methods, strategies, and procedures. You don't have to say everything perfectly every time, but do strive to make each of your comments as clear and thorough as possible.

You also need to listen to what your classmates are saying when they speak. And when I say listen, I mean really listen. I'm not talking about the kind of listening where you hear the words but let them go in one ear and out the other. What you need to do is listen so that you can figure out what the other person thinks and why. If you listen like this, you'll be ready to respond in a meaningful way so that the discussion keeps moving forward toward the mathematical truth.

The last point I want to make is that we are in this together. You have my word that your ideas will be respected by your peers and by me. I will do everything I can to make sure that you feel safe to talk about what you know and don't know. So, as we get started with this endeavor, remember what's expected of you: Talk loudly and clearly when it's your turn. When it's not, listen so that you are ready to respond in a way that brings us closer to the mathematical truth.

3. Beginning with a whole-class discussion.

After you have explicitly introduced the norms for respectful discourse, and have talked about the ways you will ask your students to talk about mathematics, you will want to introduce the norms and talk moves in an actual lesson. A good way to begin is to present the class with a math problem that can be solved in more than one way. You will then ask students to present their solution methods to the class. As they talk through their reasoning, you can introduce the talk moves of asking students to repeat in their own words what someone else has said. You can ask them to explain why they chose a particular solution path. And you can practice the now-familiar revoicing move and the use of wait time to make sure that all students have been heard and understood.

Asking students to present multiple solutions is something that many teachers do already. As students talk through their reasoning over many such sessions, they learn the importance of communicating clearly and being understood by others, and begin to use language in precise and explicit ways. Often, students will recognize flaws in their reasoning or computational procedures as they make their solution methods public. Finally, of course, students will get access to solution methods beyond their own.

In the early grades, choose a problem that lends itself to being solved by several different strategies, or that can have multiple correct answers. For example, "Jane is looking for three numbers that add up to thirty-seven. What three numbers will work?" For older students you may present a multistep problem that they can solve using a variety of forms of representation and different computational steps, such as the peach tart problem presented in Chapter 2.

Keep in mind Principle 5: Try one challenging new thing at a time. Make sure the problem is one that all of the students in your class can do. It helps to choose a type of problem with which they are familiar. You can make sure that the difficulty of the problem is manageable by choosing numbers for the problem that are "friendly" numbers. For example, in second grade, you can use the problem about Jane's three numbers, but instead of 37, choose 20 as the target number. After the students are comfortable with reporting out their solution methods, you can make the target number more difficult. In a fifth-grade discussion of the peach tart problem, use one-half of a peach per tart instead of two-thirds. The type of problem is still the same, and it will still elicit multiple solutions. However, more students are likely to participate if the computational aspects of the problem are not made more difficult by using "unfriendly" numbers.

After all the students have discussed and understood the solution methods, let them practice both the talk and the mathematics by introducing a slightly harder version of the same problem—move from one-half of a peach per tart to two-thirds of a peach per tart. If you have time, and if your students are ready, you can introduce harder numbers: seven-eighths of a peach per tart, or one and two-thirds of a peach per tart. This is one way to smoothly integrate new talk formats while not losing sight of the mathematical content.

Starting off

To start, introduce to your class what you expect them to do. As we mentioned, this serves Principles 1, 3, and 4. It helps ensure that all students can participate, as they will understand what you are doing. It also helps to ensure that students will feel safe making public contributions to the discussion. An effective way to start off is to actually model what you expect students to do. For example, you might begin this way.

> Today as we go over this problem, I'm going to ask a number of you to explain your own solution method. I want you to tell us what you did to solve the problem. Now, there are lots of ways to solve this problem, but everyone tends to have their own way, the way that seems most natural to them. Today we want to hear about as many solution methods as we can. If we can do that, we'll all learn new ways to think about problems like this. I'll go first and show you what I mean.

You would then slowly work through an explanation of one solution method, using the board as appropriate, going slowly enough that everyone can follow.

You might then ask: "Does anyone else have a *different* way of solving the problem? Let's take some time to solve the problem. You can work with your partner to find a solution method that's different from the one I just presented. Then I'll ask partners to present their solution method."

Slow it down and ask for repetitions

It is likely that many of the students' contributions will be hard for others (and possibly for you) to understand. Resist the urge to pass quickly over the unclear explanations. As students make their contributions, take the time to ask them to clarify their ideas so that they are as understandable as possible. For example, you might revoice what students say and then check with them to make sure you have correctly paraphrased their idea: "OK, Gloria, so you're saying that you first added ten and ten, and then you saw that you still had a long way to go to reach thirty-seven? Is that right?" When Gloria assents, you might then record that part of her solution on the board:

$$10 + 10 = 20$$

Then say: "So what did you do next? You said that a little bit quickly so I want to make sure that everyone understands."

In addition to your own revoicing, ask students to repeat what others have said. You can ask for exact repetitions ("Solange, can you repeat what Donny just said?") or you can ask for paraphrases ("Donny, can you put what Michael said into different words?"). If a student offers a particularly interesting or complex explanation, you can ask several students to put it into their own words. This will give all students a chance to hear it and think about it several times. You can also ask the original speaker whether the new renditions of his or her contribution are in fact what he or she intended to say ("Michael, is that what you intended to say?"). As students realize that their contributions are actually being listened to and understood by their classmates, their motivation for participating increases.

Encourage many contributions

As students continue to add their strategies, at some point you may feel that there are no other distinct solution methods. But recall that in this session, your purpose is to give students practice in talking out loud about their mathematical reasoning. So don't stop just yet. Address the students: "OK, we have four different solution methods up here on the board. This first one is Gloria's. Did anyone else use a strategy that is similar to Gloria's? Solange, can you tell us what you did?" If Solange says that her solution is just like Gloria's, ask her to put it into her own words. Continue to elicit solution methods from students in this way. You may find that some did add a new twist that you didn't anticipate. Mathematically, this practice is valuable for several reasons. Not only do students get a chance to hear new strategies that differ from their own, they also begin to develop a sense of classes of solution methods, and of what is mathematically the same and different.

You may end up spending one entire mathematics class on a whole-class discussion of solution methods for one problem. It may feel strange, but it's time well spent. If this is the first time you have used this practice, it might be enough to simply go through all the solution methods in the class. If you have time, you may want to let the students try another, mathematically more challenging version of the problem. In either case, what is most important is that the talk is aimed at deepening the understanding of each student.

Keep the discourse respectful and keep everyone focused
As you go through the process of letting each student get the feel of making their reasoning public, you will be presented with a number of opportunities to reinforce the classroom norms that will support respectful and engaged talk. To create an environment of respect, you must first make sure that students actually attend to one another's contributions. Of course, it is appropriate and wise to remind students that you expect them to listen to one another. But there are several other ways that you can push students to internalize their own responsibility to abide by these norms. One is to remind students, when they make their contributions, that they must speak loudly enough for others to hear them.

At first this may seem intrusive. A quiet student is struggling to make his or her reasoning clear, and you are asking him or her to speak louder. For many of us, this strategy may even seem cruel—it's not considered polite to force someone to speak up if they don't want to. However, one of the purposes of schooling is to gradually, over a span of years, enable students to do things that they would not be inclined to do on their own. We have seen some remarkable results come from years of gentle prompting to speak up so others can hear. Gradually, students gain the confidence to communicate their thoughts and eventually, as their confidence grows, their desire to communicate and think with others also grows.

This is a rewarding outcome, but it doesn't happen overnight. So you must persist and be flexible. After you ask a student to speak up, if he or she gives it a try but is still too quiet to hear, you revoice what the student said, making sure that everyone can hear. As the student's contribution is taken seriously, with your help in making it available, the student will begin to gain the confidence that his or her contributions really do matter.

Asking students to repeat what another has said has several benefits. It lets all students know that they are responsible for listening to and understanding other students' ideas, allows all students to hear the solution method more than once, and keeps the discussion going, since it gives everyone more time to reflect on what is being said. As you practice this consistently, reminding students that you will call on them to repeat in their own words what others have said, they come to expect your request and begin to pay closer attention to what their peers are saying. Finally, this move helps you avoid the common situation in which students are partially tuned out, simply awaiting their turn to talk, rather than listening to or building on what others have said. Your goal is for students gradually to come to treat one another as partners in mathematical thinking and reasoning.

The following example illustrates some of these problems and strategies in a whole-class discussion in which Mrs. Cardello is eliciting multiple solution methods from her fifth-grade class. The teacher posed a question for the students: "Which is bigger, three-fourths or seven-eighths?" The teacher asks Juan to give his answer and explain how he got that answer.

1. Juan: So first I thought about a rectangle and how if I divided it into four pieces then three would be colored in. And then I thought about the same rectangle, but cut into eight pieces, and I thought about what it would look like if seven were colored in, and I just knew that that one would be more.

2. Mrs. C: So who can put that into their own words for us? How about Gina?

3. Gina: Well, Juan said that he compared how each one would look if you colored in the parts that are the numerator.

4. Mrs. C: OK, that went by kind of fast for me. Let's see if we can put Juan's solution on the board. Gina, can you go over again what Juan did? Tell me what to draw up here. [Mrs. Cardello draws according to Gina's description (see Figure 9–1).]

5. Gina: OK, first he took the three-fourths and drew a picture of a rectangle and cut it into fourths. Then he colored in the three-fourths. Then he drew the same size rectangle and cut it into eight pieces. Then he colored in the seven-eighths of that rectangle and he saw it was more.

6. Mrs. C: OK, I see, so Gina said that you colored in the number of

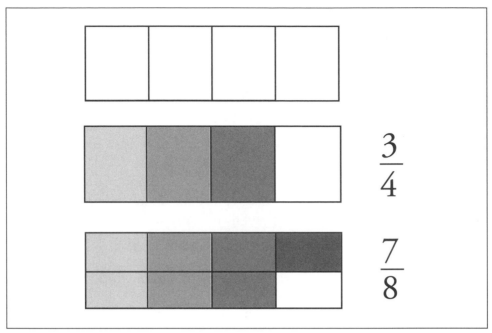

FIGURE 9–1 Mrs. Cardello's depiction of Juan's solution.

parts corresponding to the numerator. Juan, is that right? Is that your solution method?

7. Juan: Yes, but I didn't draw it, I just pictured it in my mind.

8. Mrs. C: OK, good, but we need to picture it up here so that we can be sure we understand you. Did anyone use a different approach? Sheila?

9. Sheila: Well, I changed both of them into the same denominator, so three-fourths became six-eighths and seven-eighths became just what it was, and then seven is bigger than six.

10. Mrs. C: Patty, can you repeat what Sheila said in your own words?

11. Patty: [Looks embarrassed.] I didn't hear her.

12. Mrs. C: OK, remember that it's really important to pay attention to what's going on, otherwise you'll miss the explanation and you won't be able to use that knowledge in your own work. Patty, ask Sheila to repeat what she said.

13. Patty: Can you repeat what you said please?

14. Sheila: I said that I took both the three-fourths and the seven-eighths and I changed them into the same denominator. That way I could compare them. So three-fourths became

six-eighths and seven-eighths stayed the same, so I could see that seven-eighths is bigger than six-eighths.

15. Mrs. C: OK, Patty, can you put that in your own words?

16. Patty: Well, so Sheila converted the two fractions to the same denominator and then she compared the numerators to see which one was bigger.

17. Mrs. C: OK, so Juan used a strategy of visualizing the two fractions as parts of a whole and comparing them, and Sheila used the strategy of finding a common denominator for both fractions and comparing the size of the numerator. Did anyone else use a different strategy?

Notice that in this example, in the final turn, Mrs. Cardello repeats the strategies used by both students, summarizing for the class what they have seen so far.

4. Revoicing in small-group discussion.

As you begin to use talk in your classroom, you may wish to have students first discuss in small groups. Small groups have advantages and disadvantages. Many researchers have found that they give shy or less-advanced students a chance to participate that is not available in large groups. On the other hand, small-group work can sometimes put such students at more of a disadvantage, unless the groups are carefully structured and monitored. For example, low-status students may especially suffer in small-group work. Finally, teachers obviously cannot be everywhere at once, and so small-group talk may not yield consistent results. Nevertheless, it can be a particularly good venue for you to begin to practice the revoicing move. Give the students a problem, selected according to the same criteria for a whole-class discussion. Make sure it's a problem that is familiar to the students, and for which most students will be likely to find some solution. Make sure that multiple solution methods are possible. Ask the students to take ten minutes to solve the problem in groups of three or four.

Focus on understanding, not correcting

As students discuss the problem in their small groups, circulate around the room, listening. After five minutes or so, interact with different groups. Ask: "What solutions are you coming up with?" Or: "Can you explain to me what you all are doing to solve the problem?" When they tell you, repeat their solution back to them to check if you understand it. You can say, for example: "So you're saying that [fill in with their solution method]. Is that right?" This will get them to start realizing that they are responsible for putting together coherent explanations of their methods. Just as important, it gives you time to process what they are saying. As students see you struggling to understand what they are saying, they will start to try harder to communicate clearly with you.

There will be times when you cannot understand what students are saying to you. Resist the temptation to avoid the situation and move along. Both students and teacher can feel embarrassment when a student cannot be understood, but unless you persist in trying to get clarification, students will not learn that you intend to take their explanations seriously. One strategy is to draw on others in the group. If one student has given the explanation and you cannot follow it, first ask the student to clarify. If you still cannot understand, ask another student, saying: "Well, this is complicated, and I'm still not sure I understand. Can you put what he said in your own words, Jamal?" Try to get each student in the group to explain it in their own words.

It is important in small-group discussion, just as in whole-class discussion, that you focus the talk on promoting understanding. Many students have the habit of simply waiting for the teacher, or another student, to show them how to solve a problem. Resist the urge to show a group how to solve the problem. Instead, say: "Repeat the problem to me so that I'm sure that we both have the same understanding of what it is." Or: "Tell me what you know about the problem so far." Or: "What do you think you might do first?" Put the responsibility on their shoulders to make the effort of working on the problem. Also, refrain from telling groups whether their solutions are correct or incorrect. Instead, tell them that their solutions and explanations are the material you will use in a whole-class discussion.

Some groups may finish solving a problem well before other groups are done. A common technique that teachers use is to ask the group to solve the problem in another way. You might also suggest that the students who are finished talk with one another about how they will present their solution method: Who will introduce it and describe it? What should they write on the board? They might even practice delivering their explanation out loud.

If you choose to start with small-group discussion, you may then profitably follow it up with a large-group discussion like the one described in Section 3, beginning with a whole-class discussion.

5. Using partner talk.

Many teachers are familiar with the general idea of this talk format, and often ask their students to "turn and talk" or "talk to your neighbor." This format has several benefits. It allows students to practice their ideas—to put them into words— before they face the entire class. It allows students to hear how one other student is thinking about the problem, perhaps giving them confidence that they too have a workable idea or giving them an idea of how to proceed if they are stuck.

Imagine that you are returning to a lesson from the previous day, in which students were solving a difficult problem on their own. You noticed that some students were shy about presenting their solution methods. You also noticed that because of the difficulty of the problem, students talked quite incoherently the first few times they tried to describe their strategies. You now want to give students a chance to practice talking about their solutions with one other person before you ask them to talk to the whole class. You can begin the lesson by reminding students about where you left off, and tell them that you will be asking them to report on their solutions, but that first they will have time for three to five minutes of partner talk. Tell them to refresh their memories and practice describing their solutions clearly by talking to their partner for a few minutes. Also tell them to ask questions whenever they're not sure about what their partners are saying.

During the three to five minutes in which they are talking to their partners, circulate and listen to their strategies. Listening to partners as they share strategies and solutions helps you identify students who have hit on the solutions that you think are mathematically important or interesting. Later, as you begin a whole-class discussion, you can use this information to call on particular students whose methods you think will push the content of the discussion forward in mathematically important ways.

An example of this partner-talk format is given in Chapter 2, Case 4, where Mr. Harris works with his students on division of fractions. You might wish to reread that case before going on.

6. Building and supporting an argument.

All teachers are proficient at asking questions, calling on individual students, and then evaluating whether the answer is right or wrong. Consider a sequence like this:

"Sarah, what is ninety-nine divided by eleven?"	(Teacher initiates a question.)
"Nine?"	(Student responds.)
"Yes, that's right . . ."	(Teacher evaluates the answer.)

The teacher knows the answer to the question, and the student is aiming to get the right answer. While this method—called "quizzing" by some—has many legitimate uses, it has its limits. What is missing from the quizzing sequence? There is no place for the student to do more than supply an answer to a closed question. The focus is on the right answer and not the thinking process, and there is no opportunity for other students to agree or disagree. In other words, there is no way for a more complex argument to evolve.

Teachers can foster more complex arguments by adopting moves that address these missing pieces. In a situation in which the teacher is asking a question of students, she still initiates a question, and the student still tries to respond. But instead of offering an evaluation—a "yes, that's correct" or "no, that's not correct"—the teacher then asks the student a further question, a question aimed at getting the student to give evidence or offer a rationale for his or her answer. Finally, instead of evaluating or moving on, the teacher builds on the student's answer by asking another student if she agrees or disagrees with that answer, and why.

If you have introduced norms for respectful discourse, and students are now used to externalizing their reasoning, you can work toward this emphasis on argument and reasoning. Hold a discussion in which you make extensive use of the "agree or disagree" talk move, and consistently follow it up with a request that students explain the basis for their agreement or disagreement. With older students, you may be able to adopt this practice almost from the beginning. With younger students, or with those who are less used to this kind of discourse, it may take somewhat longer.

To start, the teacher should select a problem that offers rich potential for different solution paths, and complex reasoning. Students may or may not come up with different answers. If they do, the teacher will want to address that eventually, but the purpose of this session is to focus on the development of arguments and connected reasoning. A sequence may run something like this session in a fifth grade:

1. Ms. F: So which is bigger, one-third or three-tenths? Edwina?

2. Edwina: I would say three-tenths.

3. Ms. F: OK, so what makes you think that? Give us your reasoning.

4. Edwina: Well, tenths are bigger than thirds, so three-tenths is going to be bigger than only one of thirds.

5. Ms. F: Denaldo, do you agree with what Edwina said? And tell us why you agree or don't agree.

6. Denaldo: Well, I don't agree with her answer because I think thirds are bigger than tenths. So I would say that maybe one-third is bigger, or maybe three-tenths. I'm not sure.

7. Ms. F: So you're not sure which is bigger, but you would say that tenths are not bigger than thirds. Is that right? [Denaldo nods.] Serena, do you agree or disagree? What's your view, and tell us why.

8. Serena: I agree with what Denaldo said that thirds are bigger, but I did it a different way. I know that one-third is more than three-tenths, because if you draw a picture of ten-tenths, and then you shade in three of them, that won't be equal to cutting it up into thirds. You'd still need another tiny third of a tenth.

9. Ms. F: Denaldo, do you agree with what Serena said, and could you put it into your own words?

10. Denaldo: No, I don't understand what Serena is saying.

11. Ms. F: Serena, could you draw a picture on the board so that we could understand better what you're saying?

Notice that as the students make their contributions, they are required to give a reason for their answers. Ms. Fields does not say "right" or "wrong" at this point. There are, of course, many times during a lesson at which the teacher is focused on checking for right or wrong answers, and is explicitly correcting students, but here she has a different set of purposes in mind. She wants students to

- Talk through the problem and struggle to make their thinking clear to others;
- Get into the habit of giving reasons for their answers and evidence for their claims, a crucial part of mathematical, scientific, and logical reasoning;
- Get into the habit of listening to and evaluating one another's contributions;
- Reason aloud so she can gain information about the mathematical beliefs and understandings of individual students.

Ms. Fields will build on such sequences in helping students understand the truths and conventions of the larger mathematics community.

In the short term, such sequences can reveal to the teacher whether the majority of the students understand the current question or not, and if not, where the principal problems lie. This information is important for informing the teacher's further instructional decisions. This activity has a longer-term effect as well. Over time, students become less attuned to guessing the right answer, and more attuned to actually engaging in logical reasoning. They become more interested in being able to support their answers successfully rather than simply guessing what the teacher has in mind.

Evaluating Your Progress

How can you tell when what you are doing is working? It may take months or over a year to see striking changes in students' abilities to use classroom discourse. What can you do in the meantime to help yourself see what is working and what isn't? We suggest that you find a way to keep track of your use of the principles that we introduced at the beginning of this chapter for each day that you intentionally use extensive talk in your mathematics instruction.

Perhaps the best place to start is with Principles 1 and 2: Did your class maintain the norms of respectful discourse, and was the talk consistently about mathematical reasoning, with an emphasis on understanding? Next, did you follow Principle 4, providing a clear and explicit discussion of what you expected from students in their classroom talk?

Different teachers will find different ways to keep track of this. Some will take a moment after class simply to reflect on the classroom activity, perhaps using a checklist like the one provided on the next page. Others will not have even a minute after class, and will instead spend five minutes later in the day with a "buddy"—a colleague who is also engaged in the same effort. Other teachers who find keeping a journal helpful may use some space in their journal to remind themselves of what they intended, how it played out, and what they plan to do next.

Some aspects of the process are best observed weekly rather than daily. For example, Principle 3, providing for equitable participation, may not be best evaluated on the basis of one class. Imagine that you are discussing a topic on one day and all of the volunteers are boys—not one of the girls raises a hand. If you evaluated your progress on the basis of this one day, you might be discouraged, and outside visitors might be misled. Experienced teachers know that student participation varies from day to day for a variety of reasons. It may be best in this case to keep track at slightly longer time intervals. If a whole week goes by and you see that mainly boys are responding, or mainly the white students in a diverse classroom, or mainly native speakers of English in a classroom containing many second-language learners, then it may be time to reevaluate the strategies you are using to call on students. To start out, you might keep a class list on which you can spend one minute each day, adding a check mark for each student who participates. At the end of the week, review the list for patterns and reflect. In Chapter 11, we provide additional methods you can use in your efforts to ensure equitable participation.

Self-Evaluation Checklist

1. *Establish and maintain a respectful, supportive environment.* Did you consistently require that students respect one another's contributions through asking them to listen, and to speak loudly enough so that others could hear? Did you emphasize that we agree or disagree with what others say, not with the speakers themselves? Did you enforce the norm that students may not ridicule others or make derogatory comments about others? As the weeks pass, do you see students opening up to the possibilities of talking about their ideas in a supportive environment? Do you see evidence that the norms for respectful discourse are having an effect outside of math class?

2. *Focus talk on the mathematics.* Did you consistently monitor to make sure that the preponderance of classroom talk was about mathematical ideas and reasoning? Did you plan sufficiently well that you could guide the talk in mathematically productive directions? As the weeks and months pass, do you see a change in your students' level of sophistication in talking about mathematical concepts, definitions, representations, and forms of reasoning?

3. *Provide for equitable participation in classroom talk.* Did you succeed in paying consistent attention to whether every student is benefiting from your uses of classroom discourse? Did you succeed in eliciting participation from most, if not all, students this week? As the weeks and months pass, do you see a change in the participation of students who started out only as listeners? Do you see increasing participation from students who are learning English as their second language?

4. *Explain your expectations about new forms of talk.* When introducing something new, or reviewing a practice or activity, did you explain clearly what you want students to do, and to the greatest

extent possible, and did you give them reasons for engaging in this kind of talk? Did you make sure that all students understood what was expected of them? As the weeks and months pass, do you notice that students are secure in their knowledge of what you want them to do during mathematics talk?

5. *Try one challenging new thing at a time.* When introducing a new talk move or format, did you try to make sure that the mathematical concepts or procedures you started with were well understood by all the students in the class? Conversely, when you introduced challenging new mathematical content, did you try to make sure that the talk routines you used were familiar to all the students in the class? Over the weeks, do you find yourself improving in your ability to integrate talk moves and formats with increasingly challenging mathematics?

CHAPTER
10

Planning Lessons

Now that you have started thinking about how to use productive classroom talk in mathematics, you probably have lots of practical questions about incorporating talk into your lessons. The first thing you must consider when planning a unit or a lesson is the mathematics that students will talk about. In order to maximize students' understanding, you have to be extremely clear about what mathematics you will stress or highlight. It helps to list the key concepts, problem-solving strategies, vocabulary, forms of representations, reasoning, and computational procedures that are at the heart of the topic. Once you've determined the mathematics, consider discussion questions and anticipate possible answers that might be used to help students develop understanding and proficiency. Some curriculum materials do not provide any guidance for using discussion to help students understand key ideas. However, other curriculum materials state the mathematics in the lesson and provide questions to ask students. This is a great starting place and we suggest you use these prepared questions. However, we also have found that even excellent curricula do not provide all the questions that you will want your students to consider. In many cases the questions provided are low-level, single-response questions rather than questions that force students to analyze, synthesize, or generalize. Furthermore, you have worked with the individuals in your class and are aware of your students' knowledge of related topics and of their strengths and weaknesses. Thus, you can pose pertinent questions for your students. Whatever your curriculum, this section gives guidance on how to plan lessons to get the most out of classroom talk in terms of student learning of mathematics.

Components for Effective Lesson Planning
Just as there are many factors to using talk, there are many components to effective lesson planning. The lesson plan we suggest has five different components:

- Identifying the mathematical goals;
- Anticipating confusion;
- Asking questions;
- Managing classroom talk;
- Planning the implementation.

Identifying the mathematical goals. In this part of your lesson plan you need to identify the mathematics that is most important in the lesson. In Chapters 3 through 8 we described the mathematics to be talked about: mathematical concepts; computational procedures; solution methods and problem-solving strategies; mathematical reasoning; terminology, symbols, and definitions; and forms of representation. This is a useful list to review when writing your lesson plan, but keep in mind that most lessons do not include all of these math topics.

Anticipating confusion. This section of your lesson plan is where you list the particular aspects of the mathematical content that may be potentially confusing or misconstrued by students. It helps to identify possible incorrect notions as well as common errors that might occur. By highlighting in your lesson plan the mathematics that may be problematic for students, you are more likely to make sure that students think carefully about these ideas and procedures during class.

Asking questions. You want to generate questions that will engage students in talking about what they understand or that will reveal misconceptions. These questions do not elicit single-word responses (for example, avoid questions that can be answered by "yes" or "no"). Rather, ask questions that force students to analyze, synthesize, and generalize. Sometimes teachers write what they think some of their students' likely responses will be so that they can have additional questions and counterexamples ready for use.

Managing classroom talk. In many of your lessons you will want to focus on particular principles and talk issues. This section is where you list those principles and issues such as which talk moves and formats you will use and when. This is also the place for you to record notes to yourself related to talk—vocabulary definitions or general knowledge that students may or may not have but that can be addressed through talk.

Planning the implementation. In this section you describe the sequence and content of the activities that you will use to help students make sense of the mathematics. This section is sometimes referred to as the "development" section of a lesson plan and is typically the longest.

The structure of this lesson plan may look a bit different from ones you have used before. Notice that it keeps the focus on using talk to learn mathematics. It is easy to get caught up in a discussion that sounds great and then realize at the end of the class that students probably did not learn any new mathematical content. Thinking about the mathematics before the lesson will enable you to keep the discussion focused on students' understanding of what you want them to learn. It helps move the talk forward so that the mathematical goals of the lesson are addressed. Since students' comments in math class are largely a result of their current understanding, it's important to anticipate what ideas they might have that are and are not mathematically sound. Likewise, it is essential for teachers to consider possible questions, examples, and counterexamples that will push students to reflect on their reasoning.

As explained in Chapter 2, you have a choice of moves and formats to use during instruction. Plan ahead of time which talk formats and talk moves you'll use during the lesson, choosing moves and formats that you think will lend themselves best to the mathematical ideas in the lesson. In addition, certain parts of a lesson, such as the introduction, the exploration, or the summary, are best suited for particular formats and moves. Thinking about which formats and moves to use when, saves valuable time during class and strengthens the productivity of the talk. Finally, it is helpful to identify principles, such as building a respectful, supportive environment, that you want to pay special attention to. The focus of the "Managing Classroom Talk" section will vary depending on the content of the lesson, the ages of your students, and both your experience and your students' experience with using talk.

Planning and Projecting: Creating a Road Map—A Sample Lesson Plan

Let's start with a lesson that Ms. Wong is planning for her second-grade students on area. This is the first formal lesson on area but students have had previous experience covering drawn figures with different-shaped blocks. Ms.

Wong knows that the students have little knowledge of and vocabulary associated with the topic.

In past years, Ms. Wong has used lesson plans where she describes the introduction, the exploration activities, and the summary for each lesson. In order to increase the amount of talk in this lesson, Ms. Wong adopts the talk lesson plan format given here but in order to save time simply incorporates her notes from previous years into this new lesson plan. The following is her lesson plan followed by some commentary to explain her reasoning.

IDENTIFYING THE MATHEMATICAL GOALS

- Students will learn that the surface of an object can be covered with no holes or gaps. This is called the area of the surface.
- Students will discover that some objects cover a surface more completely than others (e.g., square tiles versus circular disks).
- Students will learn that to measure area, you can count the number of square units covering the surface.
- Vocabulary: *area, covering, surface, square unit.*

ANTICIPATING CONFUSION

- Students might not realize a surface must be covered completely—they may leave holes in the surfaces, simply cover the borders, or overlap tiles.
- Students may not understand the meaning of the vocabulary.
- Students should be able to cover objects with units but may not connect this action to the idea of determining the area of the object.

ASKING QUESTIONS

- What does the word *surface* mean? Can you show me?
- What does it mean to cover something? Can all surfaces be covered with tiles? Why or why not?
- Which objects cover the surface completely? Which do not? What do you notice about the shapes of objects that cover the surface completely?
- If students are not covering the whole surface, just the border, or are leaving holes in the surface, be sure to ask these questions: This surface has a big hole in it. Why do you think I would say that it's

not completely covered? When you cover a surface with crayons and leave a hole, why would I say that it's not OK?
• What if I used rectangular tiles and our teddy-bear counters to cover the surface of the math book? Which shape would cover the surface completely? Explain your reasoning.

MANAGING CLASSROOM TALK

Formats: • Talk takes place primarily through whole-class discussion.
• Try partner talk at the beginning of the lesson and ask students to discuss what it means to cover a surface.

Moves: • Ask three or four different students the same question so that everyone has time to make sense of what is being said and students get practice in presenting.

Planning the Implementation

Introduction

Introduce the task of covering the top surface of students' math book with square tiles, circular disks, and large paper clips. Students will work in pairs. Each pair will write on a Post-it Note the number of each type of unit they used to cover their math book and will place the Post-its on the blackboard under the correct heading—square tiles, disks, or paper clips.

Use partner talk to have students discuss what I mean when I say "cover the surface of the top of the math book." Also use partner talk to ask students to estimate the number of each type of unit that covers the book prior to actually measuring. Conduct a brief whole-class discussion so that pairs can share their answers to the two partner-talk questions.

Exploration

Pairs will do the actual measuring, counting, and recording. I will circulate among pairs, listening to students' approaches and asking clarifying questions when necessary (especially when I notice any of the anticipated outcomes such as holes in the covering). I will introduce the term *area* to small groups of students who are ready to discuss their results.

Whole-Class Discussion

There are two things I want to accomplish during the discussion. First, I want many pairs to share what they discovered about covering the book's surface with different objects. In particular, I want to help students understand the difference between covering with square tiles versus covering with circles or paper clips. The goal is that students will be able to generalize that some objects cover a surface with no holes or gaps or overlaps but other objects do not cover a surface completely. I also want to introduce the term *area* to the whole class, and have them begin to link the idea of a covering of a surface to this word.

〰

What kinds of things was Ms. Wong thinking about when she wrote this lesson plan? What assumptions did she make and what did she purposely leave out? In the "Identifying the Mathematical Goals" section, Ms. Wong lists the concepts and vocabulary that she wants to develop during the lesson. At one point in her planning, Ms. Wong had two additional mathematics objectives in the lesson, but then realized that in order to address all of the objectives, there would not be time to talk about any of them.

When writing the "Anticipating Confusion" section, Ms. Wong relies on a number of resources to help her. First, she uses her experience as a classroom teacher to reflect on difficulties students in prior years had with the topic. She also examines her teacher's manual for information about possible errors or misconceptions. Ms. Wong sometimes refers to reference books that help her think about the mathematics and potential problems students will have with the topic. Finally, if the lesson is brand-new to her, after teaching it, she records her own errors and confusion as a way of gaining insight into students' minds.

The "Asking Questions" section is very important because it forces us to think about the purpose of our questioning and to consider questions that go beyond recall of knowledge. Some questions help us learn whether or not students comprehend the content of the lesson; some questions help us determine whether or not students can apply knowledge to new situations; and many discussion questions engage everyone in analyzing, synthesizing, or generalizing the topic at hand. Ms. Wong looks back at the first two components of her lesson plan when writing this section. First, she writes comprehension-type questions that she thinks might reveal students' accurate knowledge, misconceptions, or confusion about the mathematics. Second, she writes questions that might cause students some cognitive conflict—ones that she thinks will force them to reconsider any incorrect, preconceived notions. Third, she writes questions related to the mathematical objectives she identified that will lead the class to relate knowledge from several areas, to predict, or to draw conclusions. Ms. Wong saves her lesson plans from year to year and plans to note which questions were especially powerful in helping everyone make sense of the mathematics. Not surprisingly, she expects that she will drop questions that were not helpful in making the talk productive or ones that she did not use.

Ms. Wong is using two talk formats in this lesson: partner talk and whole-class discussion. She has students use partner talk as a way for everyone to share their interpretation of the meaning of *surface*. She uses whole-class discussion when she wants students to draw conclusions that everyone has agreed upon. In addition, during the whole-class discussion, she wants to remember to ask a number of students the same question. In the past, Ms. Wong did not ask more than one student to respond to the same math question but she realizes that her second graders often are confused when ideas go by too quickly. She believes that this approach will give her students more time to process the key ideas and will acclimate them to talking in mathematics class. Other times, Ms. Wong has used this section to remind herself to give enough wait time or she has listed students she needs to call upon in order to make sure that she is following Principle 3, concerning equitable participation in classroom talk.

Most lesson plans include a section on implementing the lesson. Ms. Wong's teacher guide has many suggestions for activities and sequencing which she uses. It is important to Ms. Wong that students practice sharing their discoveries about covering the surface of the book with different objects, as this talk activity is still relatively new for them. One component that she plans on incorporating into future lesson plans is a short summary section. Here is where Ms. Wong will review what the class did that day and let students know what lies ahead.

Making Decisions About Talk Formats

When planning a lesson, how do you decide when to use each of the three talk formats? We have found small-group discussion to be effective when the problems or tasks presented to students are quite difficult. The benefit of four minds instead of two focused on one problem cannot be underestimated. Also, tasks that lend themselves to a division of labor are good for small groups because students can share the results of their individual subtasks. And small-group talk can be used when students need to practice talking and listening to one another. Ms. Wong didn't use this talk format this time but could have incorporated it into her lesson when students were working in groups.

However, sometimes when small-group discussion is used, teachers become frustrated with the outcome. When students work in groups of three, four, or even five students, there are situations where some of these students do not contribute to the group work or participate in the group talk. For example, a student might sit quietly and let others solve and discuss the problems and then copy down the answers. Or a student might be totally off task, engaged in other activities, and cause problems for the group by making productive talk nearly impossible. Finally, some small groups are more interested in social talk than mathematical talk. In order for students to benefit from small-group discussion, you must construct the groups carefully, taking into consideration both the social and cognitive dynamics among students. Furthermore, you can keep changing the groups until you get groups who talk and work cooperatively.

Partner talk can be used in almost any situation: talking about vocabulary, interpreting a word problem, describing the steps in a computation, or solving a problem. In Project Challenge we used it regularly. During partner talk, the two partners must talk to each other and are forced to think and talk about the mathematics because there is no one else to do it for them. When students are engaged in trying to make sense of a situation, it is more likely that they are learning. We also used partner talk whenever students were confused or unsure of a response. If a question posed to the class did not elicit much response, we stopped the whole-class discussion and asked the students to turn and talk with a partner to discuss the solution, the word, or whatever was the issue at hand. The room would burst into talk as students shared their ideas. Partner talk provides a venue for students to try out, refine, and revise their ideas prior to presenting them to the whole class. Following partner talk, students may still be confused, but they are typically more willing to voice their confusion once they know they aren't the only ones who don't understand.

We found that it was important to choose partners carefully and to let them work together for extended periods of time—anywhere from two to eight weeks. This enabled the partners to develop some shared practices and to develop into a team. We considered the processing speed of students when partnering them—we put students who processed and computed quickly together and likewise we placed students who were easily confused together. We did not place the top-achieving students with those students working at or below grade level. Constructing partner groups by achievement levels enables you to give extra challenges to some partner teams and provide more content support for other teams. It also helps avoid the situation where one student does all the talking and thinking. As with small-group talk we moved partners around until we got the right combination: students who willingly talked together and were respectful and kind to each other.

Whole-class discussion is the talk format that can be used at the beginning of a lesson to set the stage for what is to come and to clarify the parameters of the instructional task. Whole-class discussion can also be used during the last third of the lesson as a forum for students to share what they have discovered and then both summarize and generalize the important ideas. Sometimes a full math class is spent discussing one question. One reason that whole-class discussion is used regularly is that it enables all students access to everyone's ideas and thoughts about the mathematics. Namely, by listening and contributing, students are furthering their own understanding. The class as a whole also is developing shared meaning for whatever ideas are under consideration. Finally, whole-class discussion provides the teacher with a way to assess students by asking specific students to revoice a statement or opinion, react to another student's statements, or provide their own solution methods.

Generating Good Questions

At the heart of using productive talk in instruction are the questions we pose. Our questions are the catalyst for students' thinking and talking. So how do you come up with questions that further students' mathematical knowledge? Almost every question-categorization scheme that exists, starting with Bloom's taxonomy (Anderson, Krathwohl, and Airasian 2000), makes a distinction between low-level, cognitively undemanding questions and high-level, cognitively challenging questions. The simplest, lowest-level questions ask students to recall knowledge that they already know. The most challenging questions ask students to explain a complex situation, evaluate the usefulness of a method, or synthesize a set of findings. At the far ends of the spectrum, it is fairly easy to tell the low-level question from the high-level question. For example, everyone knows that yes/no questions are less challenging in general than more open-ended "why" questions. There are many kinds of questions, however, where it is not so easy to tell what the "level" of the question really is.

Mary Kay Stein has spent many years thinking about the cognitive demands of tasks in mathematics instruction—what makes a low-level versus a high-level task. After many years of working with mathematics teachers, she has concluded that it is not always easy to tell how a question or task will pan out. Will it evoke high-level intellectual activity, a good discussion, or a conceptual breakthrough? Or will it devolve into a routine and unexciting activity? The answer depends upon the task, the teacher, and the students. If you are interested in thoughtful discussion on this matter, we recommend reading *Implementing Standards-Based Mathematics Instruction: A Casebook for Professional Development* (Stein et al. 2000).

In the meantime, though, we can suggest a strategy: Plan for high-level questions—the low-level questions will tend to take care of themselves. In other words, as you plan your lesson, try to come up with several big questions that will move students' thinking forward, questions that will require them to explain, synthesize, and make connections. You may not get all of these questions answered in one lesson, but at least they will help you define the trajectory you want to be on. The low-level questions that you must ask to check whether students remember, comprehend, or follow the discussion will emerge naturally as you pursue your larger, more complex questions.

For example, Ms. Wong asked questions to help her students generalize the fact that rectangles and squares cover surfaces more completely than circles and, in general, shapes that fit together with no holes or gaps cover a surface better than shapes that are curved, rounded, or include holes. As you write questions for each lesson, you should refer back to the mathematical goals you have defined. Make sure you are not just asking low-level questions about facts, since they usually are not conducive to discussion or debate. When asking a low-level question, consider how you can extend it so it has more than one purpose. For example, a discussion about estimating the number of beans in a jar might start out with a question designed to check students' number sense. But by asking students to explain how they decided upon their estimate, or asking them to compare their estimation technique with another student's technique, you have moved the instruction to a higher level of cognitive challenge.

Finally, when you hit upon a higher-level question that stimulates productive talk, talk that results in student advances in mathematical thinking, write it down. Share it with your colleagues. Tell your colleagues how the discussion proceeded after you introduced the question. These questions are among the valuable tools you will discover as you become more adept at using this type of instruction.

Improvising and Responding: In the Midst of the Lesson

Sometimes the lessons we design do not translate directly into practice. In fact, teachers more often than not are revising, modifying, or improvising on their lesson plans because students either know more or less than was expected. Talk lessons can sometimes lead us down paths for which we did not plan. In the following example, we see how Mrs. Carlson, a sixth-grade teacher, improvises and thus changes the direction of her lesson because of student responses. Mrs. Carlson's lesson focuses on understanding the formula for the area of a circle. Her students know how to find the area of squares, rectangles, parallelograms, and triangles. In this new lesson, students are to take a circle, cut it into small wedges, and then rearrange the wedges into a shape that approximates a parallelogram. Estimating the area of the parallelogram-like shape hopefully will help the students make sense of the circle-area formula. Following the activity, Mrs. Carlson plans to have students talk extensively about their findings.

Mrs. Carlson began the lesson by going over a few homework problems from the night before, reviewing previously introduced content such as how to find the circumference of a circle and the area of a parallelogram, and finally introducing the topic of the area of a circle. Students were seated at tables in groups of three, four, or five students. Paper circles (all the same size), protractors, and scissors were on the tables. Mrs. Carlson posed the following task to the class:

> *In order to determine the area of these paper circles, each of you is to take one, divide it into equal-size wedges, cut out the wedges, and then reconfigure the wedges into a shape that approximates a parallelogram. Without using a ruler, work together to determine the base and the height of your parallelogram-like shape and use this information to find its area. Later we will all talk about our results.*

1. Anna: How many wedges are we supposed to make?

2. Mrs. C: That is up to you. How many wedges do you think you should cut?

3. Anna: Four?

4. Ryan: I don't think that'll be enough for the new shape to look like a parallelogram. Look. [Ryan takes a circle and cuts it into fourths and puts them together for everyone to observe. See Figure 10–1.] I think we should try to cut lots of wedges.

5. Mrs. C: How many wedges could you possibly cut? Talk to the people at your table about this for a minute or so.

At the time, Mrs. Carlson didn't think her question was anything special. She thought students might agree that eight or ten or sixteen wedges would

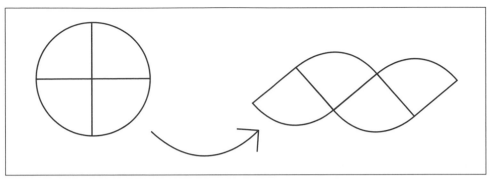

FIGURE 10–1 Ryan's attempt to make a parallelogram with four wedges cut from a circle.

be a good number for the task. She went over to one group of students and heard these suggestions:

6. Arjun: I think we can make an infinite number of wedges.

7. Kasey: No, I think three hundred sixty.

8. Alan: Wouldn't the number be one hundred eighty?

9. A.J.:   I'm confused. I can't figure out how to make more than thirty-six wedges.

Mrs. Carlson now has to make an instructional decision. Does she ignore some of the ideas that students are talking about in their small groups and focus on an answer to how many wedges the students need to cut for this task so that they can go on and complete the lesson? Or does she shift gears and have students explore through discussion the idea of determining the number of possible wedges? This is a forty-five-minute math period and with the review time at the start, about thirty minutes are left. Talk will often take classes down unanticipated paths, and it's not always clear whether or not to pursue the unexpected. In Project Challenge we tried to base our decisions on whether we felt the mathematics was important to know versus just nice to know. We often made mistakes and followed a discussion that, in retrospect, could have been skipped. However, we also had situations where we and the students learned a great deal by shifting gears. Making these types of instructional decisions is not easy. In Mrs. Carlson's case, she decides that it is worth pursuing the idea of an infinite number of wedges. She calls the class back to the whole-class discussion.

10. Mrs. C: Listening to you talk in your groups, I heard a number of possibilities for the number of wedges we might cut. I heard one hundred eighty, thirty-six, infinite, and three hundred

sixty just from one group. [Writes *180, 36, infinite, and 360* on the board.] How many wedges are in a circle? Does anyone else have a suggestion?

11. Tania: I think one hundred should also be added.

12. Mrs. C: Why?

13. Tania: Well, we know that a circle is one hundred percent, so then we can cut it into one hundred wedges, one for each percent.

14. Mrs. C: Are you thinking of a pie chart when you say that a circle is one hundred percent? [Tania nods. Mrs. Carlson adds *100* to the list on the board.] Now we have five different suggestions for how many wedges there might be. Which, if any, is correct? Talk to your partner. [Partner talk for a few minutes.] Andrew?

15. Andrew: I think that there are an infinite number of wedges possible, because you can just keep making the wedges smaller and smaller, like decimal amounts big.

16. Mrs. C: Andrew, could you explain what you mean by "decimal amounts big"?

17. Andrew: I mean we can pick a decimal amount like millionths and cut the circle into that many pieces. We could do this for every place value.

18. Swetha: I also think the number of wedges possible is infinity. You can just keep cutting more and more wedges.

19. Paul: But we can't cut that many. I think it is three hundred sixty. There are three hundred sixty degrees in a circle so that means one wedge for each degree.

20. Mrs. C: A.J., would you repeat what Paul just said?

21. A.J.: I agree with Paul. His explanation of three hundred sixty makes sense to me. Degrees are really small, so the wedges will be tiny. It will be hard to cut so many tiny wedges but I think we can do it.

22. Mrs. C: Sarah, do you want to add something?

23. Sarah: I agree with Andrew's idea. If you took each degree and cut it in half or in quarters or in eighths or any small fraction you would keep getting smaller and smaller wedges. I think there are just zillions of wedges in a circle, but they are so small we could never actually cut them out.

24. Sterling: Yeah, you can't really do that. You can't cut the wedges that small. So there are so many wedges but I don't know what to do with this problem.

Notice that two questions are being addressed: the number of wedges that can actually be cut and the number of wedges that are in a circle. It takes Mrs. Carlson a while to sort this out. As she listens to her students, she starts to understand their confusion and that she has inadvertently posed both questions during the class period. She continues to respond to the direction of the discussion, not totally clear where this might lead.

25. Mrs. C: Sarah and Sterling bring up a point for us to consider. What is possible in our minds and what is possible in reality? Namely, how many wedges are possible if we only think about it in our minds and don't try to cut them out? Talk to your partner about this.

Following more discussion, the consensus is that there are an infinite number of wedges that can be imagined. Mrs. Carlson asks everyone to summarize the points made about the number of possible wedges in their math journals. She thinks to herself that this slight diversion was well worth the discussion time. She is ready to return to her original plan. Then A.J. raises his hand and says, "I still don't understand this infinity stuff."

26. Mrs. C: OK. Who thinks they have an explanation that will help A.J. make sense of this idea? Arjun.

27. Arjun: A.J., first imagine cutting the circle into three hundred sixty wedges. Now blow up one of those tiny wedges in your mind. If you had a laser or something, could you cut each of the one-degree wedges up into smaller fractions? Yes, we could cut them into smaller and smaller wedges. You just have to imagine doing it, not it really happening.

28. Mrs. C: Andrew, do you want to add anything?

29. Andrew: Think of all the tiny decimal numbers there are. We can cut each degree into tiny decimal amounts like hundredths or thousandths or ten-thousandths. We can just keep doing this forever and if we do, the number of wedges will never end.

In many talk situations it is not the teacher who is the authority on the correctness of an answer. Instead the mathematical logic that students present is used to support answers, drive decisions, and justify conclusions. In this case, Arjun, Andrew, and others made contributions that helped A.J. better understand infinity and that supported the idea that there are an infinite number of wedges in a circle.

Mrs. Carlson realizes the period is almost over. The final thing she does before the end of the class period is to set the stage for tomorrow's lesson.

30. Mrs. C: We concluded that there are an infinite number of wedges possible in a circle but we still have the area problem to address tomorrow. So take one of the paper circles at your table and for homework please cut it into wedges that we can use to find the area. Does it make sense to cut these circles into one hundred or three hundred sixty wedges? No, so please pick a reasonable number and remember the wedges must each be the same size. Put your wedges in an envelope and bring them to class tomorrow.

Most of the discussion time was focused on the idea that there are an infinite number of wedges in a circle. Based on her knowledge of students' understanding of previous lessons, Mrs. Carlson believed that most of the students in her class understood that if they cut the circle into a large number of wedges, they could rearrange the wedges into a shape that would closely approximate a parallelogram. Thus she did not spend any time on this idea and instead adjusted the lesson to respond to the question about the number of possible wedges in a circle. In general, teachers should try to have discussions about ideas that students do not grasp. If it becomes clear that a concept or procedure is well understood, a shift in emphasis is warranted.

However, it is not always the case that teachers are clear on exactly what students do and do not understand. Mrs. Carlson may find when her students return that they do not understand how the wedges can approximate a parallelogram. Throughout this book you have read dialogues where teachers did not follow the thinking of a student. You have also seen situations where teachers ignored certain contributions in order to focus on a particular point. There isn't a road map for making instructional decisions on the fly—for deciding when to improvise and respond and when not. Nor is there one "right" direction for a discussion. Choices made by teachers bring classes down different paths and each path contributes to students' understanding of content. However, based on our experiences with classroom discourse, we suggest that if you find that a discussion has stalled or is not producing the kinds of insights you had expected, move on.

Summarizing and Solidifying: So Where Are We Now?

There are two distinct types of summarizing and solidifying that occur when using talk in lessons. One type is when either the teacher or the students summarize what occurred during the lesson. Remember that many discussions include contributions that are inarticulate, unclear in purpose, or unrelated. One job that the teacher has is to sort out the worthwhile comments (those that will help students make sense of the content) from all that was said during the discussion. Teachers often need to solidify what has been discussed in the lesson by clearly summarizing key points. Sometimes this happens in the middle of a class, sometimes at the end of the class period, and sometimes it occurs first thing the next day. When lessons take two or three days, a summary might not occur until the lesson is brought to closure. The importance of summary cannot be overestimated. It is through this process that conclusions are drawn and shared meaning among the students is developed.

Notice that Mrs. Carlson had students summarize the discussion in their math journals. The next day she will call on a few students to read what they wrote. Other times, Mrs. Carlson summarizes or asks one or two students to briefly go over the main points established in class. This does not have to take a lot of time but it is important to include.

Just as there is a need to help students summarize the important information gleaned from classroom discussions, it is also important for teachers to summarize the questions and talk moves they used in their lessons. This is a summary of instructional moves that a teacher places in his or her notes. We believe that it's essential that teachers refine their lessons from year to year. Thus, when you make changes to a planned lesson (whether because of a question that came up or because you ran out of time), it's important to go back to your original plans and add extensive notes. Mrs. Carlson's original plans did not involve talking about the number of possible wedges in a circle. However, because of what occurred in her class, she wants to include a discussion about infinity in regards to wedges in an even more focused way next year. Here are her notes.

IDENTIFYING THE MATHEMATICAL GOALS

- In theory, a circle can be cut into an infinite number of wedges.
- In reality, the number of wedges that a circle can be cut into is determined by the precision of the instruments used.

ANTICIPATING CONFUSION

- Students are likely to confuse what is physically possible and impossible.
- Students may not understand how you can make smaller and

smaller wedges—they may think 360 is the smallest number because there are 360 degrees in a circle.

- Students may not understand the concept of infinity.

ASKING QUESTIONS

- How many wedges are in a circle? or, How many wedges can you imagine there are in a circle? Convince me.
- How many wedges can we cut out of a circle? Justify your answer.
- Are the number of wedges we can cut and the number that exist the same thing? Why or why not?

MANAGING CLASSROOM TALK

- The question about the number of wedges possible creates a situation where students must take a position and either agree or disagree with each other's ideas. I need to simply present their possible answers and encourage them to use evidence to support or refute their claims.

~~~

Mrs. Carlson has solidified for herself some of the key points by taking the time to record the mathematics, the confusion, and the questions that were most helpful in moving everyone forward.

Planning talk lessons follows a cycle similar to lesson planning in general. First, teachers must plan ahead and project what will happen. They do this by analyzing the mathematics in the lesson, anticipating confusion with the mathematics, and then asking questions that will lead to either clarity or further confusion. Second, teachers must be willing to adapt portions or whole lessons as they respond to what students know and don't know. They may have to improvise, slow down, change gears, or regroup. Finally, teachers need to remember how important it is to include summaries, both of small points and of major conclusions during and after their lessons. The summaries should help both their students and the teachers themselves.

11

Troubleshooting

As experienced teachers know, any class can present obstacles or unexpected difficulties. This is particularly true when you, the teacher, decide to try something new. In our experience, students may or may not take to the methods described in this book. Some may easily begin to participate in talk, while others may seem to resist participation. As you monitor your progress, it's a good idea to keep track of the difficulties you encounter. In this section we'll talk about the most common problems and what teachers have done in the past to improve things.

My Students Won't Talk

Many students are used to a traditional classroom, in which the teacher does most of the talking and students occasionally answer questions. It's a big change to ask them to talk about their thinking and respond to other students' contributions. In some classrooms, the teacher will be met with silence at first. This can be unnerving, and even demoralizing. So the first thing to do is to ask yourself a few questions.

First, are the students silent because they have not understood a particular question? Make sure that whether the question comes from you or from another student, they have heard it a few times and have had time to think about it. If it's your question, ask several students to restate it; if it's a student's question, either revoice it yourself or ask another student to repeat it. Be sure that any question is repeated and clarified.

Second, do the students understand why you are asking them to repeat what others have said and to explain their reasoning? If you have given an introductory lesson about the reasons for these talk moves, you might revisit that. You might ask: "Why do you think I'm asking you to repeat what the previous speaker said?" Or: "Why do you think I'm asking you whether you agree with another student's reasoning?" This will give students an opportunity to review the reasons for understanding and paying attention.

If you have clarified questions and there is still no answer, it may be that your students are having an attack either of mass shyness or mass confusion. Sometimes it's hard to tell the difference. Early on in the process of starting to use talk, students may be hesitant to think out loud in front of their classmates. If you are confronted with silence from the whole class, have your students use partner talk for two minutes to clarify their thinking and practice their answers with one another. If they still don't seem to be able to talk about the ideas, you may have to step back and pose a simpler but related question. Don't give up!

If many of your students seem reluctant to speak, make sure that it is not because of a pattern of discourteous or disrespectful behavior. Even the presence of one or two students rolling their eyes at the contributions of others may be a deterrent to participation.

In some cases, reluctance to talk may be a function of an individual child's personality. In other cases it may be a family or cultural norm. In some families or communities, children are encouraged to observe and to learn through quiet apprenticeship. Children in these families or communities are not supposed to hold forth about their nascent ideas. It may be particularly frowned upon for girls to actively speak out. When you ask such children to explain their mathematical reasoning, that behavior may be in conflict with what they are used to, although they may not be able to articulate this. It will take time and patience to encourage quiet children to speak up voluntarily.

For example, one teacher we know had a group of fourth-grade girls and boys who were particularly quiet. They were eager and cooperative students but she could not get them to volunteer, and when she called on them they responded in such soft voices that no one could hear them. Repeated requests for them to speak up did not result in improvement. Finally, after several months, the teacher spoke to them outside of class as a group. She told them that their contributions were very valued and that they needed to learn to participate, even if it might seem challenging. To help get the process started, she said, she expected each of them to raise their hand at least once every lesson: to ask a question, to answer a question, or even just to request that something be repeated. The students looked relieved, she said, to have the decision to participate made for them. After that, each one started to enter into the conversation and make an effort to be heard. For these particular children, however, the process took the better part of a year.

The Same Few Students Do All the Talking

Most teachers find that when they begin the process of asking students to talk, there are a few who immediately blossom into really big talkers. As with reticence, talkativeness can be an individual personality trait or it can be a family or cultural norm. In some families and communities, children who talk a lot, who freely offer their opinions, are considered bright and personable and their talk is encouraged. When these students are asked to talk in school, they have an advantage. Just like children who have played baseball since age two have an advantage on the playground, when these children get into the game of academic talk in elementary school, they will be way ahead of others in their skills. If you have such students in your class, they will usually jump to answer your questions. Other students will quickly decide that they don't need to force themselves to do the work of participating: these two or three talkers will do the work for them!

The teacher then has a problem: the few will gladly take the floor and discuss whatever needs discussion, and the "silent majority" will become less and less willing to participate. If you see this pattern starting, it's a good idea to nip it in the bud. How? First, be determined: use your wait time. When you ask a question, and those same two or three hands go up first, keep waiting. You can say something neutral: "I want to see more hands. Let me repeat the question." Remember that repeating the question provides additional thinking time for students who may want to participate, but who don't feel ready to do so. When other students finally do raise their hands, call on several of them and have them rephrase one another's contributions. Just as we suggested meeting individually with students who are hesitant to talk, we would encourage you to meet privately with students who monopolize the floor. You might say: "I see your hand up a lot. I'm not ignoring you, but you know that every student needs to be able to participate. So since your hand is up almost all the time, you might want to think about this. Decide before you raise your hand whether this is something you really want to comment on."

Another tool you may want to consider is your inventory of turn-taking strategies. If the people who do all the talking are all boys, or all girls, you may want to introduce the "gender rule" in taking turns, and have boys and girls alternate in responding. You might decide to allow students to choose the next speaker instead of choosing the respondent yourself. Having their friends call on them can encourage students to participate more fully in discussions. (You will probably not want to rely on this strategy all of the time, but it can be useful in some circumstances.)

Sometimes you may feel that the few who raise their hands early and often are the most able, and that you want to use what they have to say. Their contributions may be the most dynamic, the most illuminating in terms of getting other students to understand the issues. We encourage you to use the insights of those students. Build on their contributions. Just make sure that you don't fall into the habit of relying on them to support your use of talk to the exclusion of other, less clear or less confident students. Your goal is to build a classroom community in which everyone can participate.

Should I Call on Students Who Do Not Raise Their Hands?

For many teachers, one of the toughest parts of using student talk in the classroom is deciding whether to call on students who never volunteer. In every classroom there will be one or two students who are truly reluctant to say anything. Are they benefiting from the use of talk in the classroom if they never talk and only listen? The little research that exists on the question seems to indicate that students certainly can benefit by listening. They can learn without talking. However, as we argued in Chapter 2, there are benefits to participating in talk, from engagement and motivation to clarification of understanding and improvement in language facility. So, how should you handle the few cases where you get the distinct feeling that you are torturing the student by waiting for him or her to answer a question?

Some teachers feel that if they call on such students they may actually harm them. In our view, if you are sensitive and supportive, you will actually help such students, rather them harm them. Once again, we recommend talking to the student privately. Ask the student about his or her concerns and reluctance. Try to come up with a plan that will let the student dip a toe in the water, so to speak. A few planned contributions can build confidence, and the student may overcome a barrier that will help him or her in other areas of life as well. Your efforts with such students may continue over a number of months. You can use a variety of strategies to help them start to participate. Call on these reluctant students right after partner talk, when they have had a chance to practice with a partner. Ask: "What did you and your partner come up with?" You may even wish to work with such students during partner talk to help them prepare what they will say.

A more general issue related to this is how we call on students every day. Should we call only on those students whose hands are raised, or should we try to distribute the turns equally throughout the class? This is a difficult issue, and different teachers will have distinct views on it. In our view, the most effective approach is to try to get all students to make a significant contribution at least once every few lessons. And in order to get them over the hurdle of speaking out loud in a group, it may also be a good idea to have each student say at least one thing every day, even a minor request for clarification.

This topic bears on your adherence to Principle 3, creating the conditions for full participation, and thus will involve your choices of turn-taking strategies. Some teachers formally incorporate a requirement that all students participate at least some of the time by using a list of student names, choosing at random from the list until everyone is called upon. While this has the advantage of making sure that a few students don't dominate all the talk, it has disadvantages as well. Some days certain students may have very valuable contributions to make about a particular topic. If they cannot contribute at will when they have something important to say, the entire enterprise may become less interesting for them. In general, you will want to strike a balance that allows equitable participation but that also allows students to retain as much sense of self-determination as possible.

My Students Will Talk, But They Won't Listen

You may be fortunate to have a class full of students who are willing to talk and share their reasoning. However, these same students may have another problem: they may be so involved in talking, they don't listen well. Instead of listening to one another's contributions and building on the idea of the preceding speaker, they may interrupt, talk over one another, and contribute ideas that all but ignore the previous contributions. Sometimes small groups of friends may talk together during large-group discussions. There may even be some discourteous or disrespectful talk about others' contributions. How can you get students to listen respectfully to one another and think together as a class?

Start by having a talk with the whole class. Remind them that each of them has the right to be heard, but that this means they have a corresponding obligation to listen. Start to rely more heavily on the move of asking students to repeat what the previous speaker has just said. If they are not able to do this, find ways of reinforcing the fact that being able to repeat what someone has said is a serious obligation.

One teacher's fourth-grade students were not very good at making their contributions connect with those of the previous speakers. He ended up with lots of disjointed talk, where one student's turn had no obvious connection to the next. For a while he tried to draw the connections for them, but finally he decided to ask them to start each turn by saying either of two things: "I agree/disagree with [the previous speaker] because . . ." or "I want to add on to what [the previous speaker] said. . . ."

We think you will find that if you are consistent, asking students to respond specifically to one another's contributions, students will begin to internalize the obligation to listen to others and think about what they have said.

"Huh?"—Responding to Incomprehensible Contributions

As we have shown in some of the examples in previous sections, students' responses are sometimes almost impossible to understand. What should one do when a student produces an unintelligible utterance? What if it is so incomprehensible that you cannot even begin to rephrase it? The temptation is simply to say, "Oh, I see. How interesting," and quickly move on to another student. This way we can avoid embarrassing ourselves and the student at the same time! However, in the long run such an approach will undermine your purposes. You want students to practice at becoming clearer in their thinking and talking. What better place to start than with a student who is unclear? You want students to learn that it is worth the struggle to try to clarify one's meaning. If you pass over students whose responses are confusing, other students will learn that it's better to avoid embarrassment than to engage in the struggle for clarity.

If you are working hard to engage students in challenging mathematics, you will not be able to avoid this problem. People—whether adults or children—who are talking about something new and complicated tend to sound unclear. As comprehension gets more difficult, fluency and clarity decrease. In our experience, when introducing a new and challenging mathematics topic, up to half of all contributions in a class may be very difficult to comprehend. So what can be done?

First, use the tool of revoicing. Try to repeat even a few words the student has said. If you can't do this, ask another student to do so. Unlikely as it seems, we have often seen students give wonderful renditions of what we found incomprehensible. In a way, this makes sense. You are up at the front of the class, trying to keep track of twenty-five different individuals and the contents of the lesson as well. Students have the benefit of being able to sit at their desks, listening. They may have understood something that got by you and are able to offer insight into what a student was saying.

There will occasionally be times when neither you nor anyone else can understand what a particular student is saying. If you need to move on, you can say to the student something like this: "Well, I guess we haven't really understood your contribution. See if you can work on it, and if you want to give it another try later, I'll come back to you." The student may or may not want to pursue it later, but at least you have conveyed the message that each student's ideas are worth struggling with.

Brilliant, But Did Anyone Understand?

Occasionally a student will make a mathematically brilliant contribution, or one that at least has the potential to open up some important issues for the class. But as you look around the room, you wonder whether you and the student are the only two people in the room who have understood what the student said. What are you to do?

First, start by asking the student to repeat. Say something like: "Wow, that sounds really interesting, but I got lost in the middle. Can you repeat that?" Next, ask several other students to revoice. This alerts them that they all have to pay attention to what has been said. Make sure that you ask the originator of the idea whether he or she agrees with the other students' interpretations. If the originator does not agree, he or she will have to repeat and clarify the idea. Even if the originator does agree, have several students in succession try to repeat the idea. If the idea is really important, having multiple students repeat it will ensure that most of them understand it, and that many of them will appreciate its significance as the discussion proceeds.

Should you pitch in at this point, attempting to give yet another rendition of what the original student said? In our view, although it's tempting to take over and revoice the student's excellent contribution yourself, we think you should refrain, if you can. By allowing other students to try first, before you step in, you focus everyone's attention on the contribution, and you allow the originator to get credit for the insight. It also reinforces the joint, collaborative nature of the discussion. You can play a role, however, in determining the extent of students' understanding and in moving the conversation forward to aspects that they still may not understand.

You may also use the board as a revoicing tool. You can scribe what other students say as they try to clarify the originator's idea. Students may also scribe or illustrate their points. Sometimes slowing down the process enough to write things down allows you to get a clearer idea of how to proceed. And getting across the importance of a difficult new idea or an original observation can take a long time. We once watched as the important idea of one student became clear to other students only over the course of two different lessons.

I Have Students at Different Levels

Most teachers are confronted with a wide range of backgrounds and abilities in their classrooms. If you are trying to get the students to focus on the same problem, what do you do if some of the students do not understand the problem? How can you have a discussion when your students are at very different levels?

Many teachers follow the practice of grouping weaker students with stronger students, because they believe that high-achieving students can help the weaker students understand the material. In our experience, in talk-intensive classrooms, this often does not work well. What happens is that high-achieving students quickly come to an understanding and present a solution, and the talk ceases long before the weaker student can participate in thinking through the problem. Even when the higher-achieving student tries to explain his or her reasoning in a sort of expository or lecture style, there is no guarantee that the weaker student will benefit. Often the weaker student takes on a very passive role as a learner, and this is the opposite of what we are trying to foster.

Therefore, the practice we have adopted is to pair students of similar ability and of compatible personality. What do we mean by similar ability and compatible personality? This is something that a teacher can discover only through getting to know the students. It doesn't necessarily mean pairing boys with boys and girls with girls, but rather is based on your intuition of which students will be able to talk to one another in a productive way. This may sometimes mean that a weaker student is paired with a student on grade level. Or a student on grade level may be paired with one of the most able students in the room. The only real proviso is to avoid pairing the very strongest students with the very weakest students.

Some teachers randomly assign partners, and this can work as well. But even in this case, you want to think carefully to avoid problems. In our experience, if you want to get the most out of this model of using talk, you might do well to pair students of similar ability, at least part of the time. Finally, you can switch partners at regular intervals, and if you see that a partnership is not working, don't be afraid to intervene and change the partners.

It's important to notice that this isn't equivalent to putting students into ability groups that are given different tasks. Everyone here is doing the same task, and when the talk begins in whole-class discussion, everyone will have taken on the same set of problems. However, it's possible to give students who understand quickly an additional question or challenge that they can do while other students work with the main assignment. This also allows the teacher to provide more scaffolding and support to groups and pairs that need it. What we are aiming for is flexible grouping based on what students know about a particular area, and based on what the teacher has perceived about their ways of interacting.

What Should I Do When They're Wrong?

Discussions like the ones you will experience are often full of mistakes of various kinds. In the process of working through a problem, students may use a word incorrectly. They may use a computational procedure incorrectly. Their answers may be wrong, sometimes strikingly wrong. Your task is to figure out how to respond. Our suggestions here fall into two broad categories: how to handle students' feelings about being wrong, and how to allocate time to their mistakes.

First, we'd like to point out that this kind of instruction requires students to agree and disagree with one another at some point. Often, in this atmosphere of inquiry, students will notice when someone says something wrong, or two students will come up with different answers. For most students, being wrong is not pleasant, and not trivial. Many students will still have the idea that success in mathematics means being right, not being a strong thinker. It is helpful to explicitly discuss the value of wrong answers, and the unavoidability of mistakes and errors. Errors can be repositioned as a source of new knowledge. Teach your students to say: "I'd like to revise my thinking" or the phrase that often pops up spontaneously in a good discussion: "I disagree with myself!"

It's very important to monitor the norms of respectful discourse at points like these, when a student has come up with a wrong answer. You do not have to avoid calling attention to a wrong answer, but you do need to continue to reassure students that it's OK to be wrong, and that all students must be sensitive to the feelings of someone who has publicly made a mistake.

Second, it will sometimes be the case that you will be in the middle of a good discussion where a student is making an important mathematical point. In the middle of making their point, they will say something incorrect—for example, "five times eight is forty-eight." You might wonder: should you stop the discussion to correct this error, at the risk of derailing a conversation where students are getting intellectually involved? We encourage you to be sensitive to the flow of discussion. If students are dealing with new and difficult ideas, and the point of the discussion is to get clarity about concepts and ideas, it might be perfectly acceptable to ignore a minor mistake. However, if you are in a review, or in a discussion in which you are going over something that has become familiar to students, that is a good time to insist on high standards of correctness.

This Discussion Is Not Going Anywhere

Sometimes you may get the impression that although your students are willing to talk and listen respectfully, the conversation is slow, repetitive, and even dull at times. If this is happening consistently, ask yourself whether you are "beating a dead horse" and going over material the majority of students have understood. If you feel that there is too much repetition, you may be asking too many students to revoice, just to be sure that they understand. Another issue may be the level of your questions. If there are too many low-level questions, you may not have appropriate fodder for a high-level, exciting discussion. It helps to work with colleagues on this issue. You might ask another teacher to come in and observe you, to see if your use of the tools of talk could be sharpened somehow.

Sometimes the problem is that students are introducing interesting but tangential questions, and although the discussion is lively, you are not making progress toward your mathematical goals. It's important to remember that you cannot follow up on every single point. In order to keep the discussion moving, you will have to ignore some things and move other topics to the forefront. This is why planning is so important—it's easy to lose sight of your goals and get offtrack with interesting but tangential questions.

Their Answers Are So Superficial!

At the beginning of this process, as you first begin to use talk intensively, students may not know how to respond. They will rely on the strategy they have used before, namely, to provide a one-word answer to the teacher's question, as in the following example:

1. Ms. G: So, what method do you think you'll use to solve this problem?
2. Phil: Add. [No response from Ms. Glass.] No, subtract!

This is a typical response from a student who has not had much experience carefully thinking through a problem and presenting reasons for his responses. What should Ms. Glass do here? One option is to ask Phil why he thinks the method should be to use subtraction. Imagine, however, that Phil responds: "I don't know." What next? Ms. Glass could refer him back to the problem, asking him again why subtraction seemed to him to be a good method. Upon rereading the problem, Phil may actually think more deeply about the problem, rather than simply trying to supply a one-word answer that in another class would be sufficient.

The principle here is that the teacher must continue to focus on reasoning: ask students to justify their decisions, whatever sort of decisions those are. Don't be afraid to press them for evidence or reasoning. Students we have worked with have told us that they appreciate the experience of being made to think more deeply. Although they do say that they feel pressured sometimes, they enjoy the fact that mathematics starts to make sense because they are forced to make sense of it.

What If the First Speaker Gives the Right Answer?

Imagine you have posed a problem to your students and after giving them time to solve the problem with a partner, you then begin the whole-class discussion. You ask, "Who can tell us how they began to solve the problem?" The first student you call on gives a coherent, articulate explanation of the correct answer. What do you do? Put aside your plans for a discussion? Move on? Not yet.

First, recall what you observed and heard when students were working in pairs to solve the problem. Did most of them solve the problem correctly before the whole-class discussion began? If so, you may wish in the whole-class discussion to ask several other students to revoice the speaker's statement and explain why they agree or disagree with its reasoning. Then, ask everyone to "turn and talk with the person next to them" about whether they agree or disagree with the speaker's comment, and listen to see if most can do so successfully. If the students can, it is not necessary to continue the discussion of a comment that most, or all, students understand. After all, classroom talk is productive when it allows students to progress in their understanding, not simply reaffirm what they already know. (If you have time, you can capitalize on their understanding by posing a similar but more difficult problem or problem extension for students to discuss. This will allow you to reach the mathematical goals of your lesson while still engaging the students in productive discourse.)

If the students you call on to respond to the speaker's comment cannot do so successfully, you may wish to use the techniques described in the section titled "Brilliant, But Did Anyone Understand?" Or, you may feel that this comment will have much greater significance if discussed later on. Perhaps students do not seem clear on the constraints of the problem, nor are they sure of what strategies to use. Maybe most have solved the problem incorrectly and need clarification of their misconceptions before discussing the correct solution. In this case you may say to the student, "You have given us a lot to think about. I know I need to back up a little bit and think more about making sense of the problem and deciding which strategy to use and why. I'm going to ask if you would be willing to offer your comment again a little later on. I know it is going to be helpful to all of us."

Further, if you wish to avoid this scenario in future discussions, use the partner-discussion time to decide who you will call on and in what order. For example, you may wish to begin the discussion by calling on several students who you heard restate the problem and question articulately and thoroughly, even though their solution strategies may have had problems. Then, you may wish to call on students who explored different ways to solve the problem, progressing in difficulty and complexity. The more you know about where students are in their understanding, the more strategically you can use their contributions in a whole-class discussion.

What Should I Do for English-Language Learners?

Three-quarters of the students that we worked with in Project Challenge were English-language learners. Yet they all made tremendous progress in classrooms using intensive talk. Teachers with ESL learners should not shy away from using this approach to mathematics, but it helps to think carefully about the demands of the talk moves and formats we have introduced here. First, make sure that you give students plenty of time. Use wait time consistently and patiently. Waiting up to thirty seconds may be necessary, and if you have many native English speakers mixed in with your ESL learners, you will have to model for them the value of waiting. Second, it may take longer into the year before such students are ready to handle the demands of talking, repeating other students' contributions, or making their own. Think carefully about putting them on the spot. But as the year progresses, do not assume that you must simply leave them out of the discussion. Talk with students outside of class to encourage them to ask a question or to request clarification.

We found in Project Challenge that the talk moves and talk formats introduced in this book actually support language learning as well as mathematical thinking. There are ideas and practices throughout the book that will help students who are learning English. In Chapters 3, 7, and 8, the emphases on definitions, concepts, and representations are particularly relevant for English-language learners. Use revoicing to help them make their contributions clear, and use revoicing to make others' contributions clearer to them. Over time, the experience of listening closely, repeating, and making their own contributions will push your students ahead in English as well as mathematics.

Reassurance from Project Challenge Students

As you begin these new practices, you may be sensitive to negative reactions from students. Many people respond to new practices with complaints or resistance. You may feel that requiring students to listen to each person's contribution is too demanding, or that waiting thirty seconds for a student's answer puts too much pressure on them. We can offer reassurance with respect to our students in Project Challenge. Recall that about 75 percent of the students in the low-income urban schools we worked in were second-language learners of English, as were the Project Challenge students. We had had concerns since the beginning of the program about the challenges they might experience in our talk-intensive classrooms. Although we had seen tremendous growth, we wanted to know how our students felt about the new approach. At the end of the fourth year of Project Challenge, we took some class time to ask our four seventh-grade classes for their reactions to our four-year focus on productive talk. The following are examples of what students said and wrote about talking and listening in the mathematics classroom.

When asked, "Was being required to listen to each other helpful or not helpful?" approximately 95 percent of the students surveyed responded " helpful." When asked why he thought listening was helpful, Anton made the following remark: "Sometimes [math] is confusing but when you listen carefully, you can figure out how to do the math slowly, or little by little, and you find out how to do it." Anton's comment is that of an experienced and effective listener. He knows that listening does not make understanding instantaneous or automatic. Rather, as he said himself, listening helps learning slowly, or little by little. And how does this happen? It happens when students have conversations about mathematics, often revoicing an idea over and over again, until peers reach a common understanding of it. The listening continues as students comment on why they agree or disagree with an idea. All the while, the listeners are learning from the students who are talking. Anton not only knows how to listen, he sees its value in his learning.

Mel offered a perspective on how talking and listening go hand-in-hand in learning mathematics. He said, "It helped us when we got to hear other people's answers. We can add things to our answers to make them better than we had originally from the question that we had to answer." Mel's comment targets one of the very core benefits of listening—helping us figure out what to say and how to say it. Mel knows that we listen not for the sake of listening, but so that we can broaden what we know about a subject and thus get better at speaking about it. He knows this because he has been encouraged and expected to listen to his classmates and then use their statements to form and articulate his own reasoning.

Brianna's comment mirrors Mel's remark. She wrote: "Listening to each other is helpful because if we don't listen to each other, how can we understand what each of us has to say?" Aaron wrote: "It's helpful because if I was not required [to listen] I wouldn't pay attention." Jan said, "You can see other people's points of view. People can correct their mistakes by hearing others." The comments are from students who have been taught to listen. But their remarks show that they understand the benefits of listening. And that's what is required if students are going to use listening as a learning tool.

When asked, "Was having to talk to others about math helpful or not helpful?" approximately 88 percent of the students responded "helpful." Jan explained that it was important to explain yourself in math class because, "In real life, if you can't explain and don't have evidence, it doesn't count." Aaron, who wrote that listening forces him to pay attention, thinks, "It's helpful [to talk] because I could ask questions." Barry said, "I like the talking to your neighbor or partner thing because if somebody doesn't really understand something and they talk to their partner, their partner can help them understand it so you get to go on without being confused or having trouble." These students can articulate the benefits of talk because they have experienced these benefits regularly and consistently in their mathematics classes. In talking about their reasoning, students come to realize that it is important to be as clear as possible, provide supporting evidence, and use talk as an opportunity to get clarification and achieve understanding.

During the discussion about talking and listening, Tina and Mrs. Anderson had an exchange that shows that even when students are uncomfortable with talk, they still see its worth. Mrs. Anderson asked Tina if she liked being called on in discussions. This is the conversation that ensued.

1. Tina: Sometimes you push me to say the answer and I really don't know the answer.

2. Mrs. A: What happens if I keep pushing you and you still don't know the answer?

3. Tina: I tell you I don't know.

4. Mrs. A: And then what happens?

5. Tina: You call on a different person.

6. Mrs. A: So how does that make you feel?

7. Tina: Better.

8. Mrs. A: And when I call on another person what are you doing?

9. Tina: Listening.

10. Mrs. A: And then do you usually raise your hand after that? [Tina shakes her head no.] Why not?

11. Tina: 'Cause you'll usually just come right back and ask me.

12. Mrs. A: And when I come back automatically, then how do you feel?

13. Tina: Better, because then I would know the answer.

It is not easy or enjoyable for students, or anyone, to admit that they do not know something. But the fact remains that not knowing answers is a normal part of life. And because it is, expressing uncertainty should be a part of talking in math class. Students should be allowed to state when they do not know or cannot explain something. Some teachers are surprised when we push revisiting a student who has admitted to not knowing an answer. They think that it puts too much pressure on a student who already has expressed that he or she lacks understanding. Tina's comments indicate that the opposite is true. Tina explains that she feels better when Mrs. Anderson goes on to speak with another student; it takes the pressure off of her. But while the other student is speaking, Tina is listening. So instead of the discussion continuing without a contribution from Tina, Mrs. Anderson "comes back to her." This gives Tina a chance to show what she has gained from listening and makes her feel better. Tina's comments suggest that students appreciate being revisited, since it gets them past the discomfort of "not knowing the answer" and onto being a contributor to the discussion.

When asked how she felt about the expectation to contribute to class discussions, Kara responded that she didn't like it. She said, "Some girls don't really know the answer or are shy and don't want to speak." When asked whether she felt that there was a payoff to speaking despite being shy or unsure, Kara said, "Sometimes it's worth it because you end up knowing the answer but you didn't know it before." Ryan told us that he did not like being called on to talk because when he was not paying attention, it was embarrassing. He then went on to say, "If I got called on and wasn't paying attention, I was afraid I would get called on again so I started paying attention." Both Kara and Ryan are quite honest in their feelings about required participation—they don't like it. But both also name benefits to it—it helps them pay attention and learn new information.

We end this chapter with one last striking example that convinced us that classroom talk, though challenging, is a rewarding endeavor. This example centers on Gayle, a Project Challenge student. When Gayle began Project Challenge in fourth grade, she did not say much at all in class. Even when working with her partner, Gayle rarely spoke. Gayle struggled on her weekly quizzes and did not seem to be benefiting from this instructional approach.

Yet over the course of fifth grade, Gayle began to change. Her fifth-grade teacher worked hard to get Gayle to speak in class. When called on, Gayle would often respond with a period of silence, which was then followed by a short, barely audible, response. Her teacher continued to call on Gayle, and each time, her responses got a little louder, a little longer, and a little more sensible. While her evolution was slow but steady, one particular example of her emergence comes to mind. Gayle's class was discussing the sum of interior angles of a triangle. In the midst of one discussion about whether or not it was necessary to measure all three angles in order to determine the measure of each, Gayle made an articulate and mathematically sound contribution. Gayle's classmates were then asked to explain why they agreed or disagreed with her comment. As they were speaking, most in support but some still dubious, Mrs. Anderson saw Gayle straighten her back, throw her shoulders back, and while maintaining a serious look on her face, beam with quiet confidence. At the end of the program, Gayle was described by her seventh-grade teacher as still quiet but articulate, responsive, and engaged. Of talking and listening, Gayle wrote, "It was helpful to listen and talk to each other because I got to listen to how people thought about problems and why they agreed or not and I got to talk to people and tell them what I thought about certain things."

Gayle's transformation occurred because she had teachers who were determined to get their students to talk productively about their mathematical understanding. The confidence Gayle exhibited in her later years in the program was the result of her experience speaking about her mathematical knowledge to a respectful, responsive audience. We know from our own experiences that while talking in mathematics class is not always easy, seeing the growth in students like Gayle makes the effort worthwhile.

PART
4

Case
Studies

12

Looking at the Shape of the Data
Grade Three

This chapter presents a case study of a talk-based lesson in Mrs. Robert's third-grade class. As in previous dialogues, Mrs. Robert and her students are fictional characters, based on the experiences of real teachers and their students. We offer this example as a realistic picture of what sometimes happens when you first strive to use the talk moves described in this book. You will see that Mrs. Robert's lesson does not go well. We have observed a fair number of disappointing talk-based lessons as teachers learned to implement this instructional format, and we want to help you avoid some typical pitfalls. We hope this case study provides insights into how to use talk effectively and persevere when a lesson doesn't quite work the way you had predicted.

How Do You Measure a Foot?
Mrs. Robert's nineteen third-grade students are in the early stages of a unit on linear measurement and data analysis. The lesson at the focus of this case study is on interpreting and analyzing data about the length of students' feet. In this lesson, the data are displayed in a line plot. The goals of the unit include using various units to measure lengths, discovering relationships among units, and exploring how students can make sense of and analyze measurement data using graphic representations. Previous lessons have given the students experiences in measuring distances by pacing, comparing and contrasting pace sizes, and exploring the relationship between size of the unit

and number of units needed to measure a given length. They have recorded the lengths they measured using their paces on line plots and looked for the "typical" pace length in the class. In this lesson, Mrs. Robert planned to have students use a twelve-inch ruler and measure student foot length in inches and then determine the typical foot length in their class.

Mrs. Robert teaches in a suburban school system that has just adopted a standards-based curriculum. Due to budget constraints, however, there has been little opportunity for professional development on how to use the new curriculum effectively. As a result, many teachers are confused about the philosophy, implementation, and goals of the new curriculum. Mrs. Robert recently attended a regional mathematics conference where she participated in a workshop on mathematical discourse. In this workshop she learned about many of the talk moves described in this book. She thought that mathematical discourse fit hand in hand with the mathematical investigations inherent in the new curriculum. After attending the workshop, Mrs. Robert was inspired, feeling that she had found a way to teach math that would be engaging and rewarding for both her and her students. She knew, however, that one workshop would not be enough to become proficient in mathematical discourse. Nonetheless, she took copious notes during the workshop and began to make changes in her teaching following the conference. A dedicated and experienced teacher, she is determined to have success using talk in her mathematics class. Her lesson shows, however, that just as she predicted, determination does not immediately equal success.

The lesson has been under way for about fifteen minutes. Mrs. Robert first reviewed with her third-grade students what they had learned about linear measurement and data representation up to that point. Then Mrs. Robert launched into the day's main lesson.

1. Mrs. R: We are going to measure the length of our feet to see if we can find the typical foot length of a member in our class. So the first thing we have to decide is whether or not we are going to take our shoes off when we measure our feet. I'd like you to talk to the person next to you about this for a moment. [There is silence in the classroom. Many students look confused. Mrs. Robert attempts to clarify.] Maybe I was not clear. Since we are going to measure our feet, we need to know whether or not to take off our shoes. Talk about that with the person next to you. [Students begin to talk. Mrs. Robert walks to another part of the room to gather the rulers. She then calls on students to share what they

talked about.] OK, Leigh what do you and your partner think?

2. Leigh: We don't know.

3. Mrs. R: What do you mean, you don't know?

4. Leigh: Well, we didn't really know what we were supposed to be talking about.

5. Mrs. R: You could have asked another student. Who can tell Leigh and her partner what you were supposed to be talking about? Joe?

6. Joe: I think we should take our shoes off.

7. Mrs. R: Hold on, Joe. I didn't ask you that. I asked if you could repeat the question I asked you all to discuss with your partners.

8. Joe: We were supposed to talk about taking our shoes off.

9. Mrs. R: Sort of. I wanted you to discuss whether or not you thought we should. [At this point, the other students seem restless and disengaged. Some are writing on a paper handed out for homework. A few are talking. Some others seem to be daydreaming.] Go ahead, Joe.

10. Joe: OK, so I think you should take your shoe off because, like, my toe is not touching my shoe so that would be wrong.

11. Mrs. R: Lara, do you agree with what Joe said? [Lara looks bewildered.] Joe, can you repeat what you said? And everyone else, you should be listening too. [Several students, but not all, seem to focus in at this point.]

12. Joe: Um . . . I forgot what I said.

13. Mrs. R: Does your partner remember?

14. Dana: Actually, I thought we should leave our shoes on. See my shoe? It's exactly the same as my foot.

15. Mrs. R: What do some other people think?

16. Barb: I think someone maybe doesn't want to take their shoes off. They shouldn't have to if they don't want to.

17. Mrs. R: Do you agree with that, Roberta?

18. Roberta: What?

19. Mrs. R: I said do you agree with what Barb said.

20. Roberta: Well, I have something else to say. My partner and I had rulers already so we measured and it was the same.

21. Mrs. R: OK, but I didn't ask you to measure yet, did I? I wanted you to talk about whether the shoes on or off mattered. Did

you hear what Barb said? [Roberta shakes her head.] Barb said that people should have a choice about leaving their shoes on or off. Do you agree with that?

22. Roberta: Yes, because it doesn't matter. [Mrs. Robert notices that Andrew is emphatically shaking his head no.]

23. Mrs. R: Andrew, do you have something to say?

24. Andrew: Yeah, they're wrong.

25. Mrs. R: Andrew, if you don't agree, you need to say, "I disagree with your idea." And tell us why you disagree.

26. Andrew: They're wrong, because look at my shoe next to my foot. [Andrew stands up, placing his stocking feet next to his shoe. The other students clamber around to get a view. In doing so, there is some chatter and pushing.] See the difference? So it does matter.

27. Mrs. R: Martin, do you agree or disagree?

28. Martin: He should put his shoe back on. His foot smells. Pee-yew! [The students burst out laughing.]

29. Mrs. R: Martin, that was inappropriate. Please apologize.

30. Martin: But it does—smell it!

31. Mrs. R: Please apologize, now!

32. Martin: Sorry. [He rolls his eyes as he says this.]

33. Mrs. R: I want everyone to go back to their seats and sit quietly for a minute. [Mrs. Robert waits as the students take their seats and are quiet.] Please turn and talk to your partner again about the decision to measure our feet with our shoes on or off. [As students talk, Mrs. Robert sees that many are still giggling about Martin's comment.] So, Tonya what do you think?

34. Tonya: It doesn't matter.

35. Mrs. R: Do you agree, Raul?

36. Raul: Yes, it doesn't matter.

37. Mrs. R: Well, since we can't seem to decide, I'll decide for you. You are going to take your shoes off to measure.

At this point, the fire alarm went off unexpectedly. It turned out to be a fire drill that Mrs. Robert had known about, but she had thought it would occur later. By the time the class got back to the room after the drill, the period was over.

Clearly, this was not what Mrs. Robert had planned for this part of the lesson. Her students were not listening to her or each other, did not know what to say or how to work together during partner talk, and did not seem to be treating each other with much respect. In addition, most of the students' comments were shallow, disjointed, and inarticulate. Mrs. Robert had begun the lesson with a review that had taken about fifteen minutes. This part of the class, discussion of the measurement question, had taken slightly over ten minutes and the lesson was going nowhere when the fire alarm rang. What did Mrs. Robert envision for the lesson? Did she anticipate that this part of the lesson would take so much time? Let's take a look at her lesson plan.

Identifying the Mathematical Goals

- Students will make conclusions about the class foot lengths by looking at the shape of the data when organized in a line plot.
- Students will determine the typical foot length in their class by looking at the value(s) with the highest frequency or where the data clumps.
- A line plot shows data, organized from least to greatest on a number line, using Xs to mark the frequency.

Vocabulary

- *Line plot* (see definition above);
- *Range* (the difference between the highest and lowest values or an expression of the difference);
- *Typical* (normal, frequent, or average).

Anticipating Confusion

- Students may think that the range of a set of data is the highest and lowest values written on the line plot.
- Students may think that the highest value in the data shows what is most typical. They may think the word *typical* means "biggest" or "most."

Asking Questions

- What do you predict will be the shortest and longest foot lengths?
- Should we leave our shoes on or take them off?
- What do you notice about the shape of our line plot? What does the shape of the line plot tell us about the data set?
- What is the range of our foot lengths? How do you know?

- What does *typical* mean? Explain.
- What is the typical foot length in our class? How do you know?

MANAGING CLASSROOM TALK

- I will focus on encouraging my students to speak loudly enough for others to hear and on getting my students to listen to one another when they speak.

Planning the Implementation

Introduction

Review what students have learned about linear measurement and displaying data in previous lessons in this unit. Explain to the students that today's task is to collect data about the lengths of their feet. Students will measure their feet in inches and then organize their data in a line plot. Explain that the purpose of this is to learn what the typical foot length is in our class. Ask the students to discuss whether or not they think they should keep their shoes on. Ask students to explain the correct way to use a ruler, compare and contrast centimeters and inches, how to figure out or remember which side of a ruler shows centimeters and which shows inches, and whether to round off to the nearest inch or half-inch. Show the students a horizontal line drawn on the blackboard and explain that the numbers written below it will stand for the lengths of their feet. Ask them to predict where the data will go and what they will look like. Ask the students what they think will be the smallest and largest foot lengths in our class.

Exploration

Students will measure the lengths of their feet. They will then come up to the board and draw an X above the appropriate number in the line plot. As students post the data, ask them why it is important to keep all of the Xs approximately the same size and distance apart. After the line plot is made, give student pairs a few moments to discuss what they observe.

Discussion

Begin the whole-class discussion by asking the students for observations about the line plot. Scribe their observations on the board as they speak. Discuss the comments that highlight the big ideas.

Seeing Mrs. Robert's lesson plan reveals just how much the beginning of the lesson went awry. Her lesson plan mentioned that she would ask students to talk about whether they should leave their shoes on or off, but this was certainly not a goal nor a major focal point of the lesson. Yet it consumed a significant amount of time during the lesson. Mrs. Robert's plan suggested that she thought students would be able to talk about the shoe issue coherently and briefly and then move on to exploring the heart of the lesson, collecting and looking at the data. This is not what happened.

Now that we have seen the discrepancy between the plan for the introduction and the implementation, let's explore possible reasons why the students' use of talk was unsuccessful. We will start with Mrs. Robert's reactions to the lesson as revealed in a conversation she had after the lesson with her mentor teacher, Mr. Brown, who has more experience using talk in math class.

Troubleshooting with a colleague

Mrs. Robert sought out Mr. Brown after the lesson because she was concerned about how the lesson had gone. She began by explaining to Mr. Brown how surprised she was at her students' inability to pay attention to what others were saying in the shoe debate. She was surprised because "the class started with a good discussion about what students remembered from previous lessons in the unit." But when Mr. Brown asked Mrs. Robert for details about this part of the lesson, it became apparent that this review was not a discussion at all. Students volunteered things that they remembered, but Mrs. Robert had not asked them to restate one another's summaries, question one another's statements, or connect their ideas to one another. It had merely been a "quizzing" session, in which students had made statements one after the other, unconnected to what previous speakers had said.

Mrs. Robert realized that she had no idea whether or not her students were even listening to one another as they reviewed previous lessons. Their performance in the shoe discussion would suggest that they were not. Mr. Brown suggested that during lesson introductions where students are asked to think about things they've learned, that they be required to relate their comments in some way to the comment of the previous speaker. Mrs. Robert thought that this was a good idea and also thought that she would try asking students to revoice one another's contributions during future reviews in order to find out if they were listening.

Next Mrs. Robert told Mr. Brown about her lack of success in using partner talk. When Mrs. Robert asked her students to talk with the person next to them about the shoe decision, the students sat silent. When she restated the question, they did start talking to their peers, but not very productively. Leigh said that she and her partner did not know what to talk about. Joe and his partner, Dana, did not reach an agreement as partners. Why did Mrs. Robert's students have so much trouble with partner talk?

Mr. Brown pointed out that Mrs. Robert's students are relatively inexperienced talkers. They may not know what to say or do when she says "turn and talk to your partner." We can't expect that students will automatically know the procedures for discourse-intensive mathematics classes. Recall that when the students began talking, Mrs. Robert stepped away to gather the rulers for the lesson. It's very likely that if she had stayed and listened to what the students were saying (and not saying) she would have seen that they were not using partner talk productively. Mr. Brown suggested that she work more actively with students during the partner-talk time. She would certainly not have time to speak with every pair, but if she spoke with two pairs each time she used partner talk, she would eventually have checked in with each group. During this time, she could observe and step in where necessary, making sure pairs were speaking to each other, responding to each other's ideas, and resolving any disputes by focusing on mathematical reasoning and making compromises.

Mr. Brown also volunteered to come in to Mrs. Robert's class: together they could model for the class how to talk during partner talk respectfully and productively. Realizing the key role that partner talk plays in productive discourse, Mrs. Robert asked him to come as soon as possible. Mrs. Robert also had an idea of her own. When she worked with a pair on using partner talk effectively, she would then ask them to briefly share with the whole class what they discussed.

Students' inability to agree or disagree with what one another said was also an obstacle during the lesson. Lara's bewildered look suggested that she did not even know where to begin answering the question. Roberta either could not or would not state why she agreed or disagreed with Barb's comment. She instead wanted to give her own reason and eventually had to admit that she did not even hear Barb's comment. When Martin was asked whether he agreed or disagreed with Andrew's comment, he responded with an inappropriate remark. Raul, when asked if he agreed with Tonya's idea, could only repeat her three-word utterance.

Keeping in mind the students' lack of experience with classroom discourse, none of this is surprising. The ability to state why one agrees or disagrees with an idea is a sophisticated one. It requires listening to what was said, making an effort to comprehend it, and trying to see how it fits in with one's own level of understanding. Although some students may be able to start off at this level, this is certainly not an "entry level" question for all students beginning to talk in math class. It's a question to aim for, but not necessarily one to start with. Mrs. Robert should probably start with getting students accustomed to listening to one another by asking them to revoice one another's contributions.

Only when students have been taught to listen to other students throughout class can they be expected to move on to agreeing and disagreeing productively. Mrs. Robert actually realized this before the lesson. Her goal for "Managing Classroom Talk" in her lesson plan was, "I will focus on encouraging my students to speak loudly enough for others to hear and on getting my students to listen to each other when they speak." Yet she seemed to have lost sight of this goal during the lesson. Mrs. Robert laughed when she reread her plan after the lesson. She admitted that she certainly forgot about this goal and aimed too high in asking students to agree and disagree. Her goal of getting students to listen to one another is the one to work on, and she will focus on this in future lessons.

Another problem in this part of the lesson is the disrespect that Andrew and Martin exhibit. Andrew is not respectful in his disagreement with Roberta's idea beginning in Line 24. Mrs. Robert encourages him to be respectful by saying, "Andrew, if you don't agree, you need to say, 'I disagree with your idea.' And tell us why you disagree." But he ignores her, beginning his comment once again with "They're wrong, because . . ." Then, his disrespect is met with further disrespect from Martin, whose comment is insulting and distracting for the entire class. Andrew's comment seems to indicate that Mrs. Robert needs to spend more time setting the ground rules for respectful and courteous talk. Without this, students will not be willing to say much of anything. In her discussion with Mr. Brown, Mrs. Robert agreed that she needs to revisit the ground rules with the entire class and the consequences if they fail to meet the expectations. She also will insist that students like Andrew disagree respectfully when they speak. This means that she will stop students every time they begin to be disrespectful and not let them continue until they have amended their statements.

Mrs. Robert was upset about Martin's comment. She is a sensitive teacher who takes students' insensitivity to one another as a sign that she has failed to create a safe environment for them. In our work, we have seen students use talk for negative purposes. Reasons for this include students not knowing how to handle a discussion that isn't focused on their ideas, students' personal conflicts with other students, and students' desire for attention. Mrs. Robert was sure that she knew why Martin made the comment about smelly feet. Martin is a very smart student. His hand is usually the first one up when she asks a question. At the beginning of the year, Mrs. Robert became accustomed to calling on him frequently. Having attended the talk workshop and having realized the importance of calling on many students, she has started to call on him less and less. Martin's reaction to this has been to fool around with friends when others are speaking, to call out, to wave his hand furiously in front of Mrs. Robert, and to yell inappropriate comments like "She never calls on me" when she calls on someone else. Mrs. Robert was confident that Martin's comment about smelly feet was his way of trying to regain attention in math class.

We have met our fair share of students like Martin. However, we have been able to help them become active, positive contributors to class discussions. Sometimes this change comes about by talking to the whole class in a very direct manner about what types of comments, gestures, actions, and sounds are and are not allowed in the class. Modeling how to speak coherently and respectfully also helps. Often we have to speak individually with the student about his or her behavior and about the class policy on respect. Finally, we sometimes have to call parents and work together with them to help their child be respectful. Students like Martin can change, but it takes positive intervention.

When Mr. Brown asked Mrs. Robert how she ended this part of the lesson, Mrs. Robert said that she decided for the class to take their shoes off. When asked why she did that, Mrs. Robert said that she felt the discussion was "dead" and that no matter what talk moves she might have attempted, she'd ultimately be unable to revive it. Besides, the clock was ticking and the data had not even been collected or analyzed. Mr. Brown agreed that her decision was reasonable. Both agreed that the fire drill was in this case a welcome interruption!

The two spent time brainstorming how Mrs. Robert might have helped the students make the decision about measuring with or without shoes on. For example, she might have put the issue to a vote and after the data were collected, discussed whether anyone wanted to change their vote. Mrs. Robert and Mr. Brown also talked about a move that might have prevented her from having to make the decision for the students. Before Mrs. Robert asked the students to talk with their partners again in Line 33, she might have helped the students pinpoint the positions taken by students up to that point, along with their reasons for those positions. This could have been done by writing the positions and their supporting reasons on the board. After partner talk, students would have had to defend one position and come up with a reason for it. These reasons would also have been posted. Mrs. Robert and Mr. Brown agreed that this may have helped the discussion progress further by giving students a way to build on each other's ideas.

Finally, Mr. Brown told Mrs. Robert that in his class, if a discussion was not progressing, he would sometimes take a more active role to get students engaged. For example, she might have posed a question that forced students to realize that no matter which decision they made, they needed to be consistent. She might have said, "Suppose that Ralph and Andrew actually have exactly the same foot length, if you measure their feet with no shoes. But suppose now that Ralph leaves his shoe on to measure and Andrew takes his off. If Ralph reports that his feet are eight inches long and Andrew reports that his are seven and a half inches, is this accurate? Why or why not?"

Mr. Brown is skilled in using classroom talk. He regularly gives his students opportunities to explain their reasoning and for peers to argue for and against ideas with reasons based on mathematical evidence. But he knows that it is his job to make sure that students make mathematical gains in his class. He knows that ultimately he is the one who determines whether a discussion is mathematically meaningful. So, when he sees that a discussion is stalled, he asks questions (like the one he suggested to Mrs. Robert) that force students to reconsider their positions. These questions do not take over the reasoning process for the students. Rather, they give them the assistance they sometimes need to build strong mathematical arguments either for or against a certain position.

Not everything about this part of the lesson was a problem. Note that none of Mrs. Robert's students refused to speak or sat quietly when called on. Certainly, many of their comments were neither meaningful nor connected, but they all said something when called on. Having seen classes where many students say nothing at all when called on, we know that this is a feature we should not undervalue.

Improvising and Responding: In the Midst of the Lesson

We wish we could say that Mrs. Robert's lesson went more smoothly the next day. As you will see, however, when she resumed the following day, the rest of the lesson was problematic as well. Mrs. Robert began by reviewing some of the important ideas from previous lessons, as well as recapping her decision from the previous day that feet should be measured with shoes off. After the problematic attempts of the previous day, she decided not to ask students to recall their reasoning about taking their shoes off or leaving them on. Instead she simply told them that in order for measurements to be comparable, each measurement had to be taken under the same conditions. Because some people have loose shoes and some have tight shoes, it would be more accurate for everyone to take off their shoes. She then continued the lesson as follows.

38. Mrs. R: Tim is passing out the rulers. You will measure your feet in inches and you should round off to the nearest half-inch. If you have any questions, you should ask me or a friend. Once you have your feet measured, you'll come up to the white board and add your data to the line plot. We have used line plots in many of the lessons so far in this unit. [She draws the line.] What do you think will be the smallest foot length? Joe?

39. Joe: Three inches.

40. Mrs. R: Okay. [She writes *3* at the left end of the line plot.] And the greatest? Tina?

41. Tina: Twelve inches?

42. Mrs. R: Okay. [She writes *12* at the right end of the line plot.] So, since we are measuring by halves, we would fill in from three to twelve by halves. So if you have a foot that is three and a half inches long, what do you do? Ralph?

43. Ralph: Put an X above three and a half?

44. Mrs. R: Yes. OK, you can start measuring and I'll stand up here to help you put the data on the line plot.

As students measure, Mrs. Robert waits at the board and looks around at the students, who seem not to be having trouble measuring. The first two students soon come to the board with their measurements. As planned, Mrs. Robert helps them put their Xs in the correct places, with the correct sizing and spacing. The third student says that she can't put her measurement up because it's 18 and there's no 18 on the line plot. Her partner has a measurement of 16; she complains that there is no place for her foot length either. While Mrs. Robert is asking them about how they got their measurements, another student asks, "What do I do if my number's not up here?" Mrs. Robert suspects that many students have measured in centimeters, so she decides that this is a perfect time to use talk to discuss the difference between inches and centimeters.

45. Mrs. R: Could everyone please stop measuring and take their seats. We seem to have a problem with our units. I asked you to find the length of your feet in inches and I think that some of you might have found your measurements in centimeters. Someone got eighteen units. Who can tell me why I think that's centimeters?

46. Jan: 'Cause the ruler only goes up to twelve on the side we were supposed to use.

47. Mrs. R: Mark, can you repeat what Jan said?

48. Mark: No.

49. Mrs. R: So ask her to repeat it.

50. Mark: Could you repeat it?

51. Jan: I said the ruler only goes up to twelve on that side.

52. Mark: She said the ruler only goes up to twelve on that side.

53. Mrs. R: And why is knowing that important?

54. Mark: [He shrugs his shoulders.]

55. Mrs. R: OK, let's back up. Someone came up to the board and reported that their foot was eighteen long. I think that that person must have measured in centimeters. And why do I think that, Jan?

56. Jan: Because the inch side only goes up to twelve.

57. Mrs. R: Go on.

58. Jan: And there is only an eighteen on the centimeter side.

59. Mrs. R: Mark, can you repeat Jan's comment?

60. Mark: She said that there is not a eighteen on the inch side and that's why you think the person measured in centimeters.

61. Mrs. R: Jan, is that what you said?

62. Jan: Yes.

63. Mrs. R: Go ahead, Carla, your hand is up.

64. Carla: That side isn't centimeters, it's mm.

65. Mrs. R: What do you mean "mm"?

66. Carla: It says "mm" on the end.

67. Andrew: That means millimeters. It's eighteen millimeters!

68. Mrs. R: So you think it's millimeters. What do some other people think?

69. Raul: It's centimeters.

70. Tonya: Mine doesn't say "mm," it says "cm."

71. Students: Where are you guys looking? I can't see. Mine doesn't say anything, it's just a bunch of lines. Which side do we look at? This is confusing. Can I come up to the board now?

72. Mrs. R: Martin, stop spinning that ruler! [Martin has made a propeller out of his ruler and a pencil.]

Mrs. Robert looks around and realizes that students have different types of rulers. Some rulers do have "mm" written at the beginning of the metric side. Some others are metric-only rulers. Mrs. Robert notices that with ten minutes left in the class, the students have neither filled in their data nor learned anything about what is typical. She is about ready to give up for the day. Feeling tired and discouraged, she takes a moment to gather her thoughts.

Before we reveal how, or whether, Mrs. Robert moved forward, let's explore what happened in this segment. First, let's recall what Mrs. Robert had planned for this part of the lesson. As she wrote under "Planning the Implementation," she was going to "ask students to explain the correct way to use a ruler, compare and contrast centimeters and inches, how to figure out or remember which side of a ruler shows centimeters and which shows inches, and whether to round off to the nearest inch or half-inch." What actually happened, however, was that she told the students to round off to the nearest half-inch and called on only one student to give a possible smallest foot length and another to give a possible greatest foot length. She accepted their suggestions without asking them for explanation, justification, or feedback from their peers. She did not review how to measure with a ruler or how to make sense of the two measurement systems displayed on the rulers. When reflecting about why her plan was so different from what took place, Mrs. Robert said that she was afraid that if she let the students discuss these issues about the ruler, it would take up too much time and, like the shoe discussion, go nowhere. So, she reverted back to an IRE (initiation, response, evaluation) technique, calling on her high-achieving students to make sure she got reasonable responses. She said that at this point in the lesson she was desperate to get the students measuring without any more delays.

We think that Mrs. Robert's reaction was both natural and reasonable. If the goal of the lesson is to make conclusions about the typical foot length, then efforts must be made to get students to reach this goal. Unfortunately, however, students were not able to reach this goal because many did not measure in inches. Possible reasons for this include misconceptions about rulers, lack of experience in using them, and the fact that the rulers were not all of the same type. Had Mrs. Robert taken the time to discuss the ruler as she had planned, it is very likely that students' difficulties and confusion would have surfaced. Once on the surface, they could have been addressed and corrected. So, Mrs. Robert was faced with a discourse dilemma: If she stopped to talk about the rulers, the students might not have had time to measure. But by not talking about the rulers, many measured using the wrong unit.

Is there a solution to such a dilemma? We think so. First, during the lesson, Mrs. Robert may have reminded herself why these questions were in her plan. Had she stopped to think about this she may have realized just how crucial the questions were to her students' success in measuring with the ruler, and might then have taken the time to discuss them. On the other hand, her decision not to discuss the ruler was not necessarily a bad one: student confusion may be used productively. Because many students did not use inches, both they and Mrs. Robert learned what they didn't understand about units of linear measurement. We believe that any time students reveal what they know and don't know about mathematics, it is beneficial to us as teachers. For Mrs. Robert, her decision not to discuss the ruler meant that students had to confront their own shortcomings with this instrument. Mrs. Robert can now use this as a "hook" for future discussion about using rulers.

Before going on, we want to point to talk moves in this part of the lesson which worked well. In Line 47, when Mark could not repeat what Jan said, Mrs. Robert had him ask Jan to repeat it. This is a good habit and an important expectation to set in the early stages of implementing classroom talk. If students are not listening, it is their job to ask another student to repeat a statement, not the teacher's job. Mrs. Robert could have asked Jan to repeat it herself but instead had Mark do it. In our experience, when teachers keep insisting that students ask each other to repeat, eventually they no longer need to be prompted to do so, but instead do so on their own. After Jan repeated her statement at Mark's request, he was able to repeat it. But by then, Jan's statement had been taken out of its original context. As a result, Mark was unable to explain the importance of the statement. This is reasonable—if he wasn't listening to Jan, it's unlikely he was listening to the question, and thus he had no idea what significance "the ruler only goes up to twelve on that side" could possibly have. Mrs. Robert handled the situation perfectly. Knowing that Jan's statement had lost meaning to Mark, it probably had lost meaning to others. But instead of taking Mark and the others off the hook by explaining to them why Jan's comment was important, she continued to hold the students accountable for this job. She did this by backing up to the question to which Jan responded, giving the reason for asking this question, and having Jan restate her comment. At this, Mark was able to revoice Jan's reasoning in a meaningful way.

It is often necessary to back up the conversation to help students get back on board. As conversations increase in complexity, the teacher must make efforts to make sure that everyone is following. This often requires extensive attention to repairs. Sometimes revoicing just one statement is not enough for a student to contribute to a discussion. Recapping a segment of a discussion and then invoking the revoicing move is a normal and necessary part of classroom talk, particularly in its initial stages.

Let's see how Mrs. Robert's lesson ended.

73. Mrs. R: First I see that I have passed out some rulers that do not even have inches marked on them at all. I apologize for that. [She collects these rulers and gives students rulers that do have inches marked on them.] We need to figure out what happened because some people got measurements like eighteen, nineteen, and twenty. Jan said that eighteen can't possibly be inches since the ruler is only twelve inches long. But we are not sure about the marks on the other side of the ruler. Let me give you this piece of information. The width of my pinky is about one centimeter. So, can you use this information to identify the marks for centimeters on the ruler? While I go and check to make sure you know how long a centimeter is, talk to the person next to you about the student whose foot is eighteen units long. Is that length of eighteen probably centimeters, millimeters, inches, or something else? [Mrs. Robert walks around the room, checking to see if everyone can correctly identify the length of 1 centimeter on the ruler. This takes five minutes.] OK, so who would like to tell us what you think? Is the eighteen millimeters or centimeters or something else?

74. Rob: It's centimeters, since eighteen millimeters is way too small.

75. Mrs. R: Grace, what did Rob just say?

76. Grace: I couldn't hear him.

77. Mrs. R: So ask him to repeat it.

78. Rob: I said—

79. Mrs. R: Wait, Rob. Grace, you need to say, "Rob, can you please repeat it?"

80. Grace: Rob, can you repeat it?

81. Rob: I said that the eighteen is centimeters, since millimeters

would be like . . . like this big. [He makes a gesture with his thumb and index finger.]

82. Grace: He said that it must be eighteen centimeters since eighteen millimeters is too small.

83. Mrs. R: And do you agree or disagree? And tell us why.

84. Grace: I agree, because on my ruler there is no way someone's foot is this small. [Gestures to the 18 mm mark.]

85. Mrs. R: How did you know to point there?

86. Grace: Those little marks are millimeters, so I counted eighteen of them right to here.

87. Mrs. R: Ralph, how does Grace know where eighteen millimeters is?

88. Ralph: [Long pause.]

89. Mrs. R: Do you need her to repeat it?

90. Ralph: Yes.

91. Mrs. R: So, ask her.

92. Ralph: Can you repeat it, Grace?

93. Grace: I just counted the little marks until I got eighteen.

94. Ralph: There's eighteen centimeters there, which are those black marks.

95. Mrs. R: Is that what you said, Grace?

96. Grace: I couldn't hear him.

97. Mrs. R: So ask him to repeat it. And from now on, try to remember that if someone is speaking and you can't hear, you need to give me the signal. [Mrs. Robert demonstrates the signal—a hand cupping an ear.]

98. Grace: Could you repeat it, Ralph?

99. Ralph: There's eighteen centimeters at that mark you pointed to.

100. Grace: No, eighteen millimeters.

101. Ralph: Yeah, eighteen millimeters.

102. Mrs. R: OK, so we are out of time. Let's summarize where we are right now. We agree that the noninch side on the ruler has marks that show centimeters and millimeters. The centimeters are the same as the width of my pinky finger. The millimeters are the little marks that show the lengths in between the centimeters. We also agree that the eighteen must be eighteen centimeters, since the ruler is only twelve inches long and it doesn't seem possible that someone had a foot that was almost two rulers long. Also, the eighteen is

probably centimeters since eighteen millimeters is way too
small. Tomorrow, we will talk some more about the ruler,
continue to measure our feet, and make our line plot.

Mrs. Robert began this part of the lesson by giving a status report on the
lesson. She corrected the ruler situation and repeated Jan's idea. She restated
for the class what they were confused about, the meaning of the marks on the
side opposite the inches, and gave them a benchmark measurement, the width
of her pinky, to aid in students' understanding. Based on students' lack of
experience exploring standard and metric units of measure, this piece of information certainly seemed to be a good way to help the students learn about the
metric side of the ruler. It would have been futile to have continued a "what
do you think they are?" discussion about the unknown marks, since it seemed
apparent that students had little previous knowledge of these metric units. In
general, it makes sense to discuss mathematical ideas of which students have
some knowledge. While Mrs. Robert's decision to check to see if each student
could identify a length of one centimeter on a ruler took time out of the lesson, it ensured that more students understood what the marks represented on
the metric side. This allowed them to figure out why some of their classmates
believed that a measure of 18 was likely centimeters.

Much of the time spent during this part of the lesson was used by students
who had to ask each other to repeat what they had said because either they weren't
listening or could not hear. Mrs. Robert lamented to Mr. Brown that she was very
frustrated by this, since it seemed to be such a tremendous waste of class time. Mr.
Brown told Mrs. Robert that he has been frustrated when students have used valuable class time asking someone to repeat something because they were not listening the first time or because the speaker was not speaking loudly enough.
However, while the students' failure to listen may waste time, Mrs. Robert's continued insistence that they ask each other to repeat is time well spent. Mr. Brown
assured Mrs. Robert that her students would get better at listening if she continued to hold them accountable for it. Through her unyielding and consistent
efforts to have students ask each other to repeat a statement that they did not hear,
her students will learn that listening is required, not requested.

In Line 83, Mrs. Robert asked Grace to state why she agreed or disagreed
with Rob's idea. Grace was able to do so coherently and reasonably. One may
wonder why Grace could do so when so many other students could not.
While two possible reasons include Grace's listening skills and her knowledge
of linear measurement, another is found upon a closer examination of the dialogue. Mrs. Robert asked Grace to agree or disagree with Rob's idea after

Grace had been able to successfully revoice the idea. This is a fine use of the "agree or disagree" talk move, as students can only agree or disagree if they have successfully heard and made sense of the comment in the first place. In the first part of the lesson, Mrs. Robert often jumped straight to the agree-or-disagree question without asking students to revoice. As a result of problems her students had with listening, they were not able to answer this question. While we would still recommend to Mrs. Robert that she focus on the revoicing talk move, we would also recommend that when she uses the agree-or-disagree question that it only follow the successful revoicing of an idea.

Summarizing and Solidifying: So Where Are We Now?

Mrs. Robert ended the lesson with a recap of what happened and an outline for what was to happen the next day. This is an important part of classroom talk. So much goes on during a class where students are using talk that it is important to leave students with focal points of the discussions. It is these focal points that allow students to see the significance of the talk, its relevance to past learning, and its linkage to future lessons. These focal points also allow students to reflect on their own learning by thinking about what they learned in the discussion and what they still have to work on. For example, a student listening to Mrs. Robert's statement may say to him or herself, "I still don't know what those little marks are but tomorrow I am going to get to listen to other people talk about it." This type of self-reflection, an essential component of learning, is one of the many benefits of classroom discourse.

Talking with her mentor, Mr. Brown, after each day's lesson, Mrs. Robert learned a great deal. She learned first and foremost that the endeavor to use talk would be a long-term effort. She learned that she would have to take it step by step and keep herself focused on the discourse goal she set for herself during each lesson. She learned firsthand the value of principles discussed in Chapter 9. She had jumped into using talk without adequately setting up the conditions for a respectful and supportive environment (Principle 1). She had not explained her expectations about the new forms of talk she was introducing (Principle 4). And she had certainly not limited herself to one new thing at a time (Principle 5). Mrs. Robert learned that her students needed to work on using partner talk productively and on listening to each other when they spoke. Feeling back in control and with plenty of good ideas running through her head, Mrs. Robert sat down and made some notes about the next day's lesson, starting once more the process of planning and projecting. Her notes included the following reminders to herself.

- Start the discussion by reminding students of their obligations to listen and speak loudly enough for others to hear. Let them know that disrespectful remarks will not be tolerated. Remind them of why the class is using talk to help support mathematics learning.
- Stop students who are not speaking loudly enough and ask them to speak up. When students offer suggestions, ask others to revoice.
- Show an overhead ruler and talk about ways to identify the "inch" side of a ruler and the "centimeter" side. Ask the students whether they think they should round off their measurements to the nearest inch or half-inch. Write these two positions on the board and as students give reasons for each position write them on the board. Again, have students revoice one another's ideas. If the discussion runs dry, use partner talk but work with a few partners on using this time effectively (e.g., hearing each other's positions and reasons, reaching an agreement or compromise, and thinking about how to phrase their statements in front of the whole class). After hearing many different reasons, put the decision to a vote, majority rules.
- After students measure their feet and post their data, share observations. Have students relate their conclusions by giving the following condition: In order to give an observation, a student must repeat the previous speaker's observation or make an observation that piggybacks off of the previous one.
- Talk about the typical foot length in the class. Ask the question, "What do you think is the typical foot length?" and then use partner talk. Work with some pairs on using the time effectively.
- Scribe students' ideas on the board and ask other students to revoice. If they can't, encourage students to ask each other to repeat without prompting them to do so. If necessary, move the discussion forward by reminding students of how they determined the typical pace length a few lessons back.
- End the class by summarizing what was learned about measuring and data collection. State some things students might still be confused about (e.g., whether the typical measure can be more than one value). Tell what is planned for tomorrow.

We think that Mrs. Robert and her students are well on the way to using talk to support the learning of mathematics. Mrs. Robert has identified the elements of the lesson that caused her students difficulties and more importantly, she has thought of specific ways to avoid such difficulties in future lessons. Further, Mrs. Robert's students are willing to talk and seem poised to learn how to talk effectively and respectfully. We would encourage Mrs. Robert to continue to try one new talk move at a time and stick to this goal during each lesson. We recommend that she continue to reflect on what worked and what did not work after her lessons. By doing this, she can learn to use talk moves that have been most effective for her class and eliminate the decisions that are reducing the effectiveness of discussions. We would also encourage her to stay as motivated as she is, since the payoff for her efforts will likely be considerable.

CHAPTER

13

Fair or Unfair
Grade Six

We will now examine a lesson on probability that Mr. Donnell planned for his second-period class of twenty-five sixth-grade students. Like Mrs. Robert in Chapter 12, Mr. Donnell is a fictional character. Also like Mrs. Robert, he is a character whose words and actions are similar to those of many teachers with whom we have worked. His students are also a synthesis of hundreds of students whom we have seen use talk to learn mathematics. The lesson is similar to dozens of lessons we have taught and observed about probability.

Mr. Donnell is an experienced teacher who has been using talk in his mathematics classes for two years. In addition, Mr. Donnell's school, which is in a suburb outside of a major city, has made a commitment to using talk to support learning in mathematics classes. So, by the time Mr. Donnell's students meet him in grade six, they are familiar with the rules of respectful, productive talk and responding to classmates' mathematical reasoning through partner talk and whole-class discussion. This by no means makes Mr. Donnell's students perfect, or even proficient, communicators in all instances. But you will see that generally they are able to communicate their reasoning quite well.

Planning and Projecting: Mr. Donnell's Lesson Plan
Mr. Donnell's students are coming to the end of a unit on probability. In this unit, they have explored the experimental and theoretical probabilities of simple, independent events involving coins, blocks in a bag, scratch-card contests, and dice. Students have collected data, interpreted the results, and calculated the experimental probabilities as decimals, fractions, and percents. They have

discussed the terms *possible*, *impossible*, *probable*, *likely*, and *certain* as they applied to their experiments and other events, such as weather, the lottery, and accidents. Students have also analyzed all possible outcomes of these simple, independent events and discussed why the experimental probability of an event was not always the same as its theoretical probability. This last issue has been particularly difficult for them to talk about and comprehend.

In this lesson, students are learning about the meaning of the word *fair*. Students play a coin-tossing game. In the game, students, playing in pairs, toss three coins twenty times. One player—the "match" player—receives a point every time the coins match (e.g., head-head-head or tail-tail-tail) and the other player—the "no-match" player—receives a point every time the coins do not match (e.g., head-head-tail). After twenty tosses, the player with the most points wins.

≈≈≈

IDENTIFYING THE MATHEMATICAL GOALS

- Students will understand that the game they are playing is not fair, since a no-match outcome is more likely than a match outcome.
- In a fair game, each player has the same chance of winning; the chances of winning and losing arc equally likely.

ANTICIPATING CONFUSION

- Students may think a game is unfair if they lose.
- Students may not understand why the experimental probability is not the same as the theoretical probability.
- Students may not understand why the coins matched so much less frequently than they did not match.

ASKING QUESTIONS

- What do you think it means to say that a game is fair?
- What conclusions can we make about this game by looking at our results?
- Do you think the game is fair? Why or why not?
- Why did so many more no-matches than matches occur? Was it just a coincidence?
- How many outcomes are possible in a throw? Are they equally likely? Why or why not?
- Are our experimental probabilities the same as the theoretical probabilities? Why or why not?

MANAGING CLASSROOM TALK

- I will work on asking students to explain why they agree or disagree with a classmate's idea. Namely, students must give evidence to back up their claims.

Planning the Implementation

Introduction

Introduce the problem to the whole class. Student pairs play a game where they toss three coins. If the coins match (either all heads or all tails), Player A gets a point. If the coins don't match (a combination of heads and tails), Player B gets a point. Whichever player has more points after twenty tosses wins. Explain that after students play this game, they will record their results in a class chart like the one below.

Group	No. of Matches	No. of No-Matches	Total Trials

FIGURE 13–1 Coin-toss results chart.

First, explain the rules of the game. Then conduct a discussion about the term *fair game*: What is a fair game? Can students give examples? What makes a game fair mathematically? Ask students to write in their notebooks a predefinition of *fair* and a prediction about whether this game will be fair or unfair.

Exploration

Have pairs play the game. I will circulate to make sure they are recording each outcome. As pairs finish, they will come up to the board and record their data on the coin-toss results chart. When everyone is finished, we will examine the class data.

Discussion

First, ask the students to summarize the data and draw conclusions about the game by using the experimental probabilities. Specifically, focus the discussion on the issue of fairness. Students will need to give evidence from the data to support whether they think the game is fair or unfair. Then, again, ask students to define the word *fair*. Second, discuss why the two outcomes have very different experimental probabilities. It will be clear that the game isn't fair, but the reason for this may not be obvious. As a class we will generate a list of all possible outcomes.

At the end of the class, summarize what was learned and what we need to work on. For homework, students will reflect upon the predefinition and prediction they made at the start of class.

Improvising and Responding: In the Midst of the Lesson

While much of what Mr. Donnell planned actually occurred in the lesson, there were also elements in the lesson that were unexpected. As you read through the lesson, think about the following questions: How, if at all, did Mr. Donnell's talk-based lesson plan help the lesson progress? How did Mr. Donnell use talk to develop students' mathematical understanding?

1. Mr. D: Raise your hand if you have ever heard the term *fair* to describe a game before. What does the term *fair game* mean?

2. Rydell: It means that there are no tricks to it. Like those amusement-park games. You never win those 'cause there are hidden tricks to them that you can't see.

3. Deanne: I heard that it was illegal for amusement parks to do that. There are people who check for that kind of cheating. So the games have to be fair.

4. Mr. D: So what do you think *fair* means, Deanne?

5. Deanne: A fair game is when there is no trick to it. You know all the rules and there are no secrets to it.

6. Mr. D: Liam, can you put Deanne's explanation of a fair game in your own words, please?

7. Liam: She thinks a game is fair if there are no tricks or secrets to it.

8. Mr. D: Is that what you think, Deanne?

9. Deanne: Yes.

10. Mr. D: Who else would like to explain what the term *fair* means? [No hands after ten seconds of wait time.] Is tossing a coin a fair way to decide who bats first in a baseball game? Why or why not?

11. Barb: Yes, that's fair because we learned that there's one way to get a head and one way to get a tail. Each outcome is equally likely, so each team has the same chance of getting to bat.

12. Mr. D: So what do you think the term *fair game* means?

13. Barb: I agree with Deanne. I think it means that there are no tricks. Like in the coin toss, there are no tricks to that. It's not like a trick coin or something that really has two heads. Both teams know for sure that there's one head and one tail.

14. Mr. D: Jose, can you repeat what Barb just said?

15. Jose: She thinks that the coin toss is fair, since the players know there's one head and one tail and they have a fifty-fifty chance of coming up.

16. Mr. D: Barb, is that what you said?

17. Barb: Yes, and also that there are no tricks to it.

18. Mr. D: Who else would like to explain the term *fair game*?

Mr. Donnell saw that no hands were raised when he asked this question. He then had students talk to their partners about the term. When he called the partners back together, he got more explanations of fair based upon trickery rather than likelihood of outcomes. He decided that it would take up too much time to get other ideas about fairness from students. While he was reluctant to move on with only one significant offering of the term's definition, he knew from experience that following the next activity, a more mathematical definition of *fairness* might be offered. He finished this phase of the lesson by saying to his students, "Well, we've heard from several people about what a fair game is. Write down what you think the term *fair game* means. It may be the same as what other students have said or it may be different. Also, based on your definition, write a prediction for whether this game will be fair. As you play the game today keep in mind two questions: Is the game fair? And what does it mean for a game to be fair? After you play, we will share our results and discuss these two questions as a whole class."

The students' ideas about fairness focused early on the issue of trickery. Mr. Donnell did not anticipate this as a misconception. In addition, when it arose, he was unsure whether or not it really was a misconception. Isn't it in fact true that a game with hidden tricks is not fair? Because Mr. Donnell did not plan to pursue a lengthy discussion of the correct definition of *fairness* at the beginning of the lesson, the students' unanticipated view of fairness did not affect the flow of the lesson. Mr. Donnell knew, however, that the issue of trickery would likely emerge at the end of the class when he did want his students to discuss the mathematical definition. Mr. Donnell used the game time to think about what he would say or do when the issue arose later in the lesson. He also made a note to add this idea to his lesson plan for next year.

Just as he had planned, Mr. Donnell relied heavily on revoicing during this discussion. He did so without making any commentary that may have influenced the students' thinking one way or another. He used revoicing to make sure that each student had some ideas about fairness to consider as they played the game. He knew that this would lead to cognitive conflict, where students' beliefs or expectations do not match reality, making the whole-class discussion at the end of the lesson potentially very rich.

When Mr. Donnell asked a student to revoice, he referred back to the original speaker to make sure that the student who did the revoicing did not misconstrue the original comment. Doing this guaranteed that a student's comment was revoiced accurately and fairly. Mr. Donnell believes that this is a good way to make sure that his class has a respectful, supportive environment. He knows from past experience that students get upset when their ideas are misinterpreted, inaccurately reworded, or changed outright. They feel that their reasoning was not given a fair chance, and thus they can be reluctant to participate in the future. Mr. Donnell uses the technique of asking, "Is this what you said?" after a student revoices, to avoid such discomfort in his students. In his classroom, all efforts to revoice must accurately reflect the mathematical reasoning of the original speaker. If they don't, the original speaker gets to restate his or her idea to provide any necessary clarification before the discussion continues.

After this discussion, Mr. Donnell's students played the game. As planned, Mr. Donnell circulated among them, discussing fairness and talking about experimental probabilities—probabilities based on the outcomes from experiments. He then recorded the class outcomes on the board in the chart shown in Figure 13–2.

19. Mr. D: Before you played the game, we discussed the term *fair game*. We did not, however, settle on a definition. Now that you've had a chance to play the game, I'd like to see if we can define the term *fair game*. What do you think it means? Based on your definition, do you think this game is fair?

20. Vivian: This game is definitely not fair. It's not even close. Look at

Group	No. of Matches	No. of No-Matches	Total Trials
1	2	18	20
2	5	15	20
3	1	19	20
4	3	17	20
5	2	18	20
6	12	8	20
7	4	16	20
8	6	14	20
9	4	16	20
10	3	17	20
11	2	18	20
12	6	14	20
Totals	50	190	240

P(match) = 50/240 or ≈ 21 %   P(no match) = 190/240 or ≈ 79 %

FIGURE 13–2   **Completed results chart.**

our chart—seventy-nine percent of the tosses were no-matches. I was the match person. I lost big-time.

21. Mr. D: So, do you think the game is not fair because you did not win? Is that what makes a game unfair?

22. Vivian: No, it's just that I didn't even come close to winning.

23. Mr. D: What do you think the term *fair game* means?

24. Vivian: It means that each person has to have a pretty good chance of winning.

25. Mr. D: Tran, do you agree or disagree with Vivian's definition?

26. Tran: I sort of agree.

27. Mr. D: Why?

28. Tran: I think that this game is not fair because we kept getting no-matches. That means that the person who gets a point for a no-match is going to get a lot more points than their opponent. That's not fair.

29. Mr. D: Vivian defines *fair game* as a game where each player has a pretty good chance of winning. Do you agree with this definition?

30. Tran: Sort of.

31. Mr. D: What do you mean, sort of?

32. Tran: Because it's not like you have to have a pretty good chance. You just have to be as likely to win as your opponent. It's not fair if the game is set up to give one person more points.

33. Mr. D: Deanne, do you agree with what Tran just said?

34. Deanne: I couldn't hear.

35. Mr. D: Well, what should you say?

36. Deanne: Tran, I couldn't hear you. Could you repeat it, please?

37. Tran: Fair means you have the same chance as your opponent. Like as you play, you are just as likely to get what you want as the other person.

38. Deanne: I agree. I think a game is fair if each person gets as many points as the other.

39. Mr. D: Tran, is that what you said?

40. Tran: No. I said that you have to have the same chance to get as many points.

41. Mr. D: Deanne, do you agree with Tran's definition of fairness? Why or why not?

42. Deanne: I agree, because in this game, like, looking at the data, the match person got almost nothing.

43. Mr. D :   Earlier you thought that a game was fair if there were no tricks. Do you still think that that's true?

44. Deanne: Yes, but I also think that fair means that each person has to have the same chance to win as the opponent.

45. Mr. D: Liam, do you agree or disagree with what Deanne just said?

46. Liam: I agree.

47. Mr. D: Why?

48. Liam: [Silence for about ten seconds.] Actually, Deanne, could you repeat it?

49. Deanne: A fair game happens when each person has the same chance of winning.

50. Liam: Oh. I disagree. I think that fair means that each person gets the same number of turns.

51. Mr. D: So do you think this game is fair?

52. Liam: Yes, because we each got ten turns.

53. Mr. D: Which player were you, the player who got a point for a match or the player who got a point for a no-match?

54. Liam: I was the match person. I lost.

55. Mr. D: And you still think it's fair even though you lost?

56. Liam: Yes. Because at the end I was getting a lot of matches. I almost made a comeback.

57. Mr. D: So, Liam thinks the game is fair since each player tossed the coins ten times. What do some other people think about this?

58. Tran: I disagree with what Liam said. Look at the data. It wasn't even close.

59. Mr. D: What do you mean?

60. Tran: There were about four times more no-matches than matches. There is no way that could be fair.

61. Mr. D: What do some other people think?

62. Lenora: Well, we don't know if we kept playing if the data would have been different. Maybe it was just this one time that the matches didn't happen.

63. Mr. D: Lenora, what do you mean it was maybe just this one time that the matches didn't happen?

64. Lenora: If we played the game again right now, maybe the match people would win.

65. Tory: I really don't think it was just a coincidence. Look at the data! There's no way this game is fair.

66. Mr. D: Why not, Tory?

67. Tory: Because the match person never really had a chance to win. They got crushed.

68. Mr. D: Okay, let's pause for a minute. The two questions we are discussing are: Is this game fair? What does the term *fair game* mean? We have heard several different answers to each of these questions. I've written them on the board as people have said them. Let's hear from some other people. Which of these do you agree with? Or, do you disagree with all of them and have a new idea of your own?

69. Barb: This game is not fair. Like I said at the beginning of class, fair means that each person has the same chance of winning. The probability to match was twenty-one percent and the probability to not match was seventy-nine percent. That doesn't seem fair.

70. Mr. D: Tracey, your hand was just raised.

71. Tracey: Oh, Barb took my answer.

72. Mr. D: If you think similarly to Barb, that's okay. You should put it in your own words. The more we hear from people, the more we will understand each other's reasoning.

73. Tracey: Well, like Barb said, to be fair, the probabilities should have been the same.

74. Mr. D: And what about the number of turns?

75. Tracey: I don't think that matters. It didn't really matter who was tossing the coins anyway.

Mr. Donnell went on to discuss fairness for another few moments. At this point, the class had not yet reached a consensus on the definition of *fairness* or whether the game was fair. They had, however, begun to think about fairness in terms of probabilities of outcomes. Mr. Donnell decided to move on to another objective of the lesson, because he knew that fairness would arise in the lesson again.

As outlined in his plan, Mr. Donnell used the agree-or-disagree question to move the discussion forward. At the beginning of the class, Mr. Donnell gave students plenty of opportunity to share their opinions about fairness either orally or in writing. As the lesson progressed, however, he wanted to be more direct. He no longer wanted opinions based on previous experiences. Rather, he wanted students to use specific evidence from the probability lessons to form a mathematically accurate definition of fairness. Vivian did so in Line 20: "This game is definitely not fair. It's not even close. Look at our chart—seventy-nine percent of the tosses were no-matches. I was the match person. I lost big-time." Mr. Donnell hoped to focus the discussion of the term *fair* on mathematical evidence.

It is interesting to note that every time Mr. Donnell asked students to agree or disagree, he required them to state *why*. Mr. Donnell knows that without the "why" part, many students bluff it, usually agreeing with an idea because it seems like the thing to do. Let's recall the exchanges with Liam beginning in Line 45.

45. Mr. D: Liam, do you agree or disagree with what Deanne just said?

46. Liam: I agree.

47. Mr. D: Why?

48. Liam: [Silence for about ten seconds.] Actually, Deanne, could you repeat it?

49. Deanne: A fair game happens when each person has the same chance of winning.

50. Liam: Oh. I disagree. I think that fair means that each person gets
              the same number of turns.

Liam was quick to say he agreed with Deanne, but then revealed that he did not really hear what Deanne said. Since it is impossible to agree with something that you did not hear in the first place, Liam was saying he agreed so that it would appear that he was listening. Then, Liam further convinced us that he was not listening when he went on to explain why he disagreed with Deanne's idea. Mr. Donnell's insistence that Liam explain why he agreed forced Liam to reengage with the lesson. Liam had to ask Deanne to repeat her comment in order to respond to Mr. Donnell's question. Then, Liam's response to Mr. Donnell's question made him an active contributor to the discussion. Mr. Donnell's decision to have Liam explain his thinking also helped to bring another misconception about fairness to the surface, whether the number of turns makes a game fair or not.

Recall that at the beginning of the class, many students defined fairness in terms of trickery. Mr. Donnell had not anticipated this and was therefore nervous about addressing it in the whole-class discussion. The misconception, however, was not much of an issue in this discussion after all. In fact, when Mr. Donnell reminded Deanne of her initial definition, in Line 43, she stated that she would now also define fairness in terms of the chances of winning. Mr. Donnell was not sure why this happened. Had the discussion and the game led Deanne toward the mathematical understanding of fairness? Or did she still hold to her original definition but sensed that the tide was moving in the other direction and therefore became reluctant to stand by it publicly? Mr. Donnell knows that knowledge often does not replace misconceptions by default. Rather, if misconceptions are not picked apart, learning will be built upon them (National Research Council 2000). Yet he wondered whether the idea of trickery was really a misconception. Fairness does depend upon an absence of trickery. Mr. Donnell decided to raise the issue of trickery in future discussions to see whether it still obscured the importance of the mathematical basis of fairness, or whether the two ideas could coexist. After all, fairness is an important and complex concept—as long as students understand the mathematical aspects of fairness in games of chance, he will have achieved his goal.

Another interesting observation about this discussion comes in Barb's last comment in Line 69. She said, "This game is not fair. Like I said at the beginning of class, fair means that each person has the same chance of winning. The probability to match was twenty-one percent and the probability to not match was seventy-nine percent. That doesn't seem fair." But in Line 13 of the discussion earlier in the class, Barb had said, "I agree with Deanne. I think it means that there are no tricks. Like in the coin toss, there are no tricks to that. It's not like a trick coin or something that really has two heads. Both teams know for sure that there's one head and one tail." Barb's comment in Line 13 shows the complexity of this topic: coin tosses do foreground the idea of probability in judgments of fairness, and the comment suggests that Barb knows that the equal probability of getting heads or tails makes it fair. However, trickery can certainly infiltrate games that use coins. Overlapping ideas of fundamentally different sorts make the term *fair* inherently complex. So, why is Barb now able to give the more mathematically correct definition? Perhaps playing the game, and participating in a discussion before and after, provided her with the additional context she needed in order to expand and generalize this aspect of her understanding of fairness.

The exchange in the discussion beginning at Line 71 highlights another technique that Mr. Donnell uses. When Tracey said that Barb "took [her] answer," Mr. Donnell asked her to restate the idea in her own words. Mr. Donnell did this because he knew that students needed to hear Barb's idea many times in order to process it. Further, he knows that in real-life conversations and debates, adults rarely say to each other that someone else "took their answers." Rather, adults will state their agreement with a previous point and put that idea in their own words. This is how people create common ground for understanding. Mr. Donnell wants his class discussions to closely mirror those of the outside world. As a result, in his class there is an emphasis on the revoicing of ideas to lend support to and further one another's learning.

After a few more comments about fair games, the class continued. Mr. Donnell worked with the class to systematically list all possible outcomes for the coin-toss game. They created the table in Figure 13–3.

The students agreed that the theoretical probability of tossing a match was $\frac{2}{8}$ or 25 percent and of tossing a no-match was $\frac{6}{8}$ or 75 percent. Following a discussion about the theoretical probability, Mr. Donnell decided to revisit the idea of fairness.

76. Mr. D: By now we agree that the chance of getting a no-match is greater than getting a match. Our theoretical probability shows this and our experimental probabilities support it. First, I want to ask you this question. Does it concern or surprise you that the experimental probabilities and theoretical probabilities aren't the same? Talk to the person next to

Coin 1	Coin 2	Coin 3	
H	H	H	Match
H	H	T	No Match
H	T	H	No Match
T	H	H	No Match
T	T	T	Match
T	T	H	No Match
T	H	T	No Match
H	T	T	No Match

FIGURE 13–3   Table listing possible coin-toss outcomes.

		you about this. [The class engages in partner talk for a minute or two, then Mr. Donnell calls on Reya.]
77.	Reya:	No, we have talked about this before. It's probability, you never know for sure what's going to happen.
78.	Mr. D:	Matt, do you agree or disagree, and tell us why.
79.	Matt:	I agree. Even if it's not the same, it's close. That's good enough.
80.	Mr. D:	What do you mean "good enough"?
81.	Matt:	Well, like, all it took was a few less no-matches and it would have been the same.
82.	Mr. D:	Sara, what do you think Matt means that it would have been the same with a few less no-matches? [Sara is Matt's partner.]
83.	Sara:	He means that if our data had a few less no-matches it would have been the same as the theoretical.
84.	Mr. D:	And does it concern you that it is not the same right now?
85.	Sara:	[Long pause.] No, that's the way it goes.
86.	Mr. D:	Now I want to ask you once again whether or not the game is fair.
87.	Barb:	I stick with what I've said all along. It's not fair because the no-match person has a better chance of winning.
88.	Mr. D:	But the match person could still win, right?
89.	Barb:	Yeah, but that would be really, really strange. And the game would still be unfair based on the probabilities.

90. Mr. D: Who thinks they can explain what Barb just said about the game being unfair based on the probabilities?

91. Liam: She means that the probability of one player winning is bigger than the probability of the other one.

92. Mr. D: Barb, is that what you think? [Barb nods her head yes.] So Liam, what do you think it means for a game to be fair?

93. Liam: It means that each person has to be as likely to win as the other.

94. Mr. D: And what about the number of turns?

95. Liam: Well, I think that matters too but the probability is what makes it fair.

96. Mr. D: I'd like everyone to turn and talk to their partners again about the question we have been discussing. Is this game fair? Why or why not? [He gives the students two minutes of partner talk and then reopens the whole-class discussion.]

97. Yajahira: My partner and I think that this game is not fair. The chance of getting a no-match was three out of four and the chance of getting a match was one out of four. That means that one person was three times as likely to win as the other. That's not fair.

98. Mr. D: Frank, can you repeat what Yajahira just said?

99. Frank: She said that the game is not fair since the chance to get a no-match was three times more likely than getting a match.

100. Mr. D: And do you and your partner agree or disagree with this? Tell us why you think so.

101. Frank: We agree. Fair would have had been fifty percent for one player and fifty percent for the other to win. In this game, one person has a better chance to win.

102. Mr. D: Let's think back to some of our other lessons. We played a game where two players took turns picking blocks out of a bag. In the bag were three blue blocks and three red blocks. If the block pulled out was red, Player A got a point. If the block pulled out was blue, Player B got a point. Think about what happened when we played this game. Was this game fair? Talk to the person next to you about this for a minute. [Students engage in partner talk for one to two minutes, then Mr. Donnell brings them back to whole-class discussion.]

103. Vivian: I think the game was fair because the red person has a fifty percent chance to win and the blue person does too.

104. Mr. D: How do you know the red person has a fifty percent chance to win?

105. Vivian: Three out of six blocks are red, that's the same as half, or fifty percent.

106. Mr. D: Tran, do you agree or disagree with what Vivian said?

107. Tran: I agree because my partner and I said that each person had the same chance of winning.

108. Mr. D: Can you think of another game that we played that was fair? Or, can you think of a game that was unfair? Be ready to convince us why they were fair or unfair. Talk to the person next to you about this. Also, look back in your notes. [Again, he provides two minutes for students to organize their answers in partner talk.] Reya, do you have a game we played?

109. Reya: The one with the spinner? That was unfair.

110. Mr. D: Reya, could you be a little more specific?

111. Reya: There was this spinner. Two sections were marked A and three were marked B. A player got a point for landing on their letter.

112. Mr. D: And why do you think that game was unfair?

113. Reya: Because the chance of landing on B was more than A.

114. Mr. D: Could everyone try to find their notes about this experiment in their notebooks? When we pooled our data, what was the experimental probability of landing on A?

115. Students: There was thirty-six percent for A and sixty-four percent for B.

116. Mr. D: And what about the theoretical probabilities?

117. Students: Two-fifths for A and three-fifths for B.

118. Mr. D: So, does this support what Reya said about the game being fair or unfair?

119. Tracey: Yes, it does. The B person has more of a chance to win. That's not fair.

120. Mr. D: Did we play a spinner game that was fair?

121. Yajahira: Yes, that spinner cut in fourths and two were red and two were blue. That's a fifty percent chance for each player and that's fair.

This discussion began with Mr. Donnell asking the class to review the theoretical probabilities of the coin game. Once he had accomplished this objective, he used the same discussion to revisit the idea of fairness. Students' comments suggested that they were making strides in understanding this term. Then, Mr. Donnell sought to strengthen their understanding of the term *fair* by asking them to recall other games that were either fair or unfair. Again, he required students to explain their reasoning. As students began to generalize their understanding of a mathematical term across contexts, their learning became more solid.

In this lesson, Mr. Donnell repeatedly asked students to agree or disagree with each other's ideas. The purpose of this question was to narrow in on the mathematical meaning of fairness so that the class could continue to move toward a more mathematical understanding of the term. The students' comments revealed that this was indeed happening. While there was no guarantee that every student "had it," yet they did seem to be headed in the right direction. Note that this forward movement occurred because of the discussion, not what Mr. Donnell said or did not say. In fact, he said very little in any of these discussions, acting instead as a facilitator. At no point did he forcefully tell the students the correct definition or give praise to any of the students who clearly articulated what it meant to be fair. He did not have to. The students appraised the value of each comment based upon what had been said so far, their experiences with the game, and their past knowledge about probability.

Summarizing and Solidifying: So Where Are We Now?
Mr. Donnell knows that since his students now have a mathematically sound definition of fairness, they are ready to expand their understanding by adjusting the relationship between likelihood and payout. Mr. Donnell will start tomorrow's lesson by reviewing what students learned and what they are still confused about from this lesson. Then he will proceed to the next lesson where students must make this game fair by adapting rules or giving different points for matches and no matches.

Mr. Donnell was pleased with the way this lesson went. He was particularly impressed by his students' abilities to explain why they agreed with one another in a reasonable and respectful manner. Compared with Mrs. Robert's class in Chapter 12, his students showed less of a need to revoice statements first or have the speaker repeat a comment. We attribute this to the students' experiences with classroom talk—Mr. Donnell's students had more experience than Mrs. Robert's students. As a result, they could agree and disagree without much need for prompting. Mr. Donnell was also pleased with the progress his students made in their understanding of the term *fair*. They sought to define *fair* in terms of the mathematics of the lesson. They listened to one another's comments and agreed or disagreed with them on the basis of their reasoning, not personal opinion or bias.

We are confident in saying that you will have fewer classes like Mrs. Robert's and more like Mr. Donnell's as you and your students gain more experience with classroom talk. However, even when you feel like you and your students have hit your stride with talk, there will certainly be days reminiscent of the early ones. When this happens, we encourage you to be reflective, as Mrs. Robert was: if possible, talk with a colleague, and think specifically about how to move forward with the discussion in the next lesson. Finally, we offer some advice that stems from the two case studies. First, heed our Principle from Chapter 9 and try one challenging new thing at a time. This is necessary for both you and your students. Second, commit to the implementation of classroom talk. Don't expect overnight miracles, but don't give up, either. Students will only get better with long-term, consistent implementation. Third, look forward to the days when you will be amazed at what your students say, days when their reasoning and insights will persuade you that your persistent focus on productive talk has resulted in deeper and more robust mathematics learning for all of your students.

References

The entries listed below range from popular articles and books to academic research studies. All of them offer insights into the use of classroom discourse, and many have influenced us in our own work with classroom discussions. Many are specifically about mathematics, but some address the use of academically productive talk across the curriculum.

Anderson, L., D. Krathwohl, and P. Airasian, eds. 2000. *A Taxonomy for Learning, Teaching, and Assessing: A Revision of Bloom's Taxonomy of Educational Objectives.* Upper Saddle River, NJ: Pearson Education.

Ball, D. 1993. "With an Eye on the Mathematical Horizon: Dilemmas of Teaching Elementary School Mathematics." *Elementary School Journal* 93: 373–397.

Ball, D. L. 1991. "Implementing the Professional Standards for Teaching Mathematics: What's All This Talk about Discourse?" *Arithmetic Teacher* 39(3): 44–48.

Ballenger, C. 1992. "Because You Like Us: The Language of Control." *Harvard Educational Review* 62(2): 199–208.

———. 1999. *Teaching Other People's Children: Literacy and Learning in a Bilingual Classroom.* New York: Teachers College Press.

Barnes, D. 1976. *From Communication to Curriculum.* Harmondsworth, U.K.: Penguin.

Barnes, D., and F. Todd. 1977. *Communication and Learning in Small Groups.* London: Routledge and Kegan Paul.

Beck, I., M. G. McKeown, R. L. Hamilton, and L. Kucan. 1997. *Questioning the Author: An Approach for Enhancing Student Engagement with Text.* Newark, DE: International Reading Association.

Burns, M. 2000. *About Teaching Mathematics: A K–8 Resource.* Sausalito, CA: Math Solutions Publications.

Carle, E. 2002. *Rooster's Off to See the World.* New York: Little Simon.

Cazden, C. B. 2001. *Classroom Discourse: The Language of Teaching and Learning.* Portsmouth, NH: Heinemann.

Chapin, S., and A. Johnson. 2000. *Math Matters: Understanding the Math You Teach, Grades K–6.* Sausalito, CA: Math Solutions Publications.

Cobb, P., T. Wood, and E. Yackel. 1993. "Discourse, Mathematical Thinking, and Classroom Practice." In *Contexts for Learning: Sociocultural Dynamics in Children's Development*, edited by E. A. Forman, N. Minick, and C. A. Stone (pp. 91–119). New York: Oxford University Press.

Cohen, E. G. 1994. "Restructuring the Classroom: Conditions for Productive Small Groups." *Review of Educational Research* 64(1): 1–35.

Cohen, E. G., and R. A. Lotan. 1995. "Producing Equal Status Interaction in the Heterogeneous Classroom." *American Educational Research Journal* 32(1): 99–120.

Delpit, L. 1995. *Other People's Children: Cultural Conflict in the Classroom*. New York: New Press.

Delpit, L., and J. K. Dowdy, eds. 2002. *The Skin That We Speak: Thoughts on Language and Culture in the Classroom*. New York: New Press.

Economopoulos, K., J. Mokros, R. Corwin, and S. Russell. 1995. *From Paces to Feet: Measuring and Data*. Palo Alto, CA: Dale Seymour.

Edwards, A. D., and D. P. G. Westgate. 1994. *Investigating Classroom Talk*. 2d ed. Bristol, PA: Falmer Press.

Edwards, D., and N. Mercer. 1987. *Common Knowledge: The Development of Understanding in the Classroom*. 2d ed. London and New York: Methuen.

Gallas, K. 1995. *Talking Their Ways into Science: Hearing Children's Questions and Theories, Responding with Curricula*. New York: Teachers College Press.

Gavelek, J. R., and T. E. Raphael. 1996. "Changing Talk About Text: New Roles for Teachers and Students." *Language Arts* 73: 182–192.

Godfrey, L., and M. C. O'Connor. 1995. "The Vertical Hand Span: Nonstandard Units, Expressions, and Symbols in the Classroom." *Journal of Mathematical Behavior* 14: 327–345.

Goldenberg, C. 1999. "Instructional Conversations: Promoting Comprehension Through Discussion." *The Reading Teacher* 46: 316–326.

Hatano, G., and K. Inagaki. 1991. "Sharing Cognition Through Collective Comprehension Activity." In *Perspectives on Socially Shared Cognition*, edited by L. Resnick, R. Levine, and S. Teasley. Washington, DC: APA.

Heath, S. B. 1983. *Ways with Words: Language, Life, and Work in Communities and Classrooms*. Cambridge, U.K., and New York: Cambridge University Press.

Hicks, D. 1995. "Discourse, Learning, and Teaching." *Review of Research in Education* 21: 49–95.

Hiebert, J., and T. P. Carpenter. 1992. "Learning and Teaching with Understanding." In *Handbook of Research on Mathematics Teaching and Learning*, edited by D. A. Grouws (pp. 65–97). New York: Macmillan.

Inagaki, K., E. Morita, and G. Hatano, 1999. "Teaching Learning of Evaluative Criteria for Mathematical Arguments Through Classroom Discourse: A Cross National Study." *Mathematical Thinking and Learning* 1(2): 93–111.

Jensen, R., ed. 1993. *Research Ideas for the Classroom: Early Childhood Mathematics*. New York: Macmillan.

Keefer, M. W., C. M. Zeitz, and L. B. Resnick. 2000. "Judging the Quality of Peer Led Student Dialogues." *Cognition and Instruction* 18(1): 53–81.

Khisty, L. L. 1995. "Making Inequality: Issues of Language and Meanings in Mathematics Teaching with Hispanic Students." In *New Directions for Equity in Mathematics Education*, edited by W. Secada, E. Fennema, and L. B. Adajian (pp. 279–297). Cambridge, U.K., and New York: Cambridge University Press.

Kieran, C., and L. Chalouh. 1993. "Prealgebra: The Transition from Arithmetic to Algebra." In *Research Ideas for the Classroom: Middle Grades Mathematics*, edited by D. Owens (pp. 179–198). New York: Macmillan.

Lampert, M. 1990. "Connecting Inventions with Conventions. In *Transforming Children's Mathematics Education: International Perspectives*, edited by L. P. Steffe and T. Wood (pp. 253–264). Hillsdale, NJ: Lawrence Erlbaum.

———. 2001. *Teaching Problems: A Study of Classroom Practice*. New Haven, CT: Yale University Press.

Lampert, M., and M. L. Blunk, eds. 1998. *Talking Mathematics in School: Studies of Teaching and Learning*. Cambridge, U.K., and New York: Cambridge University Press.

Lampert, M., P. Rittenhouse, and C. Crumbaugh. 1996. "Agreeing to Disagree: Developing Sociable Mathematical Discourse in School." In *Handbook of Psychology and Education: New Models of Learning, Teaching, and School*, edited by D. R. Olson and N. Torrance (pp. 731–764). Oxford, U.K.: Basil Blackwell.

Lappan, G., J. Fey, W. Fitzgerald, S. Friel, and E. Phillips. 2002. *How Likely Is It?* Upper Saddle River, NJ: Prentice Hall.

Lemke, J. 1990. *Talking Science: Language, Learning, and Values*. Norwood, NJ: Ablex.

McKeown, M. G., I. L. Beck, R. L. Hamilton, and L. Kucan. 1999. *"Questioning the Author" Accessibles: Easy-Access Resources for Classroom Challenges*. Bothell, WA: The Wright Group.

Mehan, H. 1979. *Learning Lessons: Social Organization in the Classroom*. Cambridge, MA: Harvard University Press.

Moschovich, J. 1999. "Supporting the Participation of English Language Learners in Mathematical Discussions." *For the Learning of Mathematics* 19(1): 11–19.

———. 2000. "Learning Mathematics in Two Languages: Moving from Obstacles to Resources. In *Changing the Faces of Mathematics: Multiculturalism and Gender Equity*, edited by W. Secada (pp. 85–93). Reston, VA: National Council of Teachers of Mathematics.

Moses, R. P., M. Kamii, S. Swap, and J. Howard. 1989. "The Algebra Project: Organizing in the Spirit of Ella." *Harvard Educational Review* 59(4): 423–443.

National Council of Teachers of Mathematics. 2000. *Principles and Standards for School Mathematics.* Reston, VA: National Council of Teachers of Mathematics.

National Research Council. 2000. *How People Learn.* Washington, DC: National Academy Press.

National Research Council. 2001. *Adding It Up: Helping Children Learn Mathematics,* edited by J. Kilpatrick, J. Swafford, and F. Bradford. Mathematics Learning Study Committee, Center for Education, Division of Behavioral and Social Sciences and Education. Washington, DC: National Academy Press.

Nystrand, M. 1997. *Opening Dialogue: Understanding the Dynamics of Language and Learning in the English Classroom.* New York: Teachers College Press.

O'Connor, M. C. 1998. "Language Socialization in the Mathematics Classroom: Discourse Practices and Mathematical Thinking." In *Talking Mathematics in School: Studies of Teaching and Learning,* edited by M. Lampert and M. L. Blunk (pp. 17–55). Cambridge, U.K., and New York: Cambridge University Press.

———. 2001. "'Can Any Fraction Be Turned into a Decimal?' A Case Study of a Mathematical Group Discussion." *Educational Studies in Mathematics* 46: 143–185.

O'Connor, M. C., and S. Michaels. 1996. "Shifting Participant Frameworks: Orchestrating Thinking Practices in Group Discussion." In *Child Discourse and Social Learning,* edited by D. Hicks (pp. 63–102). Cambridge, U.K., and New York: Cambridge University Press.

Orsolini, M., and C. Pontecorvo. 1992. "Children's Talk in Classroom Discussions." *Cognition and Instruction* 9: 113–136.

Owens, D., ed. 1993. *Research Ideas for the Classroom: Middle Grades Mathematics.* New York: Macmillan.

Paratore, J. R., and R. L. McCormack, eds. 1997. *Peer Talk in the Classroom: Learning from Research.* Newark, DE: International Reading Association.

Pimm, D. 1987. *Speaking Mathematically: Communication in Mathematics Classrooms.* London: Routledge & Kegan Paul.

Polya, G. 1945. *How to Solve It.* Princeton, NJ: Princeton University Press.

Rowe, M. B. 1986. "Wait Times: Slowing Down May Be a Way of Speeding Up." *Journal of Teacher Education* 37(1): 43–50.

Russell, S. J. 1999. "Mathematical Reasoning in the Elementary Grades." In *Developing Mathematical Reasoning in Grades K–12,* edited by L. V. Stiff and F. R. Curcio (pp. 1–12). Reston, VA: National Council of Teachers of Mathematics.

Russell, S. J., and R. B. Corwin. 1993. "Talking Mathematics: 'Going Slow' and 'Letting Go'." *Phi Delta Kappan* (March): 555–558.

Secada, W., E. Fennema, and L. B. Adajian, eds. 1995. *New Directions for Equity in Mathematics Education.* Cambridge, U.K., and New York: Cambridge University Press.

Sheffield, L., and D. Cruikshank. 2001. *Teaching and Learning Elementary and Middle School Mathematics.* 4th ed. New York: John Wiley & Sons.

Stacey, K., and M. MacGregor. February 1997. "Ideas About Symbolism That Students Bring to Algebra." *Mathematics Teacher* 90(2): 110–113.

Stein, M. K., M. S. Smith, M. A. Henningsen, and E. A. Silver. 2000. *Implementing Standards-Based Mathematics Instruction: A Casebook for Professional Development.* New York: Teachers College Press.

Van Zee, E. H., and J. Minstrell. 1997. "Using Questioning to Guide Student Thinking." *Journal of the Learning Sciences* 6(2): 227–269.

Van Zee, E. H., M. Iwasyk, A. Kurose, D. Simpson, and J. Wild. 2001. "Student and Teacher Questioning During Conversations About Science." *Journal of Research in Science Teaching* 38(2): 159–190.

Wagner, S., and S. Parker. 1993. "Advancing Algebra." In *Research Ideas for the Classroom: High School Mathematics*, edited by P. Wilson (pp. 119–139). New York: Macmillan.

Wells, G. 1985. *Language at Home and School.* Cambridge, U.K., and New York: Cambridge University Press.

———. 1999. *Dialogic Inquiry: Toward a Sociocultural Practice and Theory of Education.* Cambridge, U.K., and New York: Cambridge University Press.

Willes, M. 1983. *Children into Pupils: A Study of Language in Early Schooling.* London: Routledge & Kegan Paul.

Wood, T., and E. Yackel. 1990. "The Development of Collaborative Dialogue in Small Group Interactions." In *Transforming Early Childhood Mathematics Education: An International Perspective*, edited by L. P. Steffe and T. Wood (pp. 244–252). Hillsdale, NJ: Lawrence Erlbaum.

Yackel, E., P. Cobb, and T. Wood. 1991. "Small Group Interactions as a Source of Learning Opportunities in Second Grade Mathematics." *Journal for Research in Mathematics Education* 22: 390–408.

Index